D0793618

Teen Health Series

Sleep Information For Teens,
Second Edition

Sleep Information For Teens, Second Edition

Health Tips About Adolescent Sleep Requirements, Sleep Disorders, And The Effects Of Sleep Deprivation

Including Facts About Why People Need Sleep, Sleep Patterns, Circadian Rhythms, Dreaming, Insomnia, Sleep Apnea, Narcolepsy, And More

OMNIGRAPHICS
615 Griswold, Ste. 901
Detroit, MI 48226

Bibliographic Note
Because this page cannot legibly accommodate all the copyright notices, the Bibliographic Note portion of the Preface constitutes an extension of the copyright notice.

* * *

OMNIGRAPHICS
Siva Ganesh Maharaja, *Managing Editor*

* * *

Library of Congress Cataloging-in-Publication Data

Names: Omnigraphics, Inc., issuing body.

Title: Sleep information for teens: health tips about adolescent sleep requirements, sleep disorders, and the effects of sleep deprivation including facts about why people need sleep, sleep patterns, circadian rhythms, dreaming, insomnia, sleep apnea, narcolepsy, and more.

Description: Second edition. | Detroit, MI: Omnigraphics, Inc., [2018] | Series: Teen health series | Audience: Grade 9 to 12. | Includes bibliographical references and index.

Identifiers: LCCN 2017050215 (print) | LCCN 2017050810 (ebook) | ISBN 9780780814776 (eBook) | ISBN 9780780814783 (hardcover: alk. paper)

Subjects: LCSH: Sleep--Handbooks, manuals, etc. | Teenagers--Sleep--Handbooks, manuals, etc. | Sleep disorders in adolescence--Handbooks, manuals, etc.

Classification: LCC RA786 (ebook) | LCC RA786.S64 2018 (print) | DDC 618.92/8498--dc23

LC record available at https://lccn.loc.gov/2017050215

Table Of Contents

Part Three: Sleep Disorders And Related Problems

Part Six: If You Need More Information

Preface

About This Book

Teens are known for staying up late, oversleeping, and falling asleep during classes. The reason for this is the resetting of sleep cycles. Sleep cycles are regulated by an internal biological clock, and when children enter their teen years, their sleep patterns change. They tend to feel more wakeful later into the evening than when they were younger. When this natural tendency is coupled with earlier school starting times, sleep debts begin to accumulate. This lack of sleep can have a negative impact on learning, extracurricular activities, and social relationships. It can also prove to be dangerous by increasing reaction times, contributing to memory lapses, and affecting behavior and moods. When teens don't get enough sleep at night, they fall asleep at inappropriate—and even dangerous—times, such as in class or behind the wheel.

Sleep Information For Teens, *Second Edition* provides facts about sleep and sleep requirements for teens. It explains the biological processes involved in sleep and discusses circadian rhythms, dreaming, sleep hygiene, and sleep disorders, including insomnia, delayed sleep phase syndrome, sleep apnea, narcolepsy, restless legs syndrome, and enuresis (bedwetting). It further discusses about sleep deprivation, the physical and mental consequences of inadequate sleep, and provides information on current research initiatives reports some of the most recent findings. The book concludes with a directory of resources for additional information and a list of suggestions for further information about sleep and sleep disorders.

How To Use This Book

This book is divided into parts and chapters. Parts focus on broad areas of interest; chapters are devoted to single topics within a part.

Part One: Understanding Sleep describes what happens during sleep and why it is so important to health. It discusses the role circadian rhythms play in sleep regulation and talks about the benefits and potential problems related to napping, why we dream, how sleep helps with memory, and how sleep helps us to be fit.

Part Two: Sleep Habits examines circumstances and practices that influence the quantity and quality of sleep. It explains how much sleep is needed and offers suggestions for getting sufficient, restful sleep. The effects of caffeine, mental health, substance use, and posttraumatic stress on the ability to sleep are described. Sleep medications and the benefits and risks of sleep medications are also discussed.

Part Three: Sleep Disorders And Related Problems provides information about the symptoms, diagnostic procedures, and treatments for common sleep-related disorders, including insomnia, sleep apnea, and narcolepsy. It also explains other sleep-related behaviors such as nocturnal asthma, bedwetting, nightmares, parasomnias, and bruxism (teeth grinding).

Part Four: The Consequences Of Sleep Deprivation discusses the mental and physical effects of insufficient sleep and explains how a lack of sleep can impact daily functioning. It describes how sleep deprivation can lead to diminished learning and thinking skills, difficulties in handling emotions, and poor physical performance. It also discusses the role sleep deprivation plays in placing teens at increased risk for weight gain and accidents.

Part Five: Sleep Research And Clinical Trials provides statistical information and summarizes recent discoveries made by investigators who study sleep-related neurological different population and biological processes. It also provides information about current research initiatives that are underway through several agencies.

Part Six: If You Need More Information offers a directory of sleep-related resources and suggestions for further reading about sleep and sleep disorders.

Bibliographic Note

This volume contains documents and excerpts from publications issued by the following government agencies: Centers for Disease Control and Prevention (CDC); *Eunice Kennedy Shriver* National Institute of Child Health and Human Development (NICHD); Genetic and Rare Diseases Information Center (GARD); National Center for Complementary and Integrative Health (NCCIH); National Heart, Lung, and Blood Institute (NHLBI); National Institute of Diabetes and Digestive and Kidney Diseases (NIDDK); National Institute of General Medical Sciences (NIGMS); National Institute of Justice (NIJ); National Institute of Mental Health (NIMH); National Institute of Neurological Disorders and Stroke (NINDS); National Institute on Drug Abuse (NIDA); National Institutes of Health (NIH); National Women's Health Information Center (NWHIC); *NIH News in Health*; Office of Disease Prevention and Health Promotion (ODPHP); Office on Women's Health (OWH); U.S. Department of Veterans Affairs (VA); and U.S. Food and Drug Administration (FDA).

It may also contain original material produced by Omnigraphics and reviewed by medical consultants.

The photograph on the front cover is © Arieliona.

Medical Review

Omnigraphics contracts with a team of qualified, senior medical professionals who serve as medical consultants for the *Teen Health Series*. As necessary, medical consultants review reprinted and originally written material for currency and accuracy. Citations including the phrase, "Reviewed (month, year)" indicate material reviewed by this team. Medical consultation services are provided to the *Teen Health Series* editors by:

Dr. Vijayalakshmi, MBBS, DGO, MD
Dr. Senthil Selvan, MBBS, DCH, MD
Dr. K. Sivanandham, MBBS, DCH, MS (Research), PhD

About The *Teen Health Series*

At the request of librarians serving today's young adults, the *Teen Health Series* was developed as a specially focused set of volumes within Omnigraphics' *Health Reference Series*. Each volume deals comprehensively with a topic selected according to the needs and interests of people in middle school and high school. Teens seeking preventive guidance, information about disease warning signs, medical statistics, and risk factors for health problems will find answers to their questions in the *Teen Health Series*. The *Series*, however, is not intended to serve as a tool for diagnosing illness, in prescribing treatments, or as a substitute for the physician/patient relationship. All people concerned about medical symptoms or the possibility of disease are encouraged to seek professional care from an appropriate healthcare provider.

If there is a topic you would like to see addressed in a future volume of the *Teen Health Series*, please write to:

Editor
Teen Health Series
Omnigraphics
615 Griswold, Ste. 901
Detroit, MI 48226

A Note About Spelling And Style

Teen Health Series editors use *Stedman's Medical Dictionary* as an authority for questions related to the spelling of medical terms and the *Chicago Manual of Style* for questions related to grammatical structures, punctuation, and other editorial concerns. Consistent adherence is not always possible, however, because the individual volumes within the *Series* include many documents from a wide variety of different producers and copyright holders, and the editor's primary goal is to present material from each source as accurately as is possible following the terms specified by each document's producer. This sometimes means that information in different chapters may follow other guidelines and alternate spelling authorities. For example, occasionally a copyright holder may require that eponymous terms be shown in possessive forms (Crohn's disease vs. Crohn disease) or that British spelling norms be retained (leukaemia vs. leukemia).

Part One
Understanding Sleep

Chapter 1

Facts And Misperceptions About Sleep

Sleep is an important part of your daily routine—you spend about one-third of your time doing it. Quality sleep—and getting enough of it at the right times—is as essential to survival as food and water. Without sleep you can't form or maintain the pathways in your brain that let you learn and create new memories, and it's harder to concentrate and respond quickly.

Sleep is important to a number of brain functions, including how nerve cells (neurons) communicate with each other. In fact, your brain and body stay remarkably active while you sleep. Recent findings suggest that sleep plays a housekeeping role that removes toxins in your brain that build up while you are awake.

Everyone needs sleep, but its biological purpose remains a mystery. Sleep affects almost every type of tissue and system in the body—from the brain, heart, and lungs to metabolism, immune function, mood, and disease resistance. Research shows that a chronic lack of sleep, or getting poor quality sleep, increases the risk of disorders including high blood pressure, cardiovascular disease, diabetes, depression, and obesity.

Sleep is a complex and dynamic process that affects how you function in ways scientists are now beginning to understand.

About This Chapter: Text in this chapter begins with excerpts from "Brain Basics: Understanding Sleep," National Institute of Neurological Disorders and Stroke (NINDS), May 19, 2017; Text under the heading "Myths About Sleep" is excerpted from "Your Guide To Healthy Sleep," National Heart, Lung, and Blood Institute (NHLBI), August 2011. Reviewed December 2017.

What Is Sleep?

Sleep was long considered just a block of time when your brain and body shut down. Thanks to sleep research studies done over the past several decades, it is now known that sleep has distinct stages that cycle throughout the night in predictable patterns. How well rested you are and how well you function depend not just on your total sleep time but on how much sleep you get each night and the timing of your sleep stages. Sleep is divided into two basic types: rapid eye movement (REM) sleep and non-REM sleep (with three different stages).

(Source: "Your Guide To Healthy Sleep," National Heart, Lung, and Blood Institute (NHLBI).)

Anatomy Of Sleep

Several structures within the brain are involved with sleep.

The hypothalamus, a peanut-sized structure deep inside the brain, contains groups of nerve cells that act as control centers affecting sleep and arousal. Within the hypothalamus is the suprachiasmatic nucleus (SCN)—clusters of thousands of cells that receive information about light exposure directly from the eyes and control your behavioral rhythm. Some people with damage to the SCN sleep erratically throughout the day because they are not able to match their circadian rhythms with the light-dark cycle. Most blind people maintain some ability to sense light and are able to modify their sleep/wake cycle.

The brain stem, at the base of the brain, communicates with the hypothalamus to control the transitions between wake and sleep. (The brain stem includes structures called the pons, medulla, and midbrain.) Sleep-promoting cells within the hypothalamus and the brain stem produce a brain chemical called *GABA*, which acts to reduce the activity of arousal centers in the hypothalamus and the brain stem. The brain stem (especially the pons and medulla) also plays a special role in REM sleep; it sends signals to relax muscles essential for body posture and limb movements, so that we don't act out our dreams.

The thalamus acts as a relay for information from the senses to the cerebral cortex (the covering of the brain that interprets and processes information from short- to long-term memory). During most stages of sleep, the thalamus becomes quiet, letting you tune out the external world. But during REM sleep, the thalamus is active, sending the cortex images, sounds, and other sensations that fill our dreams.

The pineal gland, located within the brain's two hemispheres, receives signals from the SCN and increases production of the hormone melatonin, which helps put you to sleep once the lights go down. People who have lost their sight and cannot coordinate their natural wake-sleep cycle using natural light can stabilize their sleep patterns by taking small amounts of melatonin at the same time each day. Scientists believe that peaks and valleys of melatonin over time are important for matching the body's circadian rhythm to the external cycle of light and darkness.

The basal forebrain, near the front and bottom of the brain, also promotes sleep and wakefulness, while part of the midbrain acts as an arousal system. Release of adenosine (a chemical by-product of cellular energy consumption) from cells in the basal forebrain and probably other regions supports your sleep drive. Caffeine counteracts sleepiness by blocking the actions of adenosine.

The amygdala, an almond-shaped structure involved in processing emotions, becomes increasingly active during REM sleep.

Sleep Mechanisms

Two internal biological mechanisms–circadian rhythm and homeostasis–work together to regulate when you are awake and sleep.

Circadian rhythms direct a wide variety of functions from daily fluctuations in wakefulness to body temperature, metabolism, and the release of hormones. They control your timing of sleep and cause you to be sleepy at night and your tendency to wake in the morning without an alarm. Your body's biological clock, which is based on a roughly 24-hour day, controls most circadian rhythms. Circadian rhythms synchronize with environmental cues (light, temperature) about the actual time of day, but they continue even in the absence of cues.

Sleep-wake homeostasis keeps track of your need for sleep. The homeostatic sleep drive reminds the body to sleep after a certain time and regulates sleep intensity. This sleep drive gets stronger every hour you are awake and causes you to sleep longer and more deeply after a period of sleep deprivation.

Factors that influence your sleep-wake needs include medical conditions, medications, stress, sleep environment, and what you eat and drink. Perhaps the greatest influence is the exposure to light. Specialized cells in the retinas of your eyes process light and tell the brain whether it is day or night and can advance or delay our sleep-wake cycle. Exposure to light can make it difficult to fall asleep and return to sleep when awakened.

Night shift workers often have trouble falling asleep when they go to bed, and also have trouble staying awake at work because their natural circadian rhythm and sleep-wake cycle is disrupted. In the case of jet lag, circadian rhythms become out of sync with the time of day when people fly to a different time zone, creating a mismatch between their internal clock and the actual clock.

How Much Sleep Do You Need?

Your need for sleep and your sleep patterns change as you age, but this varies significantly across individuals of the same age. There is no magic "number of sleep hours" that works for everybody of the same age. Babies initially sleep as much as 16–18 hours per day, which may boost growth and development (especially of the brain). School-age children and teens on average need about 9.5 hours of sleep per night. Most adults need 7–9 hours of sleep a night, but after age 60, nighttime sleep tends to be shorter, lighter, and interrupted by multiple awakenings. Elderly people are also more likely to take medications that interfere with sleep.

In general, people are getting less sleep than they need due to longer work hours and the availability of round-the-clock entertainment and other activities. Many people feel they can "catch up" on missed sleep during the weekend but, depending on how sleep-deprived they are, sleeping longer on the weekends may not be adequate.

Dreaming

Everyone dreams. You spend about two hours each night dreaming but may not remember most of your dreams. Its exact purpose isn't known, but dreaming may help you process your emotions. Events from the day often invade your thoughts during sleep, and people suffering from stress or anxiety are more likely to have frightening dreams. Dreams can be experienced in all stages of sleep but usually are most vivid in REM sleep. Some people dream in color, while others only recall dreams in black and white.

The Role Of Genes And Neurotransmitters
Chemical Signals To Sleep

Clusters of sleep-promoting neurons in many parts of the brain become more active as we get ready for bed. Nerve-signaling chemicals called neurotransmitters can "switch off" or dampen the activity of cells that signal arousal or relaxation. GABA is associated with sleep, muscle relaxation, and sedation. Norepinephrine and orexin (also called hypocretin) keep some parts of the brain active while we are awake. Other neurotransmitters that shape sleep and wakefulness include acetylcholine, histamine, adrenaline, cortisol, and serotonin.

Genes And Sleep

Genes may play a significant role in how much sleep we need. Scientists have identified several genes involved with sleep and sleep disorders, including genes that control the excitability of neurons, and "clock" genes such as Per, tim, and Cry that influence our circadian rhythms and the timing of sleep. Genome-wide association studies have identified sites on various chromosomes that increase our susceptibility to sleep disorders. Also, different genes have been identified with such sleep disorders as familial advanced sleep-phase disorder, narcolepsy, and restless legs syndrome. Some of the genes expressed in the cerebral cortex and other brain areas change their level of expression between sleep and wake. Several genetic models—including the worm, fruit fly, and zebrafish—are helping scientists to identify molecular mechanisms and genetic variants involved in normal sleep and sleep disorders. Additional research will provide better understanding of inherited sleep patterns and risks of circadian and sleep disorders.

Sleep Studies

Your healthcare provider may recommend a polysomnogram or other test to diagnose a sleep disorder. A polysomnogram typically involves spending the night at a sleep lab or sleep center. It records your breathing, oxygen levels, eye and limb movements, heart rate, and brain waves throughout the night. Your sleep is also video and audio recorded. The data can help a sleep specialist determine if you are reaching and proceeding properly through the various sleep stages. Results may be used to develop a treatment plan or determine if further tests are needed.

Myths About Sleep

Myth 1: Sleep is a time when your body and brain shut down for rest and relaxation. No evidence shows that any major organ (including the brain) or regulatory system in the body shuts down during sleep. Some physiological processes actually become more active while you sleep. For example, secretion of certain hormones is boosted, and activity of the pathways in the brain linked to learning and memory increases.

Myth 2: Getting just one hour less sleep per night than needed will not have any effect on your daytime functioning. This lack of sleep may not make you noticeably sleepy during the day. But even slightly less sleep can affect your ability to think properly and respond quickly, and it can impair your cardiovascular health and energy balance as well as your body's ability to fight infections, particularly if lack of sleep continues. If you consistently do not get enough sleep, a sleep debt builds up that you can never repay. This sleep debt affects your health and quality of life and makes you feel tired during the day.

Myth 3: Your body adjusts quickly to different sleep schedules. Your biological clock makes you most alert during the daytime and least alert at night. Thus, even if you work the night shift, you will naturally feel sleepy when nighttime comes. Most people can reset their biological clock, but only by appropriately timed cues—and even then, by 1–2 hours per day at best. Consequently, it can take more than a week to adjust to a substantial change in your sleep-wake cycle—for example, when traveling across several time zones or switching from working the day shift to the night shift.

Myth 4: People need less sleep as they get older. Older people don't need less sleep, but they may get less sleep or find their sleep less refreshing. That's because as people age, the quality of their sleep changes. Older people are also more likely to have insomnia or other medical conditions that disrupt their sleep.

Myth 5: Extra sleep for one night can cure you of problems with excessive daytime fatigue. Not only is the quantity of sleep important, but also the quality of sleep. Some people sleep 8–9 hours a night but don't feel well rested when they wake up because the quality of their sleep is poor. A number of sleep disorders and other medical conditions affect the quality of sleep. Sleeping more won't lessen the daytime sleepiness these disorders or conditions cause. However, many of these disorders or conditions can be treated effectively with changes in behavior or with medical therapies. Additionally, one night of increased sleep may not correct multiple nights of inadequate sleep.

Myth 6: You can make up for lost sleep during the week by sleeping more on the weekends. Although this sleeping pattern will help you feel more rested, it will not completely make up for the lack of sleep or correct your sleep debt. This pattern also will not necessarily make up for impaired performance during the week or the physical problems that can result from not sleeping enough. Furthermore, sleeping later on the weekends can affect your biological clock, making it much harder to go to sleep at the right time on Sunday nights and get up early on Monday mornings.

Myth 7: Naps are a waste of time. Although naps are no substitute for a good night's sleep, they can be restorative and help counter some of the effects of not getting enough sleep at night. Naps can actually help you learn how to do certain tasks quicker. But avoid taking naps later than 3 p.m., particularly if you have trouble falling asleep at night, as late naps can make it harder for you to fall asleep when you go to bed. Also, limit your naps to no longer than 20 minutes, because longer naps will make it harder to wake up and get back in the swing of things. If you take more than one or two planned or unplanned naps during the day, you may have a sleep disorder that should be treated.

Myth 8: Snoring is a normal part of sleep. Snoring during sleep is common, particularly as a person gets older. Evidence is growing that snoring on a regular basis can make you sleepy during the day and increase your risk for diabetes and heart disease. In addition, some studies link frequent snoring to problem behavior and poorer school achievement in children. Loud, frequent snoring also can be a sign of sleep apnea, a serious sleep disorder that should be evaluated and treated.

Myth 9: Children who don't get enough sleep at night will show signs of sleepiness during the day. Unlike adults, children who don't get enough sleep at night typically become hyperactive, irritable, and inattentive during the day. They also have increased risk of injury and more behavior problems, and their growth rate may be impaired. Sleep debt appears to be quite common during childhood and may be misdiagnosed as attention deficit hyperactivity disorder.

Myth 10: The main cause of insomnia is worry. Although worry or stress can cause a short bout of insomnia, a persistent inability to fall asleep or stay asleep at night can be caused by a number of other factors. Certain medications and sleep disorders can keep you up at night. Other common causes of insomnia are depression, anxiety disorders, and asthma, arthritis, or other medical conditions with symptoms that tend to be troublesome at night. Some people who have chronic insomnia also appear to be more "revved up" than normal, so it is harder for them to fall asleep.

More Myths

During sleep, your brain rests. The body rests during sleep; however, the brain remains active, gets "recharged," and still controls many body functions including breathing. When we sleep, we typically drift between two sleep states, rapid eye movement (REM) and non-REM, in 90-minute cycles. Non-REM sleep has four stages with distinct features, ranging from stage one drowsiness, when one can be easily awakened, to "deep sleep" stages three and four, when awakenings are more difficult and where the most positive and restorative effects of sleep occur; however, even in the deepest non-REM sleep, our minds can still process information. REM sleep is an active sleep where dreams occur, breathing and heart rate increase and become irregular, muscles relax, and eyes move back and forth under the eyelids.

Health problems such as obesity, diabetes, hypertension, and depression are unrelated to the amount and quality of a person's sleep. Studies have found a relationship between the quantity and quality of one's sleep and many health problems. For example, insufficient sleep affects growth hormone secretion that is linked to obesity; as the amount of hormone secretion decreases, the chance for weight gain increases. Blood pressure usually falls during the sleep cycle; however, interrupted sleep can adversely affect this normal decline, leading to hypertension and cardiovascular problems. Research has also shown that insufficient sleep impairs the body's ability to use insulin, which can lead to the onset of diabetes. More and more scientific studies are showing correlations between poor and insufficient sleep and disease.

(Source: "Safety/Myths And Facts About Sleep," Natural Resources Conservation Service (NRCS), U.S. Department of Agriculture (USDA).)

Chapter 2

The Biology Of Sleep

Sleep plays a vital role in good health and well-being throughout your life. Getting enough quality sleep at the right times can help protect your mental health, physical health, quality of life, and safety.

The way you feel while you're awake depends in part on what happens while you're sleeping. During sleep, your body is working to support healthy brain function and maintain your physical health. In children and teens, sleep also helps support growth and development.

The damage from sleep deficiency can occur in an instant (such as a car crash), or it can harm you over time. For example, ongoing sleep deficiency can raise your risk for some chronic health problems. It also can affect how well you think, react, work, learn, and get along with others.

Healthy Brain Function And Emotional Well-Being

Sleep helps your brain work properly. While you're sleeping, your brain is preparing for the next day. It's forming new pathways to help you learn and remember information.

Studies show that a good night's sleep improves learning. Whether you're learning math, how to play the piano, how to perfect your golf swing, or how to drive a car, sleep helps enhance your learning and problem-solving skills. Sleep also helps you pay attention, make decisions, and be creative.

About This Chapter: Text in this chapter begins with excerpts from "Sleep Deprivation And Deficiency" National Heart, Lung, and Blood Institute (NHLBI), June 7, 2017; Text under the heading "How Sleep Resets The Brain" is excerpted from "How Sleep Resets The Brain," National Institutes of Health (NIH), February 14, 2017.

Studies also show that sleep deficiency alters activity in some parts of the brain. If you're sleep deficient, you may have trouble making decisions, solving problems, controlling your emotions and behavior, and coping with change. Sleep deficiency also has been linked to depression, suicide, and risk-taking behavior.

Children and teens who are sleep deficient may have problems getting along with others. They may feel angry and impulsive, have mood swings, feel sad or depressed, or lack motivation. They also may have problems paying attention, and they may get lower grades and feel stressed.

Role Of Adenosine

Many factors play a role in preparing your body to fall asleep and wake up. You have an internal "body clock" that controls when you're awake and when your body is ready for sleep.

The body clock typically has a 24-hour repeating rhythm (called the circadian rhythm). Two processes interact to control this rhythm. The first is a pressure to sleep that builds with every hour that you're awake. This drive for sleep reaches a peak in the evening, when most people fall asleep.

Circadian Rhythms

Circadian rhythms regulate changes in mental and physical characteristics that occur during the course of a day. The word circadian, meaning "around a day," comes from the Latin words "circa" (around) and "diem" (a day). Your body's biological clock controls most circadian rhythms. This clock is located in a region of the brain called the hypothalamus.

(Source: "Sleep," Eunice Kennedy Shriver National Institute of Child Health and Human Development (NICHD).)

A compound called adenosine seems to be one factor linked to this drive for sleep. While you're awake, the level of adenosine in your brain continues to rise. The increasing level of this compound signals a shift toward sleep. While you sleep, your body breaks down adenosine.

Internal Body Clock

A second process involves your internal body clock. This clock is in sync with certain cues in the environment. Light, darkness, and other cues help determine when you feel awake and when you feel drowsy. For example, light signals received through your eyes tell a special area in your brain that it is daytime. This area of your brain helps align your body clock with periods of the day and night.

Role Of Melatonin

Your body releases chemicals in a daily rhythm, which your body clock controls. When it gets dark, your body releases a hormone called melatonin. Melatonin signals your body that it's time to prepare for sleep, and it helps you feel drowsy. The amount of melatonin in your bloodstream peaks as the evening wears on. Researchers believe this peak is an important part of preparing your body for sleep.

> Studies suggest that melatonin may help with certain sleep disorders, such as jet lag, delayed sleep phase disorder (a disruption of the body's biological clock in which a person's sleep-wake timing cycle is delayed by 3–6 hours), sleep problems related to shift work, and some sleep disorders in children. It's also been shown to be helpful for a sleep disorder that causes changes in blind people's sleep and wake times.
>
> *(Source: "Melatonin: In Depth," National Center for Complementary and Integrative Health (NCCIH).)*

Disruption Of Sleep

Exposure to bright artificial light in the late evening can disrupt this process, making it hard to fall asleep. Examples of bright artificial light include the light from a TV screen, computer screen, or a very bright alarm clock. As the sun rises, your body releases cortisol. This hormone naturally prepares your body to wake up.

Teens And Their Preference To Go To Bed Late

The rhythm and timing of the body clock change with age. Teens fall asleep later at night than younger children and adults. One reason for this is because melatonin is released and peaks later in the 24-hour cycle for teens. As a result, it's natural for many teens to prefer later bedtimes at night and sleep later in the morning than adults.

People also need more sleep early in life, when they're growing and developing. For example, newborns may sleep more than 16 hours a day, and preschool aged children need to take naps.

Young children tend to sleep more in the early evening. Teens tend to sleep more in the morning. Also, older adults tend to go to bed earlier and wake up earlier.

The patterns and types of sleep also change as people mature. For example, newborn infants spend more time in rapid eye movement sleep (REM) sleep. The amount of slow wave sleep (a stage of non-REM sleep) peaks in early childhood and then drops sharply after puberty. It continues to decline as people age.

How Sleep Resets The Brain

People spend about a third of their lives asleep. When we get too little shut-eye, it takes a toll on attention, learning and memory, not to mention our physical health. Virtually all animals with complex brains seem to have this same need for sleep. But exactly what is it about sleep that's so essential?

Two National Institutes of Health (NIH)-funded studies in mice now offer a possible answer. The two research teams used entirely different approaches to reach the same conclusion: the brain's neural connections grow stronger during waking hours, but scale back during snooze time. This sleep-related phenomenon apparently keeps neural circuits from overloading, ensuring that mice (and, quite likely humans) awaken with brains that are refreshed and ready to tackle new challenges.

The idea that sleep is required to keep the brain wiring sharp goes back more than a decade. While a fair amount of evidence has emerged to support the hypothesis, its originators Chiara Cirelli and Giulio Tononi of the University of Wisconsin-Madison, set out in their new study to provide some of the first direct visual proof that it's indeed the case.

As published in the journal *Science*, the researchers used a painstaking, cutting-edge imaging technique to capture high-resolution pictures of two areas of the mouse's cerebral cortex, a part of the brain that coordinates incoming sensory and motor information. The technique, called serial scanning 3D electron microscopy, involves repeated scanning of small slices of the brain to produce many thousands of images, allowing the researchers to produce detailed 3D reconstructions of individual neurons.

Their goal was to measure the size of the synapses, where the ends of two neurons connect. Synapses are critical for one neuron to pass signals on to the next, and the strength of those neural connections corresponds to their size.

The researchers measured close to 7,000 synapses in all. Their images show that synapses grew stronger and larger as these nocturnal mice scurried about at night. Then, after 6–8 hours of sleep during the day, those synapses shrank by about 18 percent as the brain reset for another night of activity. Importantly, the effects of sleep held when the researchers switched the mice's schedule, keeping them up and engaged with toys and other objects during the day.

In the second *Science* report, Richard Huganir and his colleagues at Johns Hopkins University School of Medicine, Baltimore, measured changes in the levels of certain brain proteins with sleep to offer biochemical evidence for this weakening of synapses. Their findings show that levels of protein receptors found on the receiving ends of synapses dropped by 20 percent while their mice slept.

The researchers also show that the protein Homer1a—important in regulating sleep and wakefulness—rises in synapses during a long snooze, playing a critical role in the resetting process. When the protein was lacking, brains didn't reset properly during sleep. This suggests that Homer1a responds to chemical cues in the brain that signal the need to sleep.

These studies add to prior work that suggests another function of sleep is to allow glial lymphatics in the brain to clear out proteins and other toxins that have deposited during the day. All of this goes to show that a good night's sleep really can bring clarity. So, the next time you're struggling to make a decision and someone tells you to "sleep on it"—that might be really good advice.

Chapter 3

Sleep Stages And Circadian Rhythms

Sleep Stages

There are two basic types of sleep; rapid eye movement (REM) sleep and non-REM sleep (which has three different stages). Each is linked to specific brain waves and neuronal activity. You cycle through all stages of non-REM and REM sleep several times during a typical night, with increasingly longer, deeper REM periods occurring toward morning.

- **Stage 1:** Non-REM sleep is the changeover from wakefulness to sleep. During this short period (lasting several minutes) of relatively light sleep, your heartbeat, breathing, and eye movements slow, and your muscles relax with occasional twitches. Your brain waves begin to slow from their daytime wakefulness patterns.

- **Stage 2:** Non-REM sleep is a period of light sleep before you enter deeper sleep. Your heartbeat and breathing slow, and muscles relax even further. Your body temperature drops and eye movements stop. Brain wave activity slows but is marked by brief bursts of electrical activity. You spend more of your repeated sleep cycles in stage 2 sleep than in other sleep stages.

- **Stage 3:** Non-REM sleep is the period of deep sleep that you need to feel refreshed in the morning. It occurs in longer periods during the first half of the night. Your heartbeat and breathing slow to their lowest levels during sleep. Your muscles are relaxed and it may be difficult to awaken you. Brain waves become even slower.

About This Chapter: Text under the heading "Sleep Stages" is excerpted from "Brain Basics: Understanding Sleep," National Institute of Neurological Disorders and Stroke (NINDS), May 19, 2017; Text under the heading "Circadian Rhythms" is excerpted from "Circadian Rhythms," National Institute of General Medical Sciences (NIGMS), November 9, 2017.

REM sleep first occurs about 90 minutes after falling asleep. Your eyes move rapidly from side to side behind closed eyelids. Mixed frequency brain wave activity becomes closer to that seen in wakefulness. Your breathing becomes faster and irregular, and your heart rate and blood pressure increase to near waking levels. Most of your dreaming occurs during REM sleep, although some can also occur in non-REM sleep. Your arm and leg muscles become temporarily paralyzed, which prevents you from acting out your dreams. As you age, you sleep less of your time in REM sleep. Memory consolidation most likely requires both non-REM and REM sleep.

> REM sleep stimulates regions of the brain that are used for learning. Studies have shown that when people are deprived of REM sleep, they are not able to remember what they were taught before going to sleep. Lack of REM sleep has also been linked to certain health conditions, including migraines.
>
> *(Source: "Sleep,"* Eunice Kennedy Shriver *National Institute of Child Health and Human Development (NICHD).)*

Circadian Rhythms

What Are Circadian Rhythms?

Circadian rhythms are physical, mental, and behavioral changes that follow a daily cycle. They respond primarily to light and darkness in an organism's environment. Sleeping at night and being awake during the day is an example of a light related circadian rhythm. Circadian rhythms are found in most living things, including animals, plants, and many tiny microbes. The study of circadian rhythms is called chronobiology.

What Are Biological Clocks?

Biological clocks are an organism's innate timing device. They're composed of specific molecules (proteins) that interact in cells throughout the body. Biological clocks are found in nearly every tissue and organ. Researchers have identified similar genes in people, fruit flies, mice, fungi, and several other organisms that are responsible for making the clock's components.

Are Biological Clocks The Same Thing As Circadian Rhythms?

No, but they are related. Biological clocks produce circadian rhythms and regulate their timing.

What Is The Master Clock?

A master clock in the brain coordinates all the biological clocks in a living thing, keeping the clocks in sync. In vertebrate animals, including humans, the master clock is a group of about 20,000 nerve cells (neurons) that form a structure called the suprachiasmatic nucleus, or the suprachiasmatic nucleus or nuclei (SCN). The SCN is located in a part of the brain called the hypothalamus and receives direct input from the eyes.

Does The Body Make And Keep Its Own Circadian Rhythms?

Natural factors within the body produce circadian rhythms. However, signals from the environment also affect them. The main cue influencing circadian rhythms is daylight. This light can turn on or turn off genes that control the molecular structure of biological clocks. Changing the light dark cycles can speed up, slow down, or reset biological clocks as well as circadian rhythms.

Do Circadian Rhythms Affect Body Function And Health?

Yes. Circadian rhythms can influence sleep-wake cycles, hormone release, eating habits and digestion, body temperature, and other important bodily functions. Biological clocks that run fast or slow can result in disrupted or abnormal circadian rhythms. Irregular rhythms have been linked to various chronic health conditions, such as sleep disorders, obesity, diabetes, depression, bipolar disorder, and seasonal affective disorder.

How Are Circadian Rhythms Related To Sleep?

Circadian rhythms help determine our sleep patterns. The body's master clock, or SCN, controls the production of melatonin, a hormone that makes you sleepy. It receives information about incoming light from the optic nerves, which relay information from the eyes to the brain. When there is less light—like at night—the SCN tells the brain to make more melatonin so you get drowsy. Researchers are studying how shift work as well as exposure to light from mobile devices during the night may alter circadian rhythms and sleep-wake cycles.

How Are Circadian Rhythms Related To Jet Lag?

People get jet lag when travel disrupts their circadian rhythms. When you pass through different time zones, your biological clocks will be different from the local time. For example, if you fly east from California to New York, you "lose" 3 hours. When you wake up at 7:00 a.m. on the east coast, your biological clocks are still running on west coast time, so you feel the way you might feel at 4:00 a.m. Your biological clocks will reset, but this often takes a few days.

Be aware that adjusting to a new time zone may take several days. If you are going to be away for just a few days, it may be better to stick to your original sleep and wake times as much as possible, rather than adjusting your biological clock too many times in rapid succession.

(Source: "Sleep," National Heart, Lung, and Blood Institute (NHLBI).)

Chapter 4

Napping

What Is Napping?

Most mammals are polyphasic sleepers, which mean they sleep or nap multiple times during a 24-hour period. Humans, on the other hand, are monophasic sleepers since they have distinct, alternate phases of sleeping and waking. Whether this forms the natural sleep pattern for humans has not been clearly established, however, napping is an integral part of many cultures, globally.

The United States is fast becoming a nation of deprived sleepers, due primarily to a culture that often promotes a hectic lifestyle. Napping could be a solution, since sleeping for 20–30 minutes during normal waking hours has been shown to result in remarkable improvements in mood, alertness, and performance.

Importance Of Sleep

Getting a good night's sleep is important for everyone. Good sleep refreshes people, helps them perform better, and contributes significantly to health and happiness.

(Source: "Sleep Researchers Home In On The Benefits Of Napping," U.S. Department of Veterans Affairs (VA).)

About This Chapter: "Napping," © 2016 Omnigraphics. Reviewed December 2017.

Types Of Napping

There are three different ways that we usually nap:

- **Planned napping:** Also known as preparatory napping, this involves taking a nap before you are sleepy in anticipation of going to bed late. This helps you avoid feeling tired because of inadequate sleep later on.

- **Emergency napping:** You may take an emergency nap when you feel tired and unable to continue the task you were engaged in. This type of napping is very useful when you have been driving and are feeling drowsy or when you need to counter fatigue when operating dangerous machinery.

- **Habitual napping:** This is the practice of taking naps as a regular routine at a particular time of the day. Young children nap this way, and it is not uncommon in many cultures for adults to a nap after lunch.

Recommendations For Napping

- A nap of 20–30 minutes is optimal. It tends not to interfere with your regular sleep pattern and generally doesn't make you groggy.

- Sleep in a comfortable place with moderate room temperature and without much noise or light filtering in. It is most beneficial to sleep rather than just lie in bed resting.

- Do not take a nap too late in the day, because it will affect your regular sleep at night. Do not nap early in the day, either, since you may not be able to sleep well.

Seven Steps To Have The Perfect Nap

Just lying down, closing your eyes and hoping for the best won't necessarily help you nap. You should think it out and employ a strategy to help you nap better. The following steps will help you get the perfect nap:

Step 1. Decide how long you want to nap. Different durations confer their own benefits.

- 6 minutes: Provides improvement in memory functions.

- 10–15 minutes: Improves focus and productivity.

- 20–30 minutes: Optimum nap time, which results in alertness, concentration, and sharp motor skills.

- 40–60 minutes: Boosts brain power, consolidates memory for facts, places and faces, and improves learning ability.

- 90–120 minutes: Improves creativity and emotional and procedural memory.

Step 2. Nap between 1 p.m. and 3 p.m. The body has an inherent biological clock that controls the sleep-wake cycle, known as the circadian rhythm. Humans experience intense sleep in two periods every 24 hours. One is between 1–3 p.m. and the other is from 2–4 a.m. Alertness, reaction time, coordination, and mood are decreased during these periods. The lethargy experienced after lunch is actually biological in nature. A nap around this time will put you back on track. Napping between 1–3 p.m. will generally not disturb regular sleep. If you work a night shift, the best time to take a nap would be 6–8 hours after waking.

Step 3. Create a conducive atmosphere. If you are unable to fall asleep during the day, you may not be approaching napping the right way. Lighting is an important factor, since light inhibits melatonin, the sleep regulation hormone. Darken your room with window shades or use an eye mask. Lie down, rather than sitting, when you take a nap. You will fall asleep 50 percent faster. Many people find that a hammock is the best place to nap because of the gentle swaying motion that promotes sleep.

Step 4. Use an alarm. You will need to wake up in time to get back to work after a snooze, so set an alarm to wake you up.

Step 5. Try a coffee nap. If you are concerned about becoming sleepy in the afternoon, try having a cup of coffee and taking a nap. Caffeine kicks into the body in 20–30 minutes. This should give you enough time to take a nap and get rejuvenated. Combining coffee and napping can be more beneficial than doing either of them alone.

Step 6. Avoid the blahs after napping. Make sure you avoid sleep inertia. If you take a long nap, you may feel groggy after waking up, because a full sleep cycle was not completed. Avoid this by having coffee, washing your face, or exposing yourself to bright light. An alternative is to complete a full sleep cycle by taking a nap for at least 90 minutes.

Step 7. Get adequate sleep at night. Nothing replaces a good night's sleep, and emergency napping cannot be a long-term substitute for regular, deep sleep. Inadequate sleep on a regular basis can result in hypertension, diabetes, weight gain, depression, and a general feeling of unease.

Pros Of Napping

- Napping improves alertness and performance levels. It reduces mistakes and accidents. A National Aeronautics and Space Administration (NASA) study conducted on military pilots showed that 40 minutes of napping increased alertness by 100 percent and performance by 34 percent.

- Naps improve alertness for some duration after the nap and often increase alertness to some extent over the entire day.

- Napping results in relaxation and rejuvenation. It is a luxurious and pleasant experience, something similar to a mini vacation.

- Taking a nap when you are feeling drowsy behind the wheel can help you regain alertness so that you can continue to drive safely.

- Night-shift workers who nap have been shown to experience improved alertness on the job.

- A 45-minute daytime nap improves memory functioning.

- Napping reduces blood pressure.

- It reduces the risk of cardiovascular diseases.

- Temporary sleep issues due to jet lag, stress, or illnesses can often be remedied by napping.

- A quick nap is very good for mental and physical stamina.

- Napping improves mental acuity and overall health.

Cons Of Napping

- The stigma associated with napping is probably the biggest downside of napping.

  - It may be equated with laziness.

  - It is often associated with lack of ambition and low standards.

  - Napping may be seen as normal only for children, the sick, and the elderly.

When To Avoid

Don't take naps after 3 p.m. Naps can help make up for lost sleep, but late afternoon naps can make it harder to fall asleep at night.

(Source: "Tips For Getting A Good Night's Sleep," MedlinePlus, National Institutes of Health (NIH).)

- Napping can be counterproductive for people with sleep disorders or those with irregular sleep patterns.

- Naps are often not recommended for people with sleep apnea.

References

1. "Napping," National Sleep Foundation, n.d.

2. Belsky, Gail. "The Pros And Cons Of Napping," Health, n.d.

3. Brown, Brendan. "A How-To Guide To The Perfect Nap [Infographic]," Art of Well-being, February 16, 2016.

Chapter 5

Dreaming And REM Sleep

Dreaming

Everyone dreams. You spend about 2 hours each night dreaming but may not remember most of your dreams. Its exact purpose isn't known, but dreaming may help you process your emotions. Events from the day often invade your thoughts during sleep, and people suffering from stress or anxiety are more likely to have frightening dreams. Dreams can be experienced in all stages of sleep but usually are most vivid in rapid eye movement (REM) sleep. Some people dream in color, while others only recall dreams in black and white.

> It has long been believed that the stage of sleep called rapid eye movement (REM) owns our dreaming process. However, recent evidence suggests that dreams also occur during non-REM (NREM) sleep and at every stage of NREM, though not as often as in REM.
>
> *(Source: "Mapping The Brain During Sleep Yields New Insights On Dreaming And Consciousness," National Center for Complementary and Integrative Health (NCCIH).)*

What Is REM Sleep?

The brain cycles through five distinct phases during sleep: stages and rapid eye movement (REM) sleep. REM sleep makes up about 25 percent of your sleep cycle and first occurs about

About This Chapter: Text under the heading "Dreaming" is excerpted from "Brain Basics: Understanding Sleep," National Institute of Neurological Disorders and Stroke (NINDS), May 19, 2017; Text under the heading "What Is REM Sleep?" is excerpted from "What Is REM Sleep?" *Eunice Kennedy Shriver* National Institute of Child Health and Human Development (NICHD), December 5, 2012. Reviewed December 2017.

70–90 minutes after you fall asleep. Because your sleep cycle repeats, you enter REM sleep several times during the night.

During REM sleep, your brain and body are energized and dreaming occurs. REM is thought to be involved in the process of storing memories, learning, and balancing your mood, although the exact mechanisms are not well understood.

REM sleep begins in response to signals sent to and from different regions of the brain. Signals are sent to the brain's cerebral cortex, which is responsible for learning, thinking, and organizing information. Signals are also sent to the spinal cord to shut off movement, creating a temporary inability to move the muscles ("paralysis") in the arms and legs. Abnormal disruption of this temporary paralysis can cause people to move while they are dreaming. For example, this type of movement while dreaming can lead to injuries that could happen when a person runs into furniture while dreaming of catching a ball.

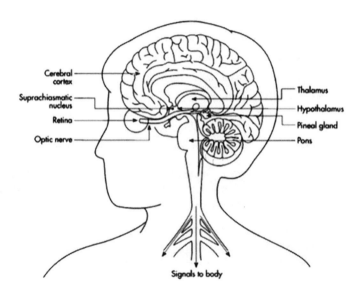

Figure 5.1. How REM Sleep Begins

(Source: "Brain Basics: Understanding Sleep," National Institute of Neurological Disorders and Stroke (NINDS).)

REM sleep stimulates regions of the brain that are used for learning. Studies have shown that when people are deprived of REM sleep, they are not able to remember what they were taught before going to sleep. Lack of REM sleep has also been linked to certain health conditions, including migraines.

The reason for dreaming during REM sleep is not understood. While some of the signals sent to the cortex during sleep are important for learning and memory, some signals seem to be random. It is these random signals that may form the basis for a "story" that the brain's cortex tries to interpret or find meaning in, resulting in dreaming.

Definition

One of the five stages of sleep. During REM sleep, the eyes move rapidly while closed and dreams occur. REM sleep is the lightest stage of sleep, during which a person may wake easily. During several hours of normal sleep, a person will go through several sleep cycles that include REM sleep and the 4 stages of non-REM (light to deep sleep). Also called rapid eye movement sleep.

(Source: "NCI Dictionary Of Cancer Terms," National Cancer Institute (NCI).)

Chapter 6

Sleep And Memory

When you learn something new, the best way to remember it is to sleep on it. That's because sleeping helps strengthen memories you've formed throughout the day. It also helps to link new memories to earlier ones. You might even come up with creative new ideas while you slumber.

Effects Of Sleep On Memory

What happens to memories in your brain while you sleep? And how does lack of sleep affect your ability to learn and remember? National Institutes of Health (NIH)-funded scientists have been gathering clues about the complex relationship between sleep and memory. Their findings might eventually lead to new approaches to help students learn or help older people hold onto memories as they age.

"We've learned that sleep before learning helps prepare your brain for initial formation of memories," says Dr. Matthew Walker, a sleep scientist at the University of California, Berkeley. "And then, sleep after learning is essential to help save and cement that new information into the architecture of the brain, meaning that you're less likely to forget it."

While you snooze, your brain cycles through different phases of sleep, including light sleep, deep sleep, and rapid eye movement (REM) sleep, when dreaming often occurs. The cycles repeat about every 90 minutes.

About This Chapter: This chapter includes text excerpted from "Sleep On It—How Snoozing Strengthens Memories," *NIH News in Health*, National Institutes of Health (NIH). April 2013. Reviewed December 2017.

> ## Deep Sleep
> Slow-wave sleep is often referred to as "deep sleep," and consists of stages 3 and 4 of non-REM sleep.
>
> *(Source: "The Connection Between Memory And Sleep," National Science Foundation (NSF).)*

The non-REM stages of sleep seem to prime the brain for learning the next day. If you haven't slept, your ability to learn new things could drop by up to 40 percent. "You can't pull an all-nighter and still learn effectively," Walker says. Lack of sleep affects a part of the brain called the hippocampus, which is key for making new memories.

You accumulate many memories, moment by moment, while you're awake. Most will be forgotten during the day. "When we first form memories, they're in a very raw and fragile form," says sleep expert Dr. Robert Stickgold of Harvard Medical School (HMS). But when you doze off, "sleep seems to be a privileged time when the brain goes back through recent memories and decides both what to keep and what not to keep," Stickgold explains. "During a night of sleep, some memories are strengthened." Research has shown that memories of certain procedures, like playing a melody on a piano, can actually improve while you sleep.

Memories seem to become more stable in the brain during the deep stages of sleep. After that, REM—the most active stage of sleep—seems to play a role in linking together related memories, sometimes in unexpected ways. That's why a full night of sleep may help with problem-solving. REM sleep also helps you process emotional memories, which can reduce the intensity of emotions.

It's well known that sleep patterns tend to change as we age. Unfortunately, the deep memory-strengthening stages of sleep start to decline in our late 30s. A study by Walker and colleagues found that adults older than 60 had a 70 percent loss of deep sleep compared to young adults ages 18–25. Older adults had a harder time remembering things the next day, and memory impairment was linked to reductions in deep sleep. The researchers are now exploring options for enhancing deep stages of sleep in this older age group.

"While we have limited medical treatments for memory impairment in aging, sleep actually is a potentially treatable target," Walker says. "By restoring sleep, it might be possible to improve memory in older people."

For younger people, especially students, Stickgold offers additional advice. "Realize that the sleep you get the night after you study is at least as important as the sleep you get the night before you study." When it comes to sleep and memory, he says, "you get very little benefit from cutting corners."

> "Sleep services all aspects of our body in one way or another: molecular, energy balance, as well as intellectual function, alertness and mood," says Dr. Merrill Mitler, a sleep expert and neuroscientist at NIH.
>
> *(Source: "The Connection Between Memory And Sleep," NIH News in Health, National Institutes of Health (NIH).)*

Sleeping To Learn

Research suggests these tips may aid students and other learners:

- Get a good night's sleep before learning. Lack of sleep can cut learning ability by up to 40 percent.

- Get a full night of sleep within 24 hours after learning to strengthen new memories and build connections between different pieces of information.

- Get enough sleep each night—7 to 8 hours for most adults. Memories won't be strengthened with 4 hours or less of nighttime sleep.

- Naps might help or hinder. A 90-minute nap can strengthen memories, but naps late in the day may make it harder to get to sleep at night.

Chapter 7

Sleep And Physical Health

Importance Of Sleep

Sleep plays a vital role in good health and well-being throughout your life. Getting enough quality sleep at the right times can help protect your mental health, physical health, quality of life, and safety.

The way you feel while you're awake depends in part on what happens while you're sleeping. During sleep, your body is working to support healthy brain function and maintain your physical health. In children and teens, sleep also helps support growth and development.

The damage from sleep deficiency can occur in an instant (such as a car crash), or it can harm you over time. For example, ongoing sleep deficiency can raise your risk for some chronic health problems. It also can affect how well you think, react, work, learn, and get along with others.

> Regular physical activity can help keep your thinking, learning, and judgment skills sharp as you age. It can also reduce your risk of depression and may help you sleep better.
>
> *(Source: "Physical Activity And Health," Centers for Disease Control and Prevention (CDC).)*

Effects Of Sleep On Physical Health

Sleep plays an important role in your physical health. For example, sleep is involved in healing and repair of your heart and blood vessels. Ongoing sleep deficiency is linked to an increased risk of heart disease, kidney disease, high blood pressure, diabetes, and stroke.

About This Chapter: This chapter includes text excerpted from "Explore Sleep Deprivation And Deficiency— Why Is Sleep Important?" National Heart, Lung, and Blood Institute (NHLBI), June 7, 2017.

Sleep deficiency also increases the risk of obesity. For example, one study of teenagers showed that with each hour of sleep lost, the odds of becoming obese went up. Sleep deficiency increases the risk of obesity in other age groups as well.

> Not getting enough sleep is linked with many chronic diseases and conditions—such as diabetes, heart disease, obesity, and depression—that threaten our nation's health. Not getting enough sleep can lead to motor vehicle crashes and mistakes at work, which cause a lot of injury and disability each year.
>
> *(Source: "Sleep And Sleep Disorders," Centers for Disease Control and Prevention (CDC).)*

Sleep helps maintain a healthy balance of the hormones that make you feel hungry (ghrelin) or full (leptin). When you don't get enough sleep, your level of ghrelin goes up and your level of leptin goes down. This makes you feel hungrier than when you're well-rested.

Sleep also affects how your body reacts to insulin, the hormone that controls your blood glucose (sugar) level. Sleep deficiency results in a higher than normal blood sugar level, which may increase your risk for diabetes.

> ## What Is Insulin?
>
> Insulin is a hormone made in the pancreas, an organ located behind the stomach. The pancreas contains clusters of cells called islets. Beta cells within the islets make insulin and release it into the blood. Insulin plays a major role in metabolism—the way the body uses digested food for energy.
>
> *(Source: "Prediabetes And Insulin Resistance," National Institute of Diabetes and Digestive and Kidney Diseases (NIDDK).)*

Sleep also supports healthy growth and development. Deep sleep triggers the body to release the hormone that promotes normal growth in children and teens. This hormone also boosts muscle mass and helps repair cells and tissues in children, teens, and adults. Sleep also plays a role in puberty and fertility.

Your immune system relies on sleep to stay healthy. This system defends your body against foreign or harmful substances. Ongoing sleep deficiency can change the way in which your immune system responds. For example, if you're sleep deficient, you may have trouble fighting common infections.

Scientific evidence is building that sleep has powerful effects on immune functioning. Studies show that sleep loss can affect different parts of the immune system, which can lead to the development of a wide variety of disorders. Sleep loss is also related to a higher risk for infection.

(Source: "Sleep And The Immune System," National Institute for Occupational Safety and Health (NIOSH), Centers for Disease Control and Prevention (CDC).)

Part Two
Sleep Habits

Chapter 8

How Much Sleep Do You Need?

People will often cut back on their sleep for work, for family demands, or even to watch a good show on television. But if not getting enough sleep is a regular part of your routine, you may be at an increased risk for obesity, diabetes, high blood pressure, coronary heart disease and stroke, poor mental health, and even early death. Even one night of short sleep can affect you the next day. Not surprisingly, you're more likely to feel sleepy. On top of that, you're more likely to be in a bad mood, be less productive at work, and to be involved in a motor vehicle crash.

Teen Sleep Habits

Almost 70 percent of high school students are not getting the recommended hours of sleep on school nights, according to a study by the Centers for Disease Control and Prevention (CDC). Researchers found insufficient sleep (<8 hours on an average school night) to be associated with a number of unhealthy activities, such as:

- Drinking soda or pop 1 or more times per day (not including diet soda or diet pop)
- Not participating in 60 minutes of physical activity on 5 or more of the past 7 days
- Using computers 3 or more hours each day
- Being in a physical fight 1 or more times
- Cigarette use
- Alcohol use

About This Chapter: Text in this chapter begins with excerpts from "Are You Getting Enough Sleep?" Centers for Disease Control and Prevention (CDC), April 24, 2017; Text beginning with the heading "How Much Sleep Do I Need?" is excerpted from "How Much Sleep Is Enough?" National Heart, Lung, and Blood Institute (NHLBI), June 7, 2017.

- Marijuana use
- Current sexual activity
- Feeling sad or hopeless
- Seriously considering attempting suicide

Adolescents not getting sufficient sleep each night may be due to changes in the sleep/wake-cycle as well as everyday activities, such as employment, recreational activities, academic pressures, early school start times, and access to technology.

(Source: "Teen Sleep Habits—What Should You Do?" Centers for Disease Control and Prevention (CDC).)

How Much Sleep Do I Need?

The amount of sleep you need each day will change over the course of your life. Although sleep needs vary from person to person, the table below shows general recommendations for different age groups. Table 8.1 reflects recent American Academy of Sleep Medicine (AASM) recommendations that the American Academy of Pediatrics (AAP) has endorsed.

Table 8.1. Recommended Amount Of Sleep

Age	Recommended Amount Of Sleep
Infants aged 4–12 months	12–16 hours a day (including naps)
Children aged 1–2 years	11–14 hours a day (including naps)
Children aged 3–5 years	10–13 hours a day (including naps)
Children aged 6–12 years	9–12 hours a day
Teens aged 13–18 years	8–10 hours a day

If you routinely lose sleep or choose to sleep less than needed, the sleep loss adds up. The total sleep lost is called your sleep debt. For example, if you lose 2 hours of sleep each night, you'll have a sleep debt of 14 hours after a week.

Is Napping Helpful?

Some people nap as a way to deal with sleepiness. Naps may provide a short-term boost in alertness and performance. However, napping doesn't provide all of the other benefits of nighttime sleep. Thus, you can't really make up for lost sleep. Some people sleep more on their days off than on work days. They also may go to bed later and get up later on days off. Sleeping more on days off might be a sign that you aren't getting enough sleep. Although extra sleep on days off might help you feel better, it can upset your body's sleep-wake rhythm.

What About Sleep Quality?

Getting enough sleep is important, but good sleep quality is also essential. Signs of poor sleep quality include feeling sleepy or tired even after getting enough sleep, repeatedly waking up during the night, and having symptoms of sleep disorders (such as snoring or gasping for air). Better sleep habits may improve the quality of your sleep. If you have symptoms of a sleep disorder, such as snoring or being very sleepy during the day after a full night's sleep, make sure to tell your doctor.

(Source: "Are You Getting Enough Sleep?" Centers for Disease Control and Prevention (CDC).)

How Can A Sleep Diary Be Of Help To Me?

Bad sleep habits and long-term sleep loss will affect your health. If you're worried about whether you're getting enough sleep, try using a sleep diary for a couple of weeks.

Write down how much you sleep each night, how alert and rested you feel in the morning, and how sleepy you feel during the day. Show the results to your doctor and talk about how you can improve your sleep.

What Is A Sleep Diary?

A sleep diary is designed to gather information about your daily sleep pattern. It is necessary for you to complete your sleep diary every day. If possible, the sleep diary should be completed within one hour of getting out of bed in the morning.

(Source: "Sleep Diary Instructions," U.S. Department of Veterans Affairs (VA).)

How Can Sleep Deficiency Affect Us?

Sleeping when your body is ready to sleep also is very important. Sleep deficiency can affect people even when they sleep the total number of hours recommended for their age group.

For example, people whose sleep is out of sync with their body clocks (such as shift workers) or routinely interrupted (such as caregivers or emergency responders) might need to pay special attention to their sleep needs.

If your job or daily routine limits your ability to get enough sleep or sleep at the right times, talk with your doctor. You also should talk with your doctor if you sleep more than 8 hours a night, but don't feel well rested. You may have a sleep disorder or other health problem.

Chapter 9

The Benefits Of Slumber

We have so many demands on our time—jobs, family, errands—not to mention finding some time to relax. To fit everything in, we often sacrifice sleep. But sleep affects both mental and physical health. It's vital to your well-being.

Of course, sleep helps you feel rested each day. But while you're sleeping, your brain and body don't just shut down. Internal organs and processes are hard at work throughout the night.

"Sleep services all aspects of our body in one way or another: molecular, energy balance, as well as intellectual function, alertness and mood," says Dr. Merrill Mitler, a sleep expert and neuroscientist at National Institutes of Health (NIH).

When you're tired, you can't function at your best. Sleep helps you think more clearly, have quicker reflexes and focus better. "The fact is, when we look at well-rested people, they're operating at a different level than people trying to get by on one or two hours less nightly sleep," says Mitler.

"Loss of sleep impairs your higher levels of reasoning, problem-solving, and attention to detail," Mitler explains. Tired people tend to be less productive at work. They're at a much higher risk for traffic accidents. Lack of sleep also influences your mood, which can affect how you interact with others. A sleep deficit over time can even put you at greater risk for developing depression.

About This Chapter: This chapter includes text excerpted from "The Benefits Of Slumber" *NIH News in Health*, National Institutes of Health (NIH), April 2013. Reviewed December 2017.

But sleep isn't just essential for the brain. "Sleep affects almost every tissue in our bodies," says Dr. Michael Twery, a sleep expert at NIH. "It affects growth and stress hormones, our immune system, appetite, breathing, blood pressure, and cardiovascular health."

Research shows that lack of sleep increases the risk for obesity, heart disease, and infections. Throughout the night, your heart rate, breathing rate, and blood pressure rise and fall, a process that may be important for cardiovascular health. Your body releases hormones during sleep that help repair cells and control the body's use of energy. These hormone changes can affect your body weight.

"Ongoing research shows a lack of sleep can produce diabetic-like conditions in otherwise healthy people," says Mitler.

Recent studies also reveal that sleep can affect the efficiency of vaccinations. Twery described research showing that well-rested people who received the flu vaccine developed stronger protection against the illness.

Why You Need A Good Night's Sleep

A good night's sleep consists of four to five sleep cycles. Each cycle includes periods of deep sleep and rapid eye movement (REM) sleep, when we dream. "As the night goes on, the portion of that cycle that is in REM sleep increases. It turns out that this pattern of cycling and progression is critical to the biology of sleep," Twery says.

Although personal needs vary, on average, adults need seven to eight hours of sleep per night. Babies typically sleep about 16 hours a day. Young children need at least 10 hours of sleep, while teenagers need at least 9 hours. To attain the maximum restorative benefits of sleep, getting a full night of quality sleep is important, says Twery.

Sleep can be disrupted by many things. Stimulants such as caffeine or certain medications can keep you up. Distractions such as electronics—especially the light from TVs, cell phones, tablets, and e-readers—can prevent you from falling asleep.

As people get older, they may not get enough sleep because of illness, medications or sleep disorders. By some estimates, about 70 million Americans of all ages suffer from chronic sleep problems. The 2 most common sleep disorders are insomnia and sleep apnea.

People with insomnia have trouble falling or staying asleep. Anxiety about falling asleep often makes the condition worse. Most of us have occasional insomnia. But chronic insomnia—lasting at least 3 nights per week for more than a month—can trigger serious daytime problems such as exhaustion, irritability, and difficulty concentrating.

Common therapies include relaxation and deep-breathing techniques. Sometimes medicine is prescribed. But consult a doctor before trying even over-the-counter (OTC) sleep pills, as they may leave you feeling unrefreshed in the morning.

People with sleep apnea have a loud, uneven snore (although not everyone who snores has apnea). Breathing repeatedly stops or becomes shallow. If you have apnea, you're not getting enough oxygen, and your brain disturbs your sleep to open your windpipe.

Apnea is dangerous. "There's little air exchange for 10 seconds or more at a time," explains Dr. Phyllis Zee, a sleep apnea expert at Northwestern University. "The oxygen goes down and the body's fight or flight response is activated. Blood pressure spikes, your heart rate fluctuates and the brain wakes you up partially to start your breathing again. This creates stress."

Apnea can leave you feeling tired and moody. You may have trouble thinking clearly. "Also, apnea affects the vessels that lead to the brain so there is a higher risk of stroke associated with it," Zee adds.

If you have mild sleep apnea, you might try sleeping on your side, exercising or losing weight to reduce symptoms. A continuous positive airway pressure (CPAP) machine, which pumps air into your throat to keep your airway open, can also help. Another treatment is a bite plate that moves the lower jaw forward. In some cases, however, people with sleep apnea need surgery.

"If you snore chronically and wake up choking or gasping for air, and feel that you're sleepy during the day, tell your doctor and get evaluated," Zee advises.

NIH is currently funding several studies to gain deeper insights into sleep apnea and other aspects of sleep. One five-year study of 10,000 pregnant women is designed to gauge the effects of apnea on the mother's and baby's health. Zee says this study will shed more light on apnea and the importance of treatment.

Good sleep is critical to your health. To make each day a safe, productive one, take steps to make sure you regularly get a good night's sleep.

Chapter 10

Bedding And Sleep Environment

Although sleep is vital to emotional and physical health, millions of people do not get the recommended 8 hours of sleep per night. Some have chronic, long-term sleep disorders, while others experience occasional trouble sleeping. Sleep deprivation can lead to daytime drowsiness, poor concentration, stress, irritability, and a weakened immune system.

Among the many factors that can impact the amount and quality of sleep, bedding and the sleep environment are perhaps the easiest to control or change. Choosing a high-quality mattress, selecting the right pillow, and creating a comfortable, inviting sleep sanctuary can help people improve their sleep as well as their overall quality of life.

Environmental factors—such as light, noise, temperature, color, accessories, and bedding—play an important role in the sleep experience. Choosing comfortable bedding, making sure the bedroom temperature is neither too hot nor too cold, and eliminating sources of distracting noise or light can make a big difference in helping people get a good night's sleep. The goal is to turn the bedroom into a soothing, relaxing, indulgent escape from the everyday pressures and hassles of life. Inviting colors and attractive accessories are available from many sources to fit any space or budget.

Have A Good Sleeping Environment

Get rid of anything in your bedroom that might distract you from sleep, such as noises, bright lights, an uncomfortable bed, or a TV or computer in the bedroom. Also, keeping the temperature in your bedroom on the cool side can help you sleep better.

(Source: "Your Guide To Healthy Sleep," National Heart, Lung, and Blood Institute (NHLBI).)

About This Chapter: "Bedding And Sleep Environment," © 2016 Omnigraphics. Reviewed December 2017.

Choosing A Mattress

The centerpiece of any bedroom, and the most important aspect of ensuring a comfortable, high-quality night's sleep, is the mattress. Mattresses generally have a lifespan of 5–7 years, depending on usage, before the comfort and support they offer begins to decline. At this point, experts recommend evaluating the mattress and comparing it to newer models. A mattress is likely to need replacing if it shows signs of wear, such as sagging, lumps, or exposed springs. A new mattress may also be warranted if users tend to sleep better elsewhere or frequently wake up with numbness, stiffness, or pain. Research has shown that 70 percent of people report significant improvements in sleep comfort, 62 percent report improvements in sleep quality, and more than 50 percent report reductions in back pain and spine stiffness when sleeping on a new mattress rather than one that is five years old.

The search for a new mattress begins at a reputable mattress store with educated salespeople who can explain the various options and guide customers through the purchasing process. Since quality mattresses are major expenditures, it is important for customers to test different types and models to find the one that best meets their personal needs. Testing a mattress involves lying down for several minutes in various sleep positions while concentrating on the feel of each surface.

The main qualities to look for in a new mattress include comfort, support, durability, and size. Many types of cushioning materials are available to create a soft, plush feel. Beneath the surface, the mattress and foundation should provide gentle support that keeps the spine in alignment. The quality of materials and construction determine the durability of the mattress. The main mattress sizes, from smallest to largest, are:

- twin (38" x 75")
- full or double (53" x 75")
- queen (60" x 80")
- California king (72" x 84")
- king (76" x 80")

Since twin- and full-sized mattresses are only 75" long, they may be too short to accommodate taller adults. If two people will be sharing a bed, experts recommend buying a queen-sized or larger mattress. King-sized mattresses provide maximum sleeping space. Since an average person shifts position 40–60 times per night, many people feel that a larger mattress provides them with greater freedom to move around comfortably.

There are many different types of mattresses to choose from, including:

- Innerspring, which features tempered steel coils for support beneath layers of insulation and cushioning for comfort;

- Foam, which can be made of solid foam or layers of different kinds of foam, including visco-elastic "memory" foam that molds to individual sleepers;

- Airbeds, which feature an air-filled core rather than springs for support and are usually adjustable to fit sleepers' preferences;

- Waterbeds, which feature a water-filled core for support beneath layers of upholstery for comfort and insulation;

- Adjustable beds, which feature an electric motor to allow sleepers to change the position of the head and foot of the bed to increase comfort; and

- Futons, which offer a space-saving alternative by converting into a sofa during the day.

Caring For A Mattress

After purchasing a new mattress, proper care is key to getting the most out of the investment. The first step is to ensure that the mattress and foundation are properly installed. If they have a slight "new product" odor, proper ventilation should solve the problem within a few hours. Although it is not illegal to remove the tag, it is best to leave it attached to the mattress in case it is required for a warranty claim.

Sleep sets retain their comfort and support longer if they are placed on a sturdy, high-quality bed frame. Boards should never be placed beneath the mattress to increase support. Instead, the mattress should be replaced when it reaches that stage. To keep the mattress fresh and prevent stains, it is important to use a washable mattress pad. If the mattress should require cleaning, the recommended methods are vacuuming or spot cleaning with mild soap and cold water. Mattresses should never be dry cleaned, which can damage the material, or soaked with water.

Basic mattress care involves not allowing children to jump on the bed, which can damage its interior construction. In addition, periodically rotating the mattress from top to bottom and end to end will help extend its useful life. For other issues, it is best to follow the manufacturer's guidelines.

Choosing A Pillow

Pillows, like mattresses, need to be replaced periodically to ensure that they provide adequate support and comfort. The useful life of a pillow depends on its quality and the amount of use it receives. Most pillows should be replaced on an annual basis. A pillow generally must be replaced when it becomes lumpy or shows signs of dirt, stains, or wear and tear. An easy test to see whether a pillow has lost its capacity to support the head involves folding it in half and squeezing the air out. If it springs back to its original shape quickly, it still retains its support. If not, it may be time to buy a new pillow.

Ideally, a pillow should support the head in the same position as if the person were standing with an upright posture. Different amounts of cushioning are available for different sleeping positions. People who sleep on their side may want a firm pillow, while people who sleep on their back may want a somewhat softer pillow. A wide variety of pillows are available to fit any budget. Some of the different types of pillows include feather, down, memory foam, microbead, neck, lumbar, body, and wedge. Special pillows are also available for people who are pregnant or have sleep apnea.

References

1. "The Better Sleep Guide," Better Sleep Council, n.d.
2. "Pillows," Better Sleep Council, n.d.

Chapter 11

What To Do If You Can't Sleep

It's important to practice good sleep hygiene, but if your sleep problems persist or if they interfere with how you feel or function during the day, you should seek evaluation and treatment by a physician, preferably one familiar with assessing and treating sleep disorders. Before visiting your physician, keep a diary of your sleep habits for about ten days to discuss at the visit.

Include the following in your sleep diary, when you:

- Go to bed.

- Go to sleep.

- Wake up.

- Get out of bed.

- Take naps.

- Exercise.

- Consume alcohol.

- Consume caffeinated beverages.

About This Chapter: Text in this chapter begins with excerpts from "Sleep And Sleep Disorders—What Should I Do If I Can't Sleep," Centers for Disease Control and Prevention (CDC), July 1, 2013. Reviewed December 2017; Text under the heading "Take Action!" is excerpted from "Get Enough Sleep," Office of Disease Prevention and Health Promotion (ODPHP), U.S. Department of Health and Human Services (HHS), October 26, 2017.

Take Action!

Making small changes to your daily routine can help you get the sleep you need.

Change what you do during the day.

- Try to spend some time outdoors every day.

- Plan your physical activity for earlier in the day, not right before you go to bed.

- Stay away from caffeine (including coffee, tea, and soda) late in the day.

- If you have trouble sleeping at night, limit daytime naps to 20 minutes or less.

- If you drink alcohol, drink only in moderation. This means no more than 1 drink a day for women and no more than 2 drinks a day for men. Alcohol can keep you from sleeping well.

- Don't eat a big meal close to bedtime.

- Quit smoking. The nicotine in cigarettes can make it harder for you to sleep.

Create a good sleep environment.

- Make sure your bedroom is dark. If there are streetlights near your window, try putting up light-blocking curtains.

- Keep your bedroom quiet.

- Consider keeping electronic devices—like TVs, computers, and smartphones—out of the bedroom.

Set a bedtime routine.

- Go to bed at the same time every night.

- Get the same amount of sleep each night.

- Avoid eating, talking on the phone, or reading in bed.

- Avoid using computers or smart phones, watching TV, or playing video games at bedtime.

If you are still awake after staying in bed for more than 20 minutes, get up. Do something relaxing, like reading or meditating, until you feel sleepy.

Seek Doctor's Help

See a doctor if you continue to have trouble sleeping. If you consistently find yourself feeling tired or not well rested during the day despite spending enough time in bed at night, you may have a sleep disorder. Your family doctor or a sleep specialist should be able to help you.

(Source: "Your Guide To Healthy Sleep," National Heart, Lung, and Blood Institute (NHLBI).)

Chapter 12

Caffeine: What You Should Know

What Is Caffeine?[1]

Caffeine is a bitter substance that occurs naturally in more than 60 plants including:

- Coffee beans

- Tea leaves

- Kola nuts, which are used to flavor soft drink colas

- Cacao pods, which are used to make chocolate products

There is also synthetic (man-made) caffeine, which is added to some medicines, foods, and drinks. For example, some pain relievers, cold medicines, and over-the-counter (OTC) medicines for alertness contain synthetic caffeine. So do energy drinks and "energy-boosting" gums and snacks.

Most people consume caffeine from drinks. The amount of caffeine in different drinks can vary a lot, but it is generally:

- An 8-ounce cup of coffee: 95–200 mg

- A 12-ounce can of cola: 35–45 mg

About This Chapter: This chapter includes text excerpted from documents published by three public domain sources. Text under headings marked 1 are excerpted from "Caffeine," MedlinePlus, National Institutes of Health (NIH), April 2, 2015; Text under heading marked 2 is excerpted from "Information About Lifestyle Practices That Can Affect Your Sleep," U.S. Department of Veterans Affairs (VA), May 8, 2017; Text under heading marked 3 is excerpted from "Caffeine And Kids: FDA Takes A Closer Look," U.S. Food and Drug Administration (FDA), November 29, 2017.

- An 8-ounce energy drink: 70–100 mg

- An 8-ounce cup of tea: 14–60 mg

How Caffeine Affects Sleep[2]

• Caffeine is a stimulant that interferes with the natural sleep cycle.

• Do not drink or eat products with caffeine after lunch.

• Some medications contain caffeine or other stimulants so check labels and talk with

your healthcare provider and pharmacist.

What Are Caffeine's Effects On The Body?[1]

Caffeine has many effects on your body's metabolism. It:

- Stimulates your central nervous system, which can make you feel more awake and give you a boost of energy

- Is a diuretic, meaning that it helps your body get rid of extra salt and water by urinating more

- Increases the release of acid in your stomach, sometimes leading to an upset stomach or heartburn

- May interfere with the absorption of calcium in the body

- Increases your blood pressure

Within one hour of eating or drinking caffeine, it reaches its peak level in your blood. You may continue to feel the effects of caffeine for 4–6 hours.

Caffeine: Breaking Down The Buzz

Caffeine has a perk-up effect because it blocks a brain chemical, adenosine, which causes sleepiness. On its own, moderate amounts of caffeine rarely cause harmful long-term health effects, although it is definitely possible to take too much caffeine and get sick as a result.

Consuming too much caffeine can make you feel jittery or jumpy—your heart may race and your palms may sweat, kind of like a panic attack. It may also interfere with your sleep, which is especially important while your brain is still developing.

(Source: "The Buzz On Caffeine," National Institute on Drug Abuse (NIDA) for Teens.)

What Are The Side Effects From Too Much Caffeine?[1]

For most people, it is not harmful to consume up to 400 mg of caffeine a day. If you do eat or drink too much caffeine, it can cause health problems, such as:

- Restlessness and shakiness

- Insomnia

- Headaches

- Dizziness

- Rapid or abnormal heart rhythm

- Dehydration

- Anxiety

- Dependency, so you need to take more of it to get the same results

Some people are more sensitive to the effects of caffeine than others.

What Are Energy Drinks, And Why Can They Be A Problem?[1]

Energy drinks are beverages that have added caffeine. The amount of caffeine in energy drinks can vary widely, and sometimes the labels on the drinks do not give you the actual amount of caffeine in them. Energy drinks may also contain sugars, vitamins, herbs, and supplements.

Companies that make energy drinks claim that the drinks can increase alertness and improve physical and mental performance. This has helped make the drinks popular with American teens and young adults. There's limited data showing that energy drinks might temporarily improve alertness and physical endurance. There is not enough evidence to show that they enhance strength or power. But what we do know is that energy drinks can be dangerous because they have large amounts of caffeine. And since they have lots of sugar, they can contribute to weight gain and worsen diabetes.

Sometimes young people mix their energy drinks with alcohol. It is dangerous to combine alcohol and caffeine. Caffeine can interfere with your ability to recognize how drunk you are, which can lead you to drink more. This also makes you more likely to make bad decisions.

Who Should Avoid Or Limit Caffeine?[1]

You should check with your healthcare provider about whether you should limit or avoid caffeine if you:

- Are a child or teen. Neither should have as much caffeine as adults. Children can be especially sensitive to the effects of caffeine.

- Are pregnant, since caffeine passes through the placenta to your baby.

- Are breastfeeding, since a small amount of caffeine that you consume is passed along to your baby.

- Have sleep disorders, including insomnia.

- Have migraines or other chronic headaches.

- Have anxiety.

- Have gastroesophageal reflux disease (GERD) or ulcers.

- Have fast or irregular heart rhythms.

- Have high blood pressure.

- Take certain medicines or supplements, including stimulants, certain antibiotics, asthma medicines, and heart medicines. Check with your healthcare provider about whether there might be interactions between caffeine and any medicines and supplements that you take.

What Is Caffeine Withdrawal?[1]

If you have been consuming caffeine on a regular basis and then suddenly stop, you may have caffeine withdrawal. Symptoms can include:

- Headaches

- Drowsiness

- Irritability

- Nausea

- Difficulty concentrating

These symptoms usually go away after a couple of days.

What's The Safe Amount Of Daily Caffeine?[3]

For healthy adults, the U.S. Food and Drug Administration (FDA) has cited 400 milligrams a day—that's about four or five cups of coffee—as an amount not generally associated with dangerous, negative effects. FDA has not set a level for children; however, the American Academy of Pediatrics (AAP) discourages the consumption of caffeine and other stimulants by children and adolescents.

Chapter 13

Caffeine And Nicotine And Their Impact Upon Sleep

Caffeine has been called the most popular drug in the world. Millions of people consume it on a daily basis in the form of coffee, tea, soft drinks, energy drinks, chocolate, or certain medications. Many people depend on it to help them feel alert and energized throughout the day at work or at school. Some people become addicted to it and experience withdrawal symptoms such as headaches, fatigue, anxiety, and irritability if they do not get their daily dose. Yet most people do not think of caffeine as a drug or realize that it can interfere with sleep.

Caffeine is typically absorbed into the bloodstream within 15 minutes after it is consumed, although it takes about an hour to reach peak levels. It acts as a stimulant to increase the heart rate and blood pressure and promote the production of adrenaline. As a result, caffeine temporarily increases alertness and reduces fatigue by suppressing sleep-inducing chemicals. These effects can last for 4–6 hours, although it takes a full 24 hours for the body to completely eliminate caffeine.

By stimulating the body to remain awake, caffeine can also weaken the body's ability to sleep. Consuming too much caffeine may cause insomnia. Most people can safely consume up to 250 milligrams per day, which is equivalent to 2–3 cups of coffee, without affecting their sleep. Consumption of 500 milligrams or more per day is considered excessive and can impair sleep.

Caffeine affects sleep in three ways: by making it harder to fall asleep, by reducing the quality of sleep, and by causing nocturia (frequent nighttime urination). These effects are particularly severe if the caffeine is consumed within 4–6 hours of bedtime. People with caffeine in

---

About This Chapter: "Caffeine And Nicotine And Their Impact Upon Sleep," © 2016 Omnigraphics. Reviewed December 2017.

their bloodstream are likely to feel jittery, anxious, or wired when they try to go to sleep. If they do manage to fall asleep, the stimulant effects of caffeine will make it difficult for their body to enter a deep, restorative phase of sleep. Finally, they are likely to wake up multiple times during the night to use the bathroom due to the diuretic effects of caffeine.

Although some people have a higher tolerance for caffeine than others, anyone who experiences difficulty sleeping may benefit from limiting caffeine consumption to less than 200 milligrams per day or eliminating it entirely. In addition, any caffeine consumption should take place early in the day—and at least 6 hours before bedtime. Ironically, cutting down on caffeine intake can cause withdrawal symptoms that can temporarily interfere with sleep. Although these symptoms subside over time as the body adjusts, people who are addicted to caffeine may want to reduce their consumption gradually rather than suddenly. Most people who eliminate caffeine find that they experience improvements in sleep afterward.

Nicotine And Sleep

Like caffeine, nicotine is absorbed into the bloodstream quickly and acts as a stimulant, increasing the heart rate and breathing rate and releasing stress hormones in the body. The stimulant effects of nicotine persist for several hours, affecting brain waves, body temperature, and other systems. These effects make it more difficult to fall asleep and stay asleep. As a result, smokers tend to sleep lightly and spend less time in deep, restorative sleep than nonsmokers.

In addition to sleep disruptions from the stimulant effects of nicotine, which tend to occur in the early part of the night, smokers may also experience withdrawal symptoms closer to morning that interfere with sleep. These symptoms may include headaches, nausea, diarrhea or constipation, irritability, anxiety, fatigue, and depression. Although quitting smoking is the best way to avoid the negative effects of nicotine on sleep, the effects can be reduced by avoiding nicotine for at least 2 hours before bedtime.

References

1. "Caffeine, Food, Alcohol, Smoking, And Sleep," Sleep Health Foundation, May 21, 2013.

2. Stewart, Kristin. "The Chemistry Of Caffeine, Nicotine, And Sleep," Everyday Health, January 7, 2013.

Chapter 14

Inadequate Sleep And Adolescent Substance Use

Sleep Disturbances And Substance Use

Many Americans suffer from unhealthy sleep-related behaviors. The prevalence of insomnia symptoms (difficulty initiating or maintaining sleep) in the general population is estimated at 33 percent, with an estimated 6 percent having a diagnosis of insomnia. According to a 12-state survey conducted by the Centers for Disease Control and Prevention (CDC):

- 35.3 percent of survey respondents obtain less than 7 hours of sleep on average during a 24-hour period.

- 48 percent snore.

- 37.9 percent unintentionally fall asleep during the day.

Substance/medication-induced sleep disorder is recognized in the *Diagnostic and Statistical Manual of Mental Disorders, Fifth Edition*. Substance use can exacerbate sleep difficulties, which in turn present a risk factor for substance use or relapse to use. The types of sleep problems vary by substance used and can include insomnia, sleep latency (the time it takes to fall asleep), disturbances in sleep cycles and sleep continuity, orhypersomnia (excessive daytime sleepiness). Specific findings on the relationship between sleep disturbances and substance use are presented below.

About This Chapter: Text under the heading "Sleep Disturbances And Substance Use" is excerpted from "Treating Sleep Problems Of People In Recovery From Substance Use Disorders," Substance Abuse and Mental Health Services Administration (SAMHSA), 2014. Reviewed December 2017; Text under the heading "A Study On Link Between Inadequate Sleep And Adolescent Substance Use" is excerpted from "The Concerning Link Between Inadequate Sleep And Adolescent Substance Use," National Institute on Drug Abuse (NIDA), July 10, 2017.

Alcohol Abuse

Insomnia and other sleep disturbances are common symptoms of alcohol dependence. Many people with alcohol use disorder (AUD) have insomnia before entering treatment. Reported rates of sleep problems among people with AUD in treatment range from 25 to 72 percent. Some people in recovery from AUD may continue to have sleep problems, including insomnia or sleep-disordered breathing (such as sleep apnea), for weeks, months, or sometimes years after initiating abstinence.

Illicit Drug Use

Sleep disturbances are common among people abstaining from chronic substance use. People stopping marijuana use can experience sleep problems in the first days of withdrawal, and these problems can last for weeks. People in detoxification from opioids often report symptoms of insomnia. A study that objectively measured sleep in people who chronically use cocaine found that sleep quality deteriorated during a period of abstinence, even though the subjects perceived their sleep to be improving. Another study of people in withdrawal from cocaine found that three-quarters experienced poor sleep quality. In a study of college students, those who reported a history of nonmedical psycho stimulant use or current use reported worse subjective and overall sleep quality and more sleep disturbance compared with those who had not used such substances.

A Study On Link Between Inadequate Sleep And Adolescent Substance Use

Children and adolescents require more sleep than adults. The American Academy of Pediatrics (AAP) defines a sufficient night's sleep for an adolescent as 8.5–9.5 hours per night. But according to data from the national Youth Risk Behavior Survey (YRBS), just over a quarter of middle and high-school students (27.5%) got 8 hours or more of sleep on the average night in 2015, and most got much less. Researchers have found striking links between insufficient sleep and a range of adverse outcomes in adolescents, including obesity, poor school performance, and behavioral problems including substance use.

Key Findings

For instance, a 2012 longitudinal study of youth (average age 14.7 years) participating in two Minnesota cohort studies found that less sleep—both weekday and total—at baseline was associated with more past-month cigarette and marijuana use 2 years later. Analysis of data on eighth graders from the 2010 and 2012 Fairfax County Youth Survey—an annual survey of middle and high school students in one of the largest school systems of the country—clearly showed that shorter sleep duration correlates with higher incidence in several risky behaviors. For example, students who reported getting 6 hours of sleep per night were three times as likely to have initiated drug use than those who got 8 or 9 hours of sleep per night.

Link Between Insufficient Sleep And Substance Use

Given this striking correlation, it is important to study the neurobiological mechanisms that link insufficient sleep and substance use. Sleep-deprivation-induced impairment of emotion regulation and executive function such as inhibitory control is likely involved. It has been found that adults who are sleep deprived show reduced availability (down-regulation) of dopamine D2 receptors in part of the brain's reward circuit, the ventral striatum. Reduced availability of D2 receptors in the ventral striatum could be expected to increase the risk for behaviors like drug use that produce large surges of dopamine to compensate for this deficit.

Reduced hours of sleep mediated the low levels of D2 receptors in individuals suffering from cocaine use disorder. Down-regulation of dopamine D2 receptors in the striatum has also been associated with impairment in prefrontal regions necessary for exerting self-control and other executive functions.

The impact of lack of sleep on dopamine receptors suggests that stimulant misuse and impaired sleep could be a vicious cycle: Stimulants impair sleep, and reduced sleep produces changes in the brain that predispose to further drug use and addiction. Two-way interactions between reduced sleep and substance use are also possible with other substances. The Minnesota study, for instance, identified a bidirectional relationship between greater cigarette use and greater weekend oversleep (sleeping late on weekends to compensate for less weekday sleep) and between greater marijuana use and less total sleep.

The mechanisms underlying these relationships are still unknown, but a longitudinal study in late-elementary schoolchildren found relationships between sleep patterns (reduced total sleep and later bedtimes and wake times on weekends) in 4th grade and cigarette or alcohol use in 6th grade, mediated by sleep-related deficits in inhibitory control.

Summing Up

From school start times that are too early to the nighttime use of computers and cell phones, today's adolescents face many challenges to getting a good night's sleep. The clear links between lack of quality sleep and risk behaviors like substance use make this a crucial target for prevention efforts. Recognizing the many health risks known to be linked to poor or insufficient sleep, the AAP has pressed for later start times (no earlier than 8:30 a.m.) in middle school and high schools. Parents should be aware of how important it is for their teenage children to get a full night's sleep every night, as a protective factor against substance use as well as other adverse impacts on their health and success.

Chapter 15

Sleep And Mental Health

Your mind and body will feel better if you sleep well. Your body needs time every day to rest and heal. If you often have trouble sleeping—either falling asleep, or waking during the night and being unable to get back to sleep—one or several of the following ideas might be helpful to you:

- Go to bed at the same time every night and get up at the same time every morning. Avoid "sleeping in" (sleeping much later than your usual time for getting up). It will make you feel worse.

- Establish a bedtime "ritual" by doing the same things every night for an hour or two before bedtime so your body knows when it is time to go to sleep.

- Avoid caffeine, nicotine, and alcohol.

- Eat on a regular schedule and avoid a heavy meal prior to going to bed. Don't skip any meals.

- Eat plenty of dairy foods and dark green leafy vegetables.

- Exercise daily, but avoid strenuous or invigorating activity before going to bed.

- Play soothing music on a tape or compact disc (CD) that shuts off automatically after you are in bed.

- Try a turkey sandwich and a glass of milk before bedtime to make you feel drowsy.

About This Chapter: This chapter includes text excerpted from "Good Mental Health," Office on Women's Health (OWH), U.S. Department of Health and Human Services (HHS), March 29, 2010. Reviewed December 2017.

- Try having a small snack before you go to bed, something like a piece of fruit and a piece of cheese, so you don't wake up hungry in the middle of the night. Have a similar small snack if you awaken in the middle of the night.

- Take a warm bath or shower before going to bed.

- Place a drop of lavender oil on your pillow.

- Drink a cup of herbal chamomile tea before going to bed.

Teens Need More Sleep Than Children And Adults

Although it may seem like teens are lazy, science shows that melatonin levels (or the "sleep hormone" levels) in the blood naturally rise later at night and fall later in the morning than in most children and adults. This may explain why many teens stay up late and struggle with getting up in the morning. Teens should get about 9–10 hours of sleep a night, but most teens don't get enough sleep. A lack of sleep makes paying attention hard, increases impulsivity and may also increase irritability and depression.

(Source: "The Teen Brain: 6 Things To Know," National Institute of Mental Health (NIMH).)

You need to see your doctor if:

- You often have difficulty sleeping and the solutions listed above are not working for you

- You awaken during the night gasping for breath

- Your partner says that your breathing stops when you are sleeping

- You snore loudly

- You wake up feeling like you haven't been asleep

- You fall asleep often during the day

Sleep Affects Mood

Insufficient sleep can make you irritable and is linked to poor behavior and trouble with relationships, especially among children and teens. People who chronically lack sleep are also more likely to become depressed.

(Source: "Your Guide To Healthy Sleep," National Heart, Lung, and Blood Institute (NHLBI).)

Chapter 16

Stress And Sleep

Stress is a complex biological response that is designed to help people focus their attention, energy, and physical resources to deal with a problem or threat. Everyone faces sources of stress in their daily lives, such as traffic jams, work deadlines, relationship issues, or hectic schedules. In fact, surveys show that 70 percent of American adults experience stress, anxiety, or worry on a daily basis. Most people report that stress interferes with their lives, particularly by reducing the quantity and quality of their sleep.

People under stress often have trouble falling asleep because their minds race with thoughts rather than shutting down. Sleep usually gives the brain a chance to rest by switching functions over from the active sympathetic nervous system to the calmer parasympathetic nervous system. Excessive worry prevents this switch from happening, so the brain remains on high alert. Stress also reduces the quantity of sleep by causing people to awaken frequently or toss and turn restlessly during the night. Among American adults, 43 percent report lying awake at night due to stress, with over half experiencing this problem more than once per week.

Stress also impacts the quality of sleep. Around 42 percent of American adults report feeling less satisfied with the quality of their sleep when they are under stress. In addition, people who experience ongoing stress have an increased risk of developing sleep disorders and insomnia. In fact, each additional source of stress in a person's life has been shown to increase their risk of insomnia by 19 percent. As a result, people with high levels of stress report sleeping only 6.2 hours per night on average, with only 33 percent feeling that they get enough sleep. People with lower levels of stress, on the other hand, sleep an average of 7.1 hours per night, and 79 percent feel that they get enough sleep.

About This Chapter: "Stress And Sleep," © 2016 Omnigraphics. Reviewed December 2017.

Compounding the problem, research indicates that sleep deprivation leads to even higher levels of stress. Among people whose sleep is affected by stress or anxiety, 75 percent report that the lack of sleep increases their levels of stress and anxiety. People with high stress are also more likely to feel the physical and emotional effects of getting too little sleep, such as fatigue, sluggishness, daytime drowsiness, trouble concentrating, irritability, lack of patience, and depression. When stress causes sleep problems, and then sleep problems increase stress levels, people become locked in a vicious cycle that can be hard to break.

Managing Stress And Improving Sleep

There are a number of stress-management tools and techniques available to help people cope with anxiety and thus improve the quantity and quality of their sleep. Some helpful approaches for dealing with stress-related sleep issues include the following:

- **Identify sources of stress.** The first step in managing stress involves figuring out its main causes, which will vary by individual. Common sources of stress include job, health, finances, trauma, and divorce.

- **Reduce exposure to stressors.** Once the main sources of stress have been identified, the next step is to find ways to handle them better. With job-related stress, for instance, it may be possible to delegate some responsibilities in order to reduce workload.

- **Adjust thought processes and expectations.** Often the way of looking at a problem or situation can determine whether or not it is stressful. It is possible to change negative thought patterns and lower expectations in order to reduce stress. It is particularly important to avoid generalizing concerns and blowing small things out of proportion. Many self-help books and websites offer tips and exercises for managing negative thoughts. For instance, one approach might be to write down worries and concerns and then throw away the paper in order to symbolically clear the mind.

- **Build a social support system.** Spending time relaxing with family and friends is a valuable way to reduce stress. Talking with supportive loved ones can also make problems seem more manageable or lead to positive new approaches and solutions.

- **Exercise.** Getting regular exercise is a proven way to relieve stress and improve mood. It can also lead to improvements in sleep, although vigorous exercise should be undertaken at least two hours before bedtime to allow body temperature to return to normal.

- **Eat a healthy diet.** A healthy diet with plenty of fruits, vegetables, whole grains, and lean proteins promotes overall health, increases energy, and helps reduce stress. On the other hand, consuming refined sugars, caffeine, and alcohol can negatively impact sleep and leave people feeling sluggish.

- **Try relaxation techniques.** Deep-breathing exercises can activate the parasympathetic nervous system and help calm nerves. Yoga, meditation, progressive muscle relaxation, and other techniques can also help quiet the mind and promote sleep.

- **Practice good sleep hygiene.** Since sleep problems increase stress levels, getting a good night's sleep is vital to effective stress management. Sleep hygiene methods that can improve the quality of sleep include making sleep a priority, blocking out 8 full hours for sleep, establishing a regular sleep schedule and a relaxing bedtime routine, avoiding naps during the day, and creating a comfortable and inviting sleep environment.

If these steps are ineffective in reducing stress and improving sleep, it may be helpful to consult with a doctor. Therapists can help patients identify sources of stress and find productive ways of dealing with them. Sleep specialists can assess patients for sleep disorders and recommend approaches or medications to address the problem. Since stress and sleep often go hand in hand, both kinds of professional help may be needed to enable people to manage stress successfully and sleep soundly through the night.

References

1. Holmes, Lindsay. "Five Ways Stress Wrecks Your Sleep (And What To Do About It)," Huffington Post, September 17, 2014.

2. "Stress And Anxiety Interfere With Sleep," Anxiety and Depression Association of America, 2016.

3. "Tips To Reduce Stress And Sleep Better," WebMD, 2016.

Chapter 17

Posttraumatic Stress Disorder Can Lead To Sleep Disturbances

Many people have trouble sleeping sometimes. This is even more likely, though, if you have posttraumatic stress disorder (PTSD). Trouble sleeping and nightmares are two symptoms of PTSD.

What Is PTSD?

PTSD (posttraumatic stress disorder) is a mental health problem that some people develop after experiencing or witnessing a life-threatening event, like combat, a natural disaster, a car accident, or sexual assault.

It's normal to have upsetting memories, feel on edge, or have trouble sleeping after this type of event. At first, it may be hard to do normal daily activities, like go to work, go to school, or spend time with people you care about. But most people start to feel better after a few weeks or months.

If it's been longer than a few months and you're still having symptoms, you may have PTSD. For some people, PTSD symptoms may start later on, or they may come and go over time.

(Source: "What Is PTSD?" National Center for Posttraumatic Stress Disorder (NCPTSD), U.S. Department of Veterans Affairs (VA).)

Why Do People With PTSD Have Sleep Problems?

- **They may be "on alert."** Many people with PTSD may feel they need to be on guard or "on the lookout," to protect himself or herself from danger. It is difficult to have restful

About This Chapter: This chapter includes text excerpted from "Sleep And PTSD," U.S. Department of Veterans Affairs (VA), August 13, 2015.

sleep when you feel the need to be always alert. You might have trouble falling asleep, or you might wake up easily in the night if you hear any noise.

- **They may worry or have negative thoughts.** Your thoughts can make it difficult to fall asleep. People with PTSD often worry about general problems or worry that they are in danger. If you often have trouble getting to sleep, you may start to worry that you won't be able to fall asleep. These thoughts can keep you awake.

- **They may use drugs or alcohol.** Some people with PTSD use drugs or alcohol to help them cope with their symptoms. In fact, using too much alcohol can get in the way of restful sleep. Alcohol changes the quality of your sleep and makes it less refreshing. This is true of many drugs as well.

- **They may have bad dreams or nightmares.** Nightmares are common for people with PTSD. Nightmares can wake you up in the middle of the night, making your sleep less restful. If you have frequent nightmares, you may find it difficult to fall asleep because you are afraid you might have a nightmare.

- **They may have medical problems.** There are medical problems that are commonly found in people with PTSD, such as chronic pain, stomach problems, and pelvic-area problems in women. These physical problems can make going to sleep difficult.

What Can You Do If You Have Problems?

There are a number of things you can do to make it more likely that you will sleep well:

Change Your Sleeping Area

Too much noise, light, or activity in your bedroom can make sleeping harder. Creating a quiet, comfortable sleeping area can help. Here are some things you can do to sleep better:

- Use your bedroom only for sleeping and sex.

- Move the TV and radio out of your bedroom.

- Keep your bedroom quiet, dark, and cool. Use curtains or blinds to block out light. Consider using soothing music or a "white noise" machine to block out noise.

Keep A Bedtime Routine And Sleep Schedule

Having a bedtime routine and a set wake-up time will help your body get used to a sleeping schedule. You may want to ask others in your household to help you with your routine.

- Don't do stressful or energizing things within two hours of going to bed.

- Create a relaxing bedtime routine. You might want to take a warm shower or bath, listen to soothing music, or drink a cup of tea with no caffeine in it.

- Use a sleep mask and earplugs, if light and noise bother you.

- Try to get up at the same time every morning, even if you feel tired. That will help to set your sleep schedule over time, and you will be more likely to fall asleep easily when bedtime comes. On weekends do not to sleep more than an hour past your regular wake-up time.

Try To Relax If You Can't Sleep

- Imagine yourself in a peaceful, pleasant scene. Focus on the details and feelings of being in a place that is relaxing.

- Get up and do a quiet activity, such as reading, until you feel sleepy.

Watch Your Activities During The Day

Your daytime habits and activities can affect how well you sleep. Here are some tips:

- Exercise during the day. Don't exercise within two hours of going to bed, though, because it may be harder to fall asleep.

- Get outside during daylight hours. Spending time in sunlight helps to reset your body's sleep and wake cycles.

- Cut out or limit what you drink or eat that has caffeine in it, such as coffee, tea, cola, and chocolate.

- Don't drink alcohol before bedtime. Alcohol can cause you to wake up more often during the night.

- Don't smoke or use tobacco, especially in the evening. Nicotine can keep you awake.

- Don't take naps during the day, especially close to bedtime.

- Don't drink any liquids after 6 p.m. if you wake up often because you have to go to the bathroom.

Chapter 18

Exercise And Sleep

Exercise is an essential aspect of a healthy lifestyle. It not only promotes physical fitness, cardiovascular health, and weight management, but it can also help people sleep better. Regular exercise has been shown to reduce stress and anxiety, which often contribute to sleep problems. It can also improve physical health conditions that contribute to sleep disorders. For instance, exercise can help people lose weight, which can reduce the symptoms of sleep apnea. Improvements in sleep duration and quality, in turn, lead to greater energy, vitality, and mood—all of which can increase people's motivation to exercise, as well as improve their athletic performance

The link between exercise and sleep is particularly important for people who are middle-aged or older. Around half of adults in this age group experience symptoms of chronic insomnia. Regular aerobic exercise can help this population combat insomnia without medication and improve their sleep and overall health. A 2010 study followed a group of sedentary women aged 60 or older who had been diagnosed with chronic insomnia. Half of the group remained inactive, while the other half engaged in a moderate exercise program over a four-month period. By the end of the study, the women who exercised 30 minutes per day were sleeping 45–60 minutes longer each night than the women who did not exercise. They also reported sleeping more soundly, waking up fewer times during the night, and feeling more refreshed in the morning.

Enhancing The Effects Of Exercise On Sleep

Although exercise has the potential to positively impact sleep, getting the full effect depends on the timing and intensity of the workout, as well as the length of time that an exercise

About This Chapter: "Exercise And Sleep," © 2016 Omnigraphics. Reviewed December 2017.

program is sustained. The following tips can help people with sleep difficulties maximize the benefits of exercise:

- Time workouts at least 5–6 hours before bedtime, if possible. Body temperature tends to rise during exercise and slowly drop back to normal afterward. This process can take several hours. Since cooler body temperatures coincide with feelings of drowsiness, exercising too close to bedtime can interfere with sleep. On the other hand, exercising in the late afternoon or early evening can help people fall asleep faster at night.

- Exercise at a moderate intensity. It is not necessary to exercise at peak intensity or to the point of exhaustion to see improvements in sleep. In fact, moderate aerobic activities such as brisk walking or bicycling seem to provide the maximum benefits. Although any increase in physical activity can lead to improvements in insomnia, studies have shown that the more people exercise, the better they tend to sleep.

- Stick with the program for at least three months. For people with insomnia or other sleep issues, research has shown that it takes time for an exercise regimen to show results. At first, they may not sleep any better than they did before starting to exercise. Researchers theorize that people with existing sleep problems have highly aroused stress systems, and that it may take several months for the effects of regular exercise to overcome this stress response. Eventually, however, people with insomnia can see improvements in sleep duration and quality that are better than those offered by other treatments or medications.

Finally, it is important to note that the connection between exercise and sleep works both ways. Just as exercise can help people sleep better, getting a good night's sleep can help people feel motivated to exercise and remain active. Studies have shown that people with insomnia often shorten or skip their workouts following nights when they have trouble sleeping. Sleep deprivation makes exercise feel harder and more tiring, and it can also detract from athletic performance. On the flip side, getting a good night's sleep can help athletes reach their potential. One study showed that college basketball players ran faster and made a higher percentage of shots when they got extra sleep the night before.

References

1. Andrews, Linda Wasmer. "How Exercise Helps You Get A Good Night's Sleep," Health Grades, November 10, 2014.

2. Hendrick, Bill. "Exercise Helps You Sleep," WebMD, September 17, 2010

3. Reynolds, Gretchen. "How Exercise Can Help Us Sleep Better," New York Times, August 21, 2013.

Chapter 19

How To Improve Your Sleep Habits

While you are sleeping, you are unconscious, but your brain and body functions are still active. Sleep is a complex biological process that helps you process new information, stay healthy, and feel rested.

How Much Sleep Do I Need?

The amount of sleep you need depends on several factors, including your age, lifestyle, health, and whether you have been getting enough sleep recently. The general recommendations for sleep are:

Teens: 9–10 hours a day

During puberty, teenagers' biological clocks shift, and they are more likely to go to bed later than younger children and adults, and they tend to want to sleep later in the morning. This delayed sleep-wake rhythm conflicts with the early-morning start times of many high schools and helps explain why most teenagers do not get enough sleep.

And it's not just the number of hours of sleep you get that matters. The quality of the sleep you get is also important. People whose sleep is frequently interrupted or cut short might not get enough of certain stages of sleep.

If you are wondering whether you are getting enough sleep, including quality sleep, ask yourself:

- Do you have trouble getting up in the morning?

About This Chapter: This chapter includes text excerpted from "Healthy Sleep," MedlinePlus, National Institutes of Health (NIH), April 26, 2017.

- Do you have trouble focusing during the day?

- Do you doze off during the day?

If you answered yes to these three questions, you should work on improving your sleep.

Does It Really Matter If You Get Enough Sleep?

Absolutely! Not only does the quantity of your sleep matter, but the quality of your sleep is important as well. People whose sleep is frequently interrupted or cut short might not get enough of certain stages of sleep. In other words, how well rested you are and how well you function the next day depend on your total sleep time and how much of the various stages of sleep you get each night.

(Source: "Your Guide To Healthy Sleep," National Heart, Lung, and Blood Institute (NHLBI).)

What Are The Health Effects Of Not Getting Enough Sleep?

Sleep is important for overall health. When you don't get enough sleep (sleep deprivation), it does more than just make you feel tired. It can affect your performance, including your ability to think clearly, react quickly, and form memories. This may cause you to make bad decisions and take more risks. People with sleep deprivation are more likely to get into accidents.

Sleep deprivation can also affect your mood, leading to:

- Irritability

- Problems with relationships, especially for children and teenagers

- Depression

- Anxiety

It can also affect your physical health. Research shows that not getting enough sleep, or getting poor-quality sleep, increases your risk of:

- High blood pressure

- Heart disease

- Stroke

- Kidney disease

- Obesity

- Type 2 diabetes

Not getting enough sleep can also mean that you don't get enough of the hormones that help children grow and help adults and children build muscle mass, fight infections, and repair cells. Sleep deprivation magnifies the effect of alcohol. A tired person who drinks too much alcohol will be more impaired than a well-rested person.

How Can I Get Better Sleep?

You can take steps to improve your sleep habits. First, make sure that you allow yourself enough time to sleep. With enough sleep each night, you may find that you're happier and more productive during the day.

To improve your sleep habits, it also may help to:

- Go to bed and wake up at the same time every day.

- Avoid caffeine, especially in the afternoon and evening.

- Avoid nicotine.

- Exercise regularly, but don't exercise too late in the day.

- Avoid alcoholic drinks before bed.

- Avoid large meals and beverages late at night.

- Don't take a nap after 3 p.m.

- Relax before bed, for example by taking a bath, reading or listening to relaxing music.

- Keep the temperature in your bedroom cool.

- Get rid of distractions such as noises, bright lights, and a TV or computer in the bedroom. Also, don't be tempted to go on your phone or tablet just before bed.

- Get enough sunlight exposure during the day.

- Don't lie in bed awake; if you can't sleep for 20 minutes, get up and do something relaxing.

- See a doctor if you have continued trouble sleeping. You may have a sleep disorder, such as insomnia or sleep apnea. In some cases, your doctor may suggest trying over-the-counter or prescription sleep aid. In other cases, your doctor may want you to do a sleep study, to help diagnose the problem.

Chapter 20

Sleep Medications

Sedatives And Hypnotics

Drugs for insomnia, which are also known as sedatives, hypnotics, medications for sleep, sleeping aids, or more colloquially "sleeping pills," are some of the most commonly used medications, both by prescription and over-the-counter. Insomnia affects up to 20 percent of the adult population and can be transient (<3 days), short term (3 to 30 days), or long term and chronic. Insomnia is also categorized as either primary or secondary. The drugs for insomnia are typically used for a short time only and act to decrease the latency to onset of sleep or prevent early awakening. They may improve the quality of sleep as assessed subjectively, but they usually do not usually increase sleep duration.

In many situations, insomnia need not be treated with medications; good sleep hygiene, adequate exercise, avoidance of alcohol and caffeine, and attention to the details of regular sleep habits can improve insomnia in many patients. Furthermore, while medications can be effective in the short term, they sometimes worsen or perpetuate insomnia when used for long periods.

Several types of medications are used to treat insomnia or as sleeping aids, including barbiturates, antihistamines, various herbals, benzodiazepines, and benzodiazepine receptor analogues. The benzodiazepine receptor analogues are the most frequently used drugs for insomnia and have perhaps the best record for safety and efficacy. The majority of sleeping aids have not been linked to liver injury, either in the form of clinically apparent acute liver injury or in causing transient serum enzyme elevations.

About This Chapter: This chapter includes text excerpted from "Drug Record—Sedatives And Hypnotics," LiverTox®, National Institutes of Health (NIH), October 16, 2017.

Drugs for insomnia are also referred to as sedatives, even tranquillizers. The various agents used to treat insomnia or as sleeping aids or sedatives are each described separately with annotated references.

Drug Class: Sedatives And Hypnotics

Subclasses:

- Antihistamines
  - Diphenhydramine
  - Doxylamine
  - Hydroxyzine
- Barbiturates
  - Amobarbital
  - Butabarbital
  - Phenobarbital
  - Secobarbital
- Benzodiazepines
  - Diazepam
  - Estazolam
  - Flurazepam
  - Quazepam
  - Temazepam
  - Triazolam
- Benzodiazepine receptor agonists
  - Eszopiclone
  - Zaleplon
  - Zolpidem
- Herbals
  - Chamomile (Matricaria recutita)

- Hops (Humulus lupulus)
- Lavender (Lavandula angustifolia)
- Passionflower (Passiflora incarnata)
- Valerian (Valeriana officinalis)
- Melatonin and its analogues
  - Melatonin
  - Ramelteon
  - Tasimelteon
- Miscellaneous agents
  - Buspirone
  - Chloral hydrate
  - Doxepin
  - Meprobamate
  - Oxybate (narcolepsy agent)
  - Suvorexant

Chapter 21

Sleep Medications: Benefits And Risks

Medicines To Help You Sleep

There are medicines that may help you fall asleep or stay asleep. You need a doctor's prescription for some sleep drugs. You can get other over-the-counter (OTC) medicines without a prescription.

Prescription

Prescription sleep medicines work well for many people but they can cause serious side effects.

- Talk to your doctor about all of the risks and benefits of using prescription sleep medicines.

- Sleep drugs taken for insomnia can affect your driving the morning after use.

- Sleep drugs can cause rare side effects like:

  - Severe allergic reactions

  - Severe face swelling

  - Behaviors like making phone calls, eating, having sex, or driving while you are not fully awake

About This Chapter: Text under the heading "Medicines To Help You Sleep" is excerpted from "For Women—Sleep Problems," U.S. Food and Drug Administration (FDA), April 24, 2017; Text under the heading "Prescription Insomnia Drugs" is excerpted from "Postmarket Drug Safety Information For Patients And Providers," U.S. Food and Drug Administration (FDA), June 13, 2017; Text under the heading "Some Sleep Drugs Can Impair Driving" is excerpted from "Some Sleep Drugs Can Impair Driving," U.S. Food and Drug Administration (FDA), April 24, 2017.

Over-The-Counter (OTC)

OTC sleep drugs have side effects too. Read the **'Drug Facts Label'** to learn more about the side effects of your OTC sleep medicine.

Tips For Better Sleep

Making some changes to your night time habits may help you get the sleep you need.

- Go to bed and get up at the same times each day
- Sleep in a dark, quiet room.
- Limit caffeine.
- Don't drink alcohol before bedtime.
- Do something to help you relax before bedtime.
- Don't exercise before bedtime.
- Don't take a nap after 3 p.m.
- Don't eat a large meal before you go to sleep.
- Talk to your healthcare provider if you have trouble sleeping almost every night for more than two weeks.

Prescription Insomnia Drugs

- Ambien (zolpidem)
- Belsomra (suvorexant)
- Butisol (butabarbital)
- Doral (quazepam)
- Edluar (zolpidem)
- Estazolam
- Flurazepam
- Halcion (triazolam)
- Hetlioz (tasimelteon)
- Intermezzo (zolpidem)

- Lunesta (eszopiclone)

- Restoril (temazepam)

- Rozerem (ramelteon)

- Seconal (secobarbital)

- Silenor (doxepin)

- Sonata (zaleplon)

- Zolpimist (zolpidem)

> Some sleep disorders are caused by conditions that need to be treated with drugs, such as hot flashes, pain, anxiety, depression, or mood disorders. The drug used will depend on your type of sleep problem (such as trouble falling asleep or trouble staying asleep) and other medicines you're taking. All of your other medicines and health conditions will affect which sleeping medicines are safe and will work well for you.
>
> *(Source: "Sleep Disorders (PDQ®)–Patient Version," National Cancer Institute (NCI).)*

Some Sleep Drugs Can Impair Driving

Many people take sedatives to help them sleep. The U.S. Food and Drug Administration (FDA) is reminding consumers that some drugs to treat insomnia could make them less able the next morning to perform activities for which they must be fully alert, including driving a car.

FDA has informed manufacturers that the recommended dose should be lowered for sleep drugs approved for bedtime use that contain a medicine called zolpidem. FDA is also evaluating the risk of next-morning impairment in other insomnia medications.

People with insomnia have trouble falling or staying asleep. Zolpidem, which belongs to a class of medications called sedative-hypnotics, is a common ingredient in widely prescribed sleep medications. Some sleep drugs contain an extended-release form of zolpidem that stays in the body longer than the regular form.

FDA is particularly concerned about extended-release forms of zolpidem. They are sold as generic drugs and under the brand name Ambien CR.

AMBIEN CR And Its Side Effects

AMBIEN CR is a central nervous system (CNS) depressant and can impair daytime function in some patients even when used as prescribed. Prescribers should monitor for excess depressant effects, but impairment can occur in the absence of subjective symptoms, and may not be reliably detected by ordinary clinical exam (i.e., less than formal psychomotor testing). While pharmacodynamic tolerance or adaptation to some adverse depressant effects of AMBIEN CR may develop, patients using AMBIEN CR should be cautioned against driving or engaging in other hazardous activities or activities requiring complete mental alertness the day after use.

(Source: "AMBIEN CR (Zolpidem Tartrate Extended-Release) Tablets," U.S. Food and Drug Administration (FDA).)

New data show that the morning after use, many people who take products containing extended-release zolpidem have drug levels that are high enough to impair driving and other activities. FDA says that women are especially vulnerable because zolpidem is cleared from the body more slowly in women than in men.

FDA also found that some medicines containing the immediate-release form of zolpidem can impair driving and other activities the next morning. They are marketed as generic drugs and under the following brand names:

- Ambien (oral tablet)

- Edluar (tablet placed under the tongue)

- Zolpimist (oral spray)

FDA has informed the manufacturers of products containing zolpidem that the recommended dose for women for both immediate- and extended-release products should be lowered. FDA is also suggesting a lower dose range for men.

Drowsiness is already listed as a side effect in the drug labels of insomnia drugs, along with warnings that patients may still feel drowsy the day after taking these products. However, people with high levels of zolpidem in their blood can be impaired even if they feel wide awake. "All insomnia drugs are potent medications, and they must be used carefully," says Russell Katz, M.D., director of FDA's Division of Neurology Products (DNP).

Recommended Doses

FDA has informed manufacturers that changes to the dosage recommendations for the use of zolpidem products should be made:

- For women, dosing should be cut in half, from 10 mg to 5 mg for products containing the regular form of zolpidem (Ambien, Edluar, Zolpimist) and from 12.5 mg to 6.25 mg for zolpidem extended-release products (Ambien CR).

- For men, the lower dose of 5 mg for immediate-release zolpidem and 6.25 mg for extended-release should be considered.

Intermezzo, a more recently approved drug containing zolpidem, is used when middle-of-the-night wakening is followed by difficulty returning to sleep and at least 4 hours remain available for sleep. The recommended dose for Intermezzo remains at 1.75 mg for women and 3.5 mg for men.

Intermezzo And Its Side Effects

Intermezzo may cause serious side effects. After taking Intermezzo, you may get up out of bed while not being fully awake and do an activity that you do not know you are doing. The next morning, you may not remember that you did anything during the night. You have a higher chance for doing these activities if you drank alcohol that day or take other medicines that make you sleepy with Intermezzo.

(Source: "Intermezzo Medication Guide," U.S. Food and Drug Administration (FDA).)

FDA is evaluating the risk of next-day impairment with other insomnia drugs, both prescription and over-the-counter (OTC) drugs.

Most Widely Used Sleep Drug

Zolpidem—which has been on the market for nearly 20 years—is by far the most widely used active ingredient in prescription sleep medications, says Ronald Farkas, M.D., Ph.D., a medical team leader in FDA's neurology products division. About 9 million patients received products containing zolpidem from retail pharmacies in 2011. FDA's Adverse Event Reporting System (FAERS) has logged approximately 700 reports of zolpidem use and impaired driving ability and/or traffic accidents.

What Is FAERS?

The FDA Adverse Event Reporting System (FAERS) is a database that contains adverse event reports, medication error reports and product quality complaints resulting in adverse events that were submitted to FDA.

(Source: "Questions And Answers On FDA's Adverse Event Reporting System (FAERS)," U.S. Food and Drug Administration (FDA).)

However, FDA cannot be certain that those incidents are conclusively linked to zolpidem. Many of those reports lacked important information, such as the dose of zolpidem and the time at which it was taken, the time of the accident, and whether alcohol or other drugs had also been used.

"We have had longstanding concern about sleep medications and driving. However, only recently have data from clinical trials and specialized driving simulation studies become available that enabled FDA to better establish the risk of driving impairment and to make new recommendations about dosing," Farkas says.

An Individual Decision

FDA is urging healthcare professionals to caution patients who use these products about the risks of next-morning impairment and its effect on activities, such as driving, that require alertness.

The agency recommends that people who take sleep medications talk to their healthcare professional about ways to take the lowest effective dose. It should not be assumed that OTC sleep medicines are necessarily safer alternatives.

With zolpidem, Farkas notes that people must be aware of how this drug affects them personally. "Even with the new dosing recommendations, it's important to work with your healthcare professional to find the sleep medicine and dose that work best for you," he says.

Patients are asked to contact FDA's MedWatch program if they suffer side effects from the use of zolpidem or another insomnia medication.

Zolpidem is a medication approved by the U.S. Food and Drug Administration (FDA) for short-term treatment of insomnia and is the active ingredient in the popular sleep aids Ambien®, Ambien CR®, Edluar®, and Zolpimist®.

(Source: "Zolpidem SL Tablets (Edluar And Intermezzo) Abbreviated Review," U.S. Department of Veterans Affairs (VA).)

Part Three
Sleep Disorders And Related Problems

Chapter 22

Common Sleep Problems

Types Of Sleep Problems

At least 40 million Americans per year suffer from long-term sleep disorders. An additional 20 million experience occasional sleeping problems. Among the most common sleep disorders are insomnia, sleep apnea, restless legs syndrome, and narcolepsy.

Insomnia

At one time or another, nearly everyone experiences short-term insomnia, which can occur as a result of stress, diet, jet lag, or a number of other factors. Insomnia almost always affects job performance and a person's overall well-being. The condition increases with age and affects about 30 percent of men and 40 percent of women at some time.

For short-term cases of insomnia, healthcare providers may prescribe sleeping pills. Sleeping pills are generally not considered effective for long-term use because they stop working after several weeks of nightly use, and long-term use can interfere with sleep. For more serious or long-term cases of insomnia, researchers are examining other approaches, including the use of bright light (light therapy) to alter circadian rhythms.

Sleep Apnea

According to the National Sleep Foundation (NSF), approximately 18 million Americans have sleep apnea, but few of them have been diagnosed. Those with this condition experience

About This Chapter: This chapter includes text excerpted from "What Are Some Common Sleep Disorders?" *Eunice Kennedy Shriver* National Institute of Child Health and Human Development (NICHD), December 5, 2012. Reviewed December 2017.

What Is Insomnia?

Insomnia is a common sleep disorder. People who have insomnia have trouble falling asleep, staying asleep, or both. As a result, they may get too little sleep or have poor-quality sleep. They may not feel refreshed when they wake up.

(Source: "Insomnia," National Heart, Lung, and Blood Institute (NHLBI).)

pauses in their breathing while they are asleep. Physical changes, such as alterations in fat accumulation or loss of muscle tone with aging, can contribute to sleep apnea. Typical features of this disorder include loud snoring, obesity, and excessive daytime sleepiness. Although sleep apnea is associated with loud snoring, not all people who snore have sleep apnea.

Diagnosing sleep apnea requires monitoring people while they are sleeping and recording measurements of some of their body functions and activities during sleep. A polysomnogram is a record of a person's sleep pattern, breathing, and heart activity. A polysomnogram is produced by a sleep test, called polysomnography, which can diagnose sleep apnea. This test records a person's brain waves, heartbeat, and breathing during an entire night, allowing for a diagnosis of sleep apnea. Methods of treating sleep apnea include losing weight and preventing a person from sleeping on his or her back. Another option is a special device or surgery to correct the obstruction in the airway. People with sleep apnea should not take sedatives or sleeping pills because these medications can prevent them from waking up to breathe.

What Is Sleep Apnea?

Sleep apnea is a common disorder that causes your breathing to stop or get very shallow. Breathing pauses can last from a few seconds to minutes. They may occur 30 times or more an hour. The most common type is obstructive sleep apnea. It causes your airway to collapse or become blocked during sleep. Normal breathing starts again with a snort or choking sound. People with sleep apnea often snore loudly. However, not everyone who snores has sleep apnea.

You are more at risk for sleep apnea if you are overweight, male, or have a family history or small airways. Children with enlarged tonsils or adenoids may also get it.

(Source: "Sleep Apnea," MedlinePlus, National Institutes of Health (NIH).)

Restless Legs Syndrome (RLS)

According to the National Institute of Neurological Disorders and Stroke (NINDS), as many as 10 percent of Americans may have RLS. This condition tends to run in families and causes unpleasant sensations of crawling, prickling, or tingling in the legs and feet, with a resulting need to move the feet and legs for relief. People with RLS may move their legs constantly during the day and night, which can result in trouble sleeping.

Symptoms of RLS can occur at any age, but the most severe cases usually occur in the elderly. Many RLS patients have a disorder called periodic limb movement disorder (PLMD), which causes repetitive jerking movements of the limbs, particularly the legs. The movements occur every 20–40 seconds and can cause awakening throughout the night. Treatments prescribed for RLS and PLMD include drugs that affect dopamine, a neurotransmitter. However, because RLS and PLMD are not well understood, the reasons that drugs affecting the levels of dopamine in the brain are useful are also not well understood.

What Is Restless Legs Syndrome (RLS)?

Restless legs syndrome (RLS), also called Willis-Ekbom Disease, causes unpleasant or uncomfortable sensations in the legs and an irresistible urge to move them. Symptoms commonly occur in the late afternoon or evening hours, and are often most severe at night when a person is resting, such as sitting or lying in bed. They also may occur when someone is inactive and sitting for extended periods (for example, when taking a trip by plane or watching a movie). Since symptoms can increase in severity during the night, it could become difficult to fall asleep or return to sleep after waking up. Moving the legs or walking typically relieves the discomfort but the sensations often recur once the movement stops.

(Source: "Restless Legs Syndrome Fact Sheet," National Institute of Neurological Disorders and Stroke (NINDS).)

Narcolepsy

Approximately 0.02 to 0.067 percent of Americans are affected by narcolepsy. People with this condition experience "sleep attacks" throughout the day even though they may have had adequate sleep during the previous night. The sleep attacks last from several seconds to 30 minutes or more. In addition to falling asleep at unexpected times, people with narcolepsy may have loss of muscle control during emotional situations, hallucinations, temporary paralysis, and disrupted nighttime sleep. Narcolepsy tends to run in families with a history of sleep disorders, and it also occurs in some people who have experienced head trauma or injury.

Once diagnosed, narcolepsy can be treated with drugs that control its symptoms. Commonly prescribed drugs for this condition include stimulants and antidepressants. Because each case is different, the drug that is most effective depends on the person.

What Is Narcolepsy?

Narcolepsy is a chronic neurological disorder that affects the brain's ability to control sleep-wake cycles. People with narcolepsy usually feel rested after waking, but then feel very sleepy throughout much of the day. Many individuals with narcolepsy also experience uneven and interrupted sleep that can involve waking up frequently during the night.

(Source: "Narcolepsy Fact Sheet," National Institute of Neurological Disorders and Stroke (NINDS).)

Chapter 23

How To Discuss Sleep-Related Issues With Your Doctor

Speak Out About Your Sleep Problem

Doctors might not detect sleep problems during routine office visits because patients are awake. Thus, you should let your doctor know if you think you might have a sleep problem. For example, talk with your doctor if you often feel sleepy during the day, don't wake up feeling refreshed and alert, or are having trouble adapting to shift work.

> It's important to talk about your sleep problems with your family and the healthcare team so education and support can be given. Supportive care may improve your quality of life and ability to sleep.
>
> *(Source: "Sleep Disorders (PDQ®)–Patient Version," National Cancer Institute (NCI).)*

Keep A Note Of Your Sleep Habits

To get a better sense of your sleep problem, your doctor will ask you about your sleep habits.

Before you see the doctor, think about how to describe your problems, including:

- How often you have trouble sleeping and how long you've had the problem

- When you go to bed and get up on workdays and days off

About This Chapter: Text beginning with the heading "Speak Out Your Sleep Problem" is excerpted from "How To Discuss Sleep With Your Doctor," National Heart, Lung, and Blood Institute (NHLBI), June 7, 2017; Text beginning with the heading "Polysomnogram" is excerpted from "Diagnosing Sleep Disorders," MedlinePlus, National Institutes of Health (NIH), 2012. Reviewed December 2017.

- How long it takes you to fall asleep, how often you wake up at night, and how long it takes you to fall back asleep

- Whether you snore loudly and often or wake up gasping or feeling out of breath

- How refreshed you feel when you wake up, and how tired you feel during the day

- How often you doze off or have trouble staying awake during routine tasks, especially driving

Your doctor also may ask questions about your personal routine and habits. For example, he or she may ask about your work and exercise routines. Your doctor also may ask whether you use caffeine, tobacco, alcohol, or any medicines (including over-the-counter (OTC) medicines).

Look over this list of common signs of a sleep disorder, and talk to your healthcare provider if you have any of these signs on three or more nights a week:

- It typically takes you more than 30 minutes to fall asleep at night.
- You awaken frequently in the night and have trouble falling back to sleep.
- You awaken too early in the morning.
- You often don't feel well rested despite spending seven to eight hours or more asleep at night.
- You feel sleepy during the day and fall asleep within five minutes if you have an opportunity to nap, or you fall asleep unexpectedly or at inappropriate times during the day.
- Your bed partner reports that you snore loudly, snort, or make choking sounds while you sleep, or your partner notices your breathing stops for short periods.
- You have creeping, tingling feelings in your legs that are relieved by moving or massaging them, especially in the evening or when you try to fall asleep.
- You have vivid, dreamlike experiences while falling asleep or dozing.
- You have episodes of sudden muscle weakness when you are angry or fearful, or when you laugh.
- You feel as though you cannot move when you first wake up.
- Your bed partner notes that your legs or arms jerk often during sleep.
- You regularly depend on wake-promoting products, such as caffeinated beverages, to stay awake during the day.

(Source: "Are You Sleep-Deprived? Learn More About Healthy Sleep," MedlinePlus, National Institutes of Health (NIH).)

Maintain Sleep Diary

To help your doctor, consider keeping a sleep diary for a couple of weeks. Write down when you go to sleep, wake up, and take naps. (For example, you might note: Went to bed at 10 a.m.; woke up at 3 a.m. and couldn't fall back asleep; napped after work for 2 hours.) Also write down how much you sleep each night, how alert and rested you feel in the morning, as well as how sleepy you feel at various times during the day. Share the information in your sleep diary with your doctor.

Diagnosis Of Sleep Disorders

Doctors can diagnose some sleep disorders by asking questions about sleep schedules and habits and by getting information from sleep partners or parents. To diagnose other sleep disorders, doctors also use the results from sleep studies and other medical tests.

Sleep studies allow your doctor to measure how much and how well you sleep. They also help show whether you have sleep problems and how severe they are.

Your doctor will do a physical exam to rule out other medical problems that might interfere with sleep. You may need blood tests to check for thyroid problems or other conditions that can cause sleep problems.

Polysomnogram

A sleep recording or polysomnogram (PSG) is usually done while you stay overnight at a sleep center or sleep laboratory. Electrodes and other monitors are placed on your scalp, face, chest, limbs, and finger. While you sleep, these devices measure your brain activity, eye movements, muscle activity, heart rate and rhythm, blood pressure, and how much air moves in and out of your lungs. This test also checks the amount of oxygen in your blood. A PSG test is painless. In certain circumstances, the PSG can be done at home. A home monitor can be used to record heart rate, how air moves in and out of your lungs, the amount of oxygen in your blood, and your breathing effort.

Polysomnogram (PSG) is the most common sleep study for sleep apnea and often takes place in a sleep center or lab to record brain activity, eye movement, blood pressure and the amount of air that moves in and out of your lungs.

(Source: "Always Tired? You May Have Sleep Apnea," U.S. Food and Drug Administration (FDA).)

Multiple Sleep Latency Test (MSLT)

This daytime sleep study measures how sleepy you are and is particularly useful for diagnosing narcolepsy. The MSLT is conducted in a sleep laboratory and typically done after an overnight sleep recording (PSG). In this test, monitoring devices for sleep stage are placed on your scalp and face. You are asked to nap four or five times for 20 minutes every two hours during the day. Technicians note how quickly you fall asleep and how long it takes you to reach various stages of sleep, especially REM (rapid eye movement) sleep, during your naps. Normal individuals either do not fall asleep during these short designated naptimes or take a long time to fall asleep. People who fall asleep in less than five minutes are likely to require treatment for a sleep disorder, as are those who quickly reach REM sleep during their naps.

What Are Sleep Studies?

Sleep studies are tests that measure how well you sleep and how your body responds to sleep problems. These tests can help your healthcare provider find out whether you have a sleep disorder and how severe it is. Sleep studies are important because untreated sleep disorders can raise your risk for heart disease, high blood pressure, stroke, and other medical conditions. Sleep disorders also have been linked to an increased risk of injury, such as falling (in the elderly) and car accidents.

Research is helping to improve our understanding of the connection between sleep disorders and the impact of untreated sleep disorders on our physical, mental, and behavioral health.

Chapter 24

Insomnia

What Is Insomnia?

Insomnia is a common sleep disorder. If you have insomnia, you may:

- Lie awake for a long time and have trouble falling asleep

- Wake up a lot and have trouble returning to sleep

- Wake up too early in the morning

- Feel like you haven't slept at all

Lack of or poor quality sleep causes other symptoms that can affect daytime function. You may feel very sleepy and have low energy throughout the day. You may have trouble thinking clearly or staying focused. Or, you might feel depressed or irritable.

Insomnia is defined as short and poor quality sleep that affects your functioning during the day. Although the amount of sleep a person needs varies, most people need 7–8 hours of sleep a night to feel refreshed.

Insomnia can be mild to severe and varies in how often it occurs and how long it lasts. Acute insomnia is a short-term sleep problem that is generally related to a stressful or traumatic life

About This Chapter: Text beginning with the heading "What Is Insomnia?" is excerpted from "Insomnia," Office on Women's Health (OWH), U.S. Department of Health and Human Services (HHS), June 12, 2017; Text beginning with the heading "If You're Considering Complementary Health Approaches For Sleep Problems" is excerpted from "Sleep Disorders: In Depth," National Center for Complementary and Integrative Health (NCCIH), October 2015; Text under the heading "Mindfulness Meditation May Benefit People With Chronic Insomnia" is excerpted from "Mindfulness Meditation May Benefit People With Chronic Insomnia," National Center for Complementary and Integrative Health (NCCIH), September 1, 2014. Reviewed December 2017.

event and lasts from a few days to a few weeks. Acute insomnia might happen from time to time. With chronic insomnia, sleep problems occur at least 3 nights a week for more than a month.

What Are The Different Types Of Insomnia And What Causes Them?

There are 2 types of insomnia:

- **Primary insomnia** is not a symptom or side-effect of another medical condition. It is its own disorder. It may be lifelong or triggered by travel, shift work, stressful life events, or other factors that disrupt your sleep routine. Primary insomnia may end once the issue is resolved, or can last for years. Some people tend to be prone to primary insomnia.

- **Secondary insomnia** has an underlying cause, so it's a symptom or side-effect of something else. It is the most common type. Secondary insomnia may have a medical cause, such as:

  - Depression or anxiety

  - Chronic pain such as from fibromyalgia, migraine, or arthritis

  - Gastrointestinal problems such as heartburn

  - Sleep disorders, such as sleep apnea or restless legs syndrome

  - Stroke

  - Alzheimer disease

  - Menopause

Secondary insomnia also can result from:

- Some medicines, such as those that treat asthma, heart problems, allergies, and colds

- Caffeine, tobacco, and alcohol

- Poor sleep environment (such as too much light or noise, or a bed partner who snores)

Secondary insomnia often goes away once the underlying cause is treated, but may become a primary insomnia.

Some people with primary or secondary insomnia form habits to deal with the lack of sleep, such as worrying about sleep or going to bed too early. These habits can make insomnia worse or last longer.

How Is Insomnia Diagnosed?

Talk to your doctor if you are having problems falling or staying asleep, especially if lack of sleep is affecting your daily activities. Keep a sleep diary for 2 weeks before you see your doctor. Note the time of day you fall asleep and wake up, changes in your daily sleep routine, your bedtime routine, and how you feel during the day.

Your doctor may do a physical exam and take medical and sleep histories. He or she may also want to talk to your bed partner about how much and how well you are sleeping. In some cases, you may be referred to a specialist or a sleep center for special tests.

What Can I Do To Sleep Better?

- Try to go to sleep at the same time each night and get up at the same time each morning. Do not take naps after 3 p.m.

- Avoid caffeine, nicotine, and alcohol late in the day or at night.

- Get regular physical activity. But exercise or physical activity done too close to bedtime can make it hard to fall asleep. Make sure you eat dinner at least 2–3 hours before bedtime.

- Keep your bedroom dark, quiet, and cool. If light is a problem, try a sleeping mask. If noise is a problem, try earplugs, a fan, or a "white noise" machine to cover up the sounds.

- Follow a routine to help relax and wind down before sleep, such as reading a book, listening to music, or taking a bath.

- If you can't fall asleep within 20 minutes or don't feel drowsy, get out of bed and sit in your bedroom or another room. Read or do a quiet activity until you feel sleepy. Then try going back to bed.

- If you lay awake worrying about things, try making a to-do list before you go to bed so that you don't use time in bed for worry.

- Use your bed only for sleep and sex.

- See your doctor or a sleep specialist if you think that you have insomnia or another sleep problem.

How Is Insomnia Treated?

If insomnia is caused by a short-term change in the sleep/wake schedule, as with jet lag, your sleep schedule may return to normal on its own. Making lifestyle changes to help you sleep better can also help. If your insomnia makes it hard for you to function during the day, talk to your doctor.

Treatment for chronic insomnia begins by:

- Finding and treating any medical or mental health problems

- Stopping or reducing behaviors that may lead to the insomnia or make it worse, like drinking moderate to large amounts of alcohol at night

Other treatments are:

- Cognitive behavioral therapy (CBT)

- Medication

Cognitive Behavioral Therapy (CBT)

Research shows that CBT is an effective and lasting treatment of insomnia. CBT helps you change thoughts and actions that get in the way of sleep. This type of therapy is also used to treat conditions such as depression, anxiety, and eating disorders.

CBT consists of one or more approaches. These are:

- **Cognitive control and psychotherapy**—Controlling or stopping negative thoughts and worries that keep you awake.

- **Sleep hygiene**—Taking steps to make quality sleep more likely, such as going to bed and waking up at the same time each day, not smoking, avoiding drinking too much coffee or alcohol late in the day, and getting regular exercise.

- **Sleep restriction**—Matching the time spent in bed with the amount of sleep you need. This is achieved by limiting the amount of time spent in your bed not sleeping. You go to bed later and get up earlier then you would normally, and then slowly increase the time in bed until you are able to sleep all night.

- **Stimulus control**—Conditioning a positive response with getting into bed. For example, using the bed only for sleep and sex.

- **Relaxation training**—Reducing stress and body tension. This can include meditation, hypnosis, or muscle relaxation.

- **Biofeedback**—Measuring body actions, such as muscle tension and brain wave frequency, to help you control them.

- **Remain passively awake**—Trying not to fall asleep, thereby stopping any worries you might have about falling asleep easily.

Medication

In some cases, insomnia is treated with medicine:

- **Prescription sleep medicines**—Prescription sleep medicines can help some people get much-needed rest. Most sleep medicines are used for short-term treatment, though some people with severe chronic insomnia may benefit from longer treatment. It is important to understand the risks before using a sleep medicine. In some cases, sleep medicines may:

  - Become habit-forming

  - Mask medical problems that may be causing the insomnia, and delay treatment

  - Interact with other medicines you use and cause serious health problems

  - Cause grogginess or rebound insomnia, where the sleeping problems get worse

Uncommon side-effects of sleep medicines include:

  - Severe allergic reactions or facial swelling

  - High blood pressure, dizziness, weakness, nausea, confusion, or short-term memory loss

  - Complex sleep-related behaviors, such as binge eating or driving while asleep

- **Over-the-counter (OTC) sleep aids**—OTC sleep aids may help on an occasional sleepless night, but they are not meant for regular or long-term use. Most OTC sleep aids contain antihistamines. Antihistamines are not safe for some people to use. OTC sleep aids also can have some unpleasant side-effects, such as dry mouth, dizziness, and prolonged grogginess.

Some dietary supplements claim to help people sleep. Some are "natural" products like melatonin. Others are food supplements such as valerian (an herb) teas or extracts. The U.S. Food and Drug Administration (FDA) does not regulate dietary supplements as it does medicine. It is unclear if these products are safe or if they actually work.

Talk to your doctor about sleep problems before using an OTC sleep aid. You may have a medical issue that needs to be treated. Also, the insomnia may be better treated in other ways.

If you decide to use a sleep medicine, experts advise you to:

- Read the medication guide first.

- Use the medicine at the time of day directed by your doctor.

- Do not drive or engage in activities that require you to be alert.

- Always take the dose prescribed by your doctor.

- Tell your doctor about other medicines you use.

- Call your doctor right away if you have any problems while using the medicine.

- Avoid drinking alcohol and using drugs.

- Talk to your doctor if you want to stop using the sleep medicine. Some medicines must be stopped gradually.

Antihistamines

Antihistamines represent a class of medications that block the histamine type 1 (H1) receptors. Importantly, antihistamines do not block or decrease the release of histamine, but rather ameliorate its local actions.

(Source: "Antihistamines," LiverTox®, National Institutes of Health (NIH).)

If You're Considering Complementary Health Approaches For Sleep Problems

- Talk to your healthcare providers. Tell them about the complementary health approach you are considering and ask any questions you may have. Because trouble sleeping can be an indication of a more serious condition, and because some prescription and over-the-counter (OTC) drugs can contribute to sleep problems, it is important to discuss your sleep-related symptoms with your healthcare providers before trying any complementary health product or practice.

- Be cautious about using any sleep product—prescription medications, over-the-counter medications, dietary supplements, or homeopathic remedies. Find out about potential side effects and any risks from long-term use or combining products.

- Keep in mind that "natural" does not always mean safe. For example, kava products can cause serious harm to the liver. Also, a manufacturer's use of the term "standardized" (or "verified" or "certified") does not necessarily guarantee product quality or consistency. Natural products can cause health problems if not used correctly. The healthcare providers you see about your sleep problems can advise you.

- If you are considering a practitioner-provided complementary health practice, check with your insurer to see if the services will be covered, and ask a trusted source (such as your healthcare provider or a nearby hospital or medical school) to recommend a practitioner.

- Tell all your healthcare providers about any complementary health approaches you use. Give them a full picture of what you do to manage your health. This will help ensure coordinated and safe care.

What The Science Says About Complementary Health Approaches And Insomnia?

Research has produced promising results for some complementary health approaches for insomnia, such as relaxation techniques. However, evidence of effectiveness is still limited for most products and practices, and safety concerns have been raised about a few.

Mind And Body Practices

- There is evidence that relaxation techniques can be effective in treating chronic insomnia.

  - Progressive relaxation may help people with insomnia and nighttime anxiety.

  - Music-assisted relaxation may be moderately beneficial in improving sleep quality in people with sleep problems, but the number of studies has been small.

  - Various forms of relaxation are sometimes combined with components of cognitive behavioral therapy (CBT) (such as sleep restriction and stimulus control), with good results.

  - Using relaxation techniques before bedtime can be part of a strategy to improve sleep habits that also includes other steps, such as maintaining a consistent sleep schedule; avoiding caffeine, alcohol, heavy meals, and strenuous exercise too close to bedtime; and sleeping in a quiet, cool, dark room.

  - Relaxation techniques are generally safe. However, rare side effects have been reported in people with serious physical or mental health conditions. If you have a serious underlying health problem, it would be a good idea to consult your healthcare provider before using relaxation techniques.

- In a preliminary study, mindfulness-based stress reduction (MBSR), a type of meditation, was as effective as a prescription drug in a small group of people with insomnia.

  - Several other studies have also reported that mindfulness-based stress reduction improved sleep, but the people who participated in these studies had other health problems, such as cancer.

- Preliminary studies in postmenopausal women and women with osteoarthritis suggest that yoga may be helpful for insomnia.

- Some practitioners who treat insomnia have reported that hypnotherapy enhanced the effectiveness of cognitive behavioral therapy and relaxation techniques in their patients, but very little rigorous research has been conducted on the use of hypnotherapy for insomnia.

- A small study on massage therapy showed promising results for insomnia in postmenopausal women. However, conclusions cannot be reached on the basis of a single study.

- Most of the studies that have evaluated acupuncture for insomnia have been of poor scientific quality. The current evidence is not rigorous enough to show whether acupuncture is helpful for insomnia.

Dietary Supplements

Melatonin And Related Supplements

A 2013 evaluation of the results of 19 studies concluded that melatonin may help people with insomnia fall asleep faster, sleep longer, and sleep better, but the effect of melatonin is small compared to that of other treatments for insomnia.

Dietary supplements containing substances that can be changed into melatonin in the body—L-tryptophan and 5-hydroxytryptophan (5-HTP)—have been researched as sleep aids.

What Is Melatonin?

Melatonin is a natural hormone that plays a role in sleep. Melatonin dietary supplements have been studied for sleep disorders, such as jet lag, disruptions to the body's internal "clock," insomnia, and problems with sleep among people who work night shifts. It has also been studied for dementia symptoms.

(Source: "Melatonin Information," National Center for Complementary and Integrative Health (NCCIH).)

Herbs

- Although chamomile has traditionally been used for insomnia, often in the form of a tea, there is no conclusive evidence from clinical trials showing whether it is helpful. Some people, especially those who are allergic to ragweed or related plants, may have allergic reactions to chamomile.

- Although kava is said to have sedative properties, very little research has been conducted on whether this herb is helpful for insomnia.

- Clinical trials of valerian (another herb said to have sedative properties) have had inconsistent results, and its value for insomnia has not been demonstrated. Although few people have reported negative side effects from valerian, it is uncertain whether this herb is safe for long-term use.

- Some "sleep formula" dietary supplements combine valerian with other herbs such as hops, lemon balm, passionflower, and kava or other ingredients such as melatonin and 5-HTP. There is little evidence on these preparations from studies in people.

Mindfulness Meditation May Benefit People With Chronic Insomnia

Mindfulness meditation—and particularly a form designed for insomnia—may help people with chronic insomnia and could be a viable treatment option, according to a small study. Results of this National Center for Complementary and Integrative Health (NCCIH)-funded research were published in the journal Sleep. Findings from the study showed that the meditation-based treatments (MBSR or MBTI) provided improvement by significantly reducing total wake time and presleep arousal.

Researchers randomly assigned 54 adults with chronic insomnia to participate in one of three groups:

1. Mindfulness-based stress reduction (MBSR),

2. An adaptation of MBSR called mindfulness-based therapy for insomnia (MBTI), or

3. An 8-week self-monitoring program using sleep diaries.

The MBSR group met for 2.5 hours once weekly for 8 weeks, and participated in a 6-hour meditation retreat. The weekly meetings included meditation practice, general discussion about at-home meditation, and education on the daily applications of meditation. The MBTI group had the same amount of meditation practice as the MBSR group, but instead of a discussion on general health and education on meditation, the MBTI group learned specific behavioral strategies for insomnia (e.g., sleep hygiene, sleep restriction therapy). Participants in both meditation groups were asked to meditate 30–45 minutes at least 6 days a week. All three groups completed sleep diaries at the start of the study, at each treatment/monitoring week, at the end of the study, and at the 3-month and 6-month followup. The researchers also measured sleep using wrist monitors and overnight laboratory sleep tests at the start and end of the study and at the 6-month followup.

Findings from the study showed that the meditation-based treatments (MBSR or MBTI) provided improvement by significantly reducing total wake time and presleep arousal. Both meditation-based therapies were better than the self-monitoring on each of the patient-reported measures. Only one significant difference was found between them across the study: the MBTI group had a significantly greater reduction in the severity of insomnia compared with the MBSR group, and this difference was largest at the 3-month followup.

The researchers noted that the small number of participants, as well as the participants' lack of diversity, should be taken into consideration when interpreting the findings. They also noted that future research, with a larger sample size, comparing meditation-based therapies to standard treatment, such as cognitive-behavior therapy for insomnia, would help determine the position of meditation-based therapies among treatment options.

Chapter 25

Fatal Familial Insomnia

Fatal familial insomnia (FFI) is an inherited prion disease that mainly affects the thalamus. The thalamus is the part of the brain that controls the sleep-wake cycle, but is also known as the "relay center" of the brain because it helps the different parts of the brain communicate with each other. Like all prion diseases, FFI is a progressive neurodegenerative disease, which means over time there are fewer neurons (nerve cells). Loss of neurons in the thalamus, as well as other mechanisms not yet fully understood, cause the symptoms of FFI.

The first symptoms of FFI usually begin in mid-life and may include progressive insomnia, weight loss, lack of appetite, too high or too low body temperature, and rapidly progressive dementia. Almost all cases of FFI are caused by certain changes (mutations) in the *PRNP* gene and are inherited in an autosomal dominant manner. There are a very small number of reported sporadic cases of FFI. There is currently no effective treatment for FFI, but research for a treatment and cure is ongoing. Death usually occurs within 12–18 months of the first symptoms.

Symptoms

The first symptoms of fatal familial insomnia (FFI) usually begin between the ages of 32 and 62 (mean average 51 years), but have been reported to begin as early as 18 to as late as 72. It is important to note that insomnia is not always the first symptom of FFI; sometimes the first symptom is progressive dementia. When insomnia begins, it usually comes on suddenly

About This Chapter: This chapter includes text excerpted from "Fatal Familial Insomnia," Genetic and Rare Diseases Information Center (GARD), National Center for Advancing Translational Sciences (NCATS), December 2, 2016.

and steadily worsens over a period of a few months. Other symptoms may include panic attacks, phobias, weight loss, lack of appetite, and having a body temperature which is too low or too high (hypothermia; hyperthermia). Autonomic disorders such as high blood pressure, episodes of hyperventilation, excessive sweating and salivation, and/or erectile dysfunction may occur.

As the disease progresses, most people with FFI develop abnormal, uncoordinated movements (ataxia), hallucinations, severe confusion (delerium), and muscle twitches and jerks (myoclonus). Although the dementia may begin as forgetfulness and confusion, it leads eventually to the inability to walk and talk. Total inability to sleep is common towards the end of the course of the disease.

Cause

Fatal familial insomnia (FFI) is a very rare form of genetic prion disease. In almost every case it is caused by a very specific mutation in the *PRNP gene*. This mutation causes the prion protein (PrP) that is made from this gene to be a different shape (fold incorrectly). Since the protein has a different shape, it cannot work correctly.

The abnormally shaped PrP (prion protein) causes changes in the thalamus including the progressive loss of neurons (nerve cells). The thalamus relays messages between different parts of the brain. It manages our sleep/wake cycle; the flow of visual, auditory, and motor information; our sense of balance; how we experience pain; aspects of learning, memory, speech and understanding language; and even emotional experiences, expression, and our personalities. Losing neurons in the thalamus causes many of the symptoms of FFI because the thalamus can no longer do all of its jobs well.

Although the main target of FFI is the thalamus, other parts of the brain are affected as well including the inferior olives. The inferior olives are part of the medulla oblongata and are important for coordinating our movements (motor control). Losing neurons in the inferior olives can make it harder for a person to control their movements as seen in later stages of FFI. Medical researchers are still working to understand how the abnormally folded PrP causes the progressive changes in the thalamus and other affected brain areas.

In very rare cases of FFI, the cause is sporadic, meaning there is not a change in the PRNP gene. As of 2016, there have only been 24 reported cases of sporadic FFI. Sporadic FFI occurs when some of a person's normal PrP (prion protein) spontaneously changes into the abnormal shape which causes FFI, and then somehow changes the shape of PrP in other neurons in a chain reaction.

Inheritance

In most cases, a person with fatal familial insomnia (FFI) has inherited the genetic change from a parent with FFI. In order to have FFI, a person only needs one copy of their *PRNP* gene to carry the specific genetic change (mutation) that causes FFI. In other words, a person only needs to inherit the genetic change from one parent. In genetic terms, this is called autosomal dominant inheritance. In rare cases, FFI may result from a new (de novo) change in the *PRNP* gene, however it is not known how often a new mutation is the cause of FFI. New mutations can happen during the making of the egg or the sperm.

A person that has the genetic change that causes FFI has a 50-percent chance with each pregnancy of passing along the changed gene to his or her child.

In the rare sporadic cases of FFI, the disease is not inherited from either parent and cannot be passed down to their children.

Diagnosis

The diagnosis of fatal familial insomnia (FFI) is first suggested by rapidly progressive cognitive impairment (dementia) along with behavior or mood changes, ataxia and sleep disturbances. Further diagnosis will include a sleep study and possibly a PET scan to confirm thalamic hypometabolism (meaning the thalamus in the brain is less active than it should be). The recommended PET scan is the fluorodeoxyglucose positron emission tomography (FDG-PET).

Genetic testing can confirm the diagnosis, but in the United States is only available if the person meets one of the following three criteria:

- Family history of FFI

- Abnormal sleep study or PET scan (consistent with strong suspicion of FFI)

- Diagnosis of FFI (usually through a combination of sleep study results and PET scan results)

Carrier testing for at-risk relatives and prenatal testing are possible for families with a confirmed diagnosis of FFI.

Treatment

There is currently no cure for fatal familial insomnia (FFI) or treatment that can slow the disease progression. The management goal is to ease symptoms and keep the person with FFI as comfortable as possible. However research is ongoing and a number of potential treatments are being developed.

As of 2016, a number of treatments have had some success in slowing disease progression in animal models, including pentosan polysulfate, quinacrine (mepacrine), and amphotericin B. Sadly, the results have been less clear in clinical trials in humans. In Italy, a clinical trial trying to prevent symptoms in people known to have the genetic changes for FFI but have not yet developed symptoms is underway using doxyclycline. Most promisingly, several forms of immunotherapy have reported success. The three main research areas focus on antibody vaccines, dendritic cell vaccines, and adoptive transfer of physiological prion protein-specific CD4+ T-lymphocytes. More research is being done to study how well these treatments work (effectiveness) and if the treatments are safe, but medical researchers believe that these or similar immunotherapies may offer hope for those with FFI in the future.

Chapter 26

Circadian Rhythm Sleep-Wake Disorders

Each of us has a brain-based body clock called a circadian rhythm. This clock triggers our bodies to feel and do different things at different times of the day based on the near 24-hour light-dark cycle. For most people, daytime triggers feelings of being alert and energetic, and nighttime triggers a desire to sleep.

What Are Circadian Rhythm Sleep-Wake Disorders (CRSD)?

People with circadian rhythm sleep-wake disorders (CRSD) have sleep-wake timing that does not match the time of day and typical school, social, and work schedules. If you have ever had jet lag, you may be familiar with this: you've taken a long flight and your body clock has not adjusted to the new time zone leading to difficulty falling and staying asleep as well as sleepiness. The clock says that it is time to sleep (night), but your mind and body are wide awake or, the clock says it is time to be awake (day) but your mind and body want to sleep. People with CRSD experience this on a regular basis and this leads to impairment in daily life.

Types Of CSRD

There are seven main types of CRSD:

1. **Shift Work Disorder** affects people who work nights or frequently change their work shift. Similar to jet lag, their body clocks are unable to adjust their sleep-wake

---

About This Chapter: This chapter includes text excerpted from "Circadian Rhythm Sleep-Wake Disorders (CRSD)," U.S. Department of Veterans Affairs (VA), September 18, 2017.

schedule to their work schedule resulting in the person getting less sleep than they need. People with this condition may complain of difficulty falling and or staying asleep and excessive sleepiness.

2. **Advanced Sleep-Wake Phase Disorder** causes a tendency to fall asleep much earlier than what is typical. People with this condition may be called "early birds" or "larks" and wake up earlier than what is typical. They may complain of early morning awakening and sleepiness in the early evening.

3. **Delayed Sleep-Wake Phase Disorder** causes a tendency to stay up late with difficulty waking up when expected. People with this condition may be called "night owls" and feel most productive late at night. They may be chronically late for work or school and/or function poorly during the day.

4. **Irregular Sleep-Wake Rhythm Disorder** causes irregular sleep-wake patterns throughout a 24-hour period such that a person might sleep for at least 3 irregularly scheduled bouts. These bouts may seem like naps. People with this condition may complain of sleepiness and have difficulty participating in scheduled activities that require sustained wakefulness like work, school, and social life.

5. **Non-24 Hour Sleep-Wake Rhythm Disorder** causes periods of difficulty falling and staying asleep and or excessive daytime sleepiness alternating with periods without these symptoms. People with this condition may complain of sleepiness and have difficulty participating in scheduled activities that require regularly scheduled wakefulness like work, school, and social life.

6. **Jet Lag Disorder** occurs after transmeridian jet travel across at least two time zones. It causes difficulty falling and or staying asleep with excessive daytime sleepiness and a reduction in total sleep time. People with this condition also experience general malaise, gastrointestinal disturbance, and general difficulty functioning in work, school, and or social life within one or two days after travel. Typically, this condition is worse with eastward travel. The condition generally resolves itself, taking one or two days after travel, per time zone, for the person to adjust.

7. **CRSD** Not Otherwise Specified is a disorder reserved for people who have difficulty falling and or staying asleep on a regular schedule and who also experience daytime sleepiness and difficulty participating in scheduled activities that require sustained wakefulness like work, school, and social life, but who do not fit any of the descriptions in any of the specific CRSD. There are some medical problems and diseases that

can cause this, including some mental illnesses, Parkinson disease, Alzheimer disease, and Huntington disease.

With the exception of Jet Lag Disorder, the pattern of sleep-wake timing, and associated sleep and daytime complaints, is not temporary and must occur for at least three months to meet diagnostic criteria for any of the above-mentioned disorders.

Causes

Multiple factors coming together can cause a CRSD. Some people may have a genetic predisposition to developing a CRSD. Some medical and mental health problems are associated with increased risk for development of a CRSD. Importantly, the body clock needs appropriately-timed light exposure to work properly. Therefore, people who don't get good exposure to light during the day and or who have too much exposure to bright light during the evening may be at risk for developing a CRSD. Not surprisingly, blindness is associated with development of CRSD as is a tendency to have irregular routines in daily living. Additionally, travelling across time zones and work schedules that do not allow regular sleep and wake patterns corresponding with day and night can trigger CRSD.

Signs And Symptoms

- Difficulty falling and or staying asleep and difficulty staying awake on a typical schedule
- Impairment in school, work, social, or other life as a result of sleep problems

Tests And Diagnosis

Because people with these disorders are unable to sleep at the times when they are expected to, they frequently have signs and symptoms of insomnia, but in order for treatment of the insomnia to be successful, the underlying problem with the body clock needs to be detected and addressed as well. One key difference between insomnia and insomnia with CRSD is that if the person is allowed to sleep on their preferred sleep schedule, they might not have any trouble sleeping.

Treatment

Once diagnosed, your healthcare provider may recommend:

- **Lifestyle changes:** Adjusting exposure to daylight, making changes in the timing of daily routines, and strategically scheduling naps.

- **Bright light therapy:** This therapy synchronizes the body clock by exposing the eyes to safe levels of intense, bright light for brief durations at strategic times of day.

- **Melatonin:** Per physician guidance, taking melatonin at precise times and doses may alleviate the symptoms of some CRSD.

Chapter 27

Snoring

Snoring is the sound you make when your breathing is blocked while you are asleep. The sound is caused by tissues at the top of your airway that strike each other and vibrate. Snoring is common, especially among older people and people who are overweight.

When severe, snoring can cause frequent awakenings at night and daytime sleepiness. It can disrupt your bed partner's sleep. Snoring can also be a sign of a serious sleep disorder called sleep apnea. You should see your healthcare provider if you are often tired during the day, don't feel that you sleep well, or wake up gasping.

To reduce snoring:

- Lose weight if you are overweight. It may help, but thin people can snore, too.

- Cut down or avoid alcohol and other sedatives at bedtime

- Don't sleep flat on your back

Is Snoring A Problem?

Long the material for jokes, snoring is generally accepted as common and annoying in adults but as nothing to worry about. However, snoring is no laughing matter. Frequent, loud snoring is often a sign of sleep apnea and may increase your risk of developing cardiovascular disease (CVD) and diabetes. Snoring also may lead to daytime sleepiness and impaired performance.

About This Chapter: Text in this chapter begins with excerpts from "Snoring," MedlinePlus, National Institutes of Health (NIH), August 4, 2016; Text beginning with the heading "Is Snoring A Problem?" is excerpted from "Your Guide To Healthy Sleep," National Heart, Lung, and Blood Institute (NHLBI), August 2011. Reviewed December 2017.

Although snoring may be harmless for most people, it can be a symptom of a life threatening sleep disorder called sleep apnea, especially if it is accompanied by severe daytime sleepiness. Snoring on a frequent or regular basis has been directly associated with hypertension. Those who snore loudly, especially if pauses in the snoring are noted, should consult a physician.

(Source: "Safety/Myths And Facts About Sleep," Natural Resources Conservation Service (NRCS), U.S. Department of Agriculture (USDA).)

What Causes Snoring?

Snoring is caused by a narrowing or partial blockage of the airways at the back of your mouth, throat, or nose. This obstruction results in increased air turbulence when breathing in, causing the soft tissues in your upper airways to vibrate. The end result is a noisy snore that can disrupt the sleep of your bed partner. This narrowing of the airways is typically caused by the soft palate, tongue, and throat relaxing while you sleep, but allergies or sinus problems also can contribute to a narrowing of the airways, as can being overweight and having extra soft tissue around your upper airways.

The larger the tissues in your soft palate (the roof of your mouth in the back of your throat), the more likely you are to snore while sleeping. Alcohol or sedatives taken shortly before sleep also promote snoring. These drugs cause greater relaxation of the tissues in your throat and mouth. African Americans, Asians, and Hispanics are more likely to snore loudly and frequently compared with Caucasians, and snoring problems increase with age.

Does Everyone Who Snores Have Sleep Apnea?

Not everyone who snores has sleep apnea, but people who have sleep apnea typically do snore loudly and frequently. Sleep apnea is a serious sleep disorder, and its hallmark is loud, frequent snoring with pauses in breathing or shallow breaths while sleeping. Even if you don't

How To Reduce Snoring
The snoring usually is loudest when you sleep on your back; it might be less noisy when you turn on your side.

(Source: "Sleep Apnea," National Heart, Lung, and Blood Institute (NHLBI).)

experience these breathing pauses, snoring can still be a problem for you as well as for your bed partner. Snoring adds extra effort to your breathing, which can reduce the quality of your sleep and lead to many of the same health consequences as sleep apnea.

What Are The Risks Associated With Snoring?

In addition, snoring increases the risk of developing diabetes and heart disease. One study found that women who snored regularly were twice as likely as those who did not snore to develop diabetes, even if they were not overweight (another risk factor for diabetes). Other studies suggest that regular snoring may raise the lifetime risk of developing high blood pressure, heart failure, and stroke.

How Does Snoring Cause Problems In Children?

Snoring also can be a problem in children. As many as 10–15 percent of young children, who typically have enlarged adenoids and tonsils (both tissues in the throat), snore on a regular basis. Several studies show that children who snore (with or without sleep apnea) are more likely than those who do not snore to score lower on tests that measure intelligence, memory, and attention span. These children also have more problematic behavior, including hyperactivity. The end result is that children who snore don't perform in school as well as those who do not snore. Strikingly, snoring was linked to a greater drop in IQ than that seen in children who had elevated levels of lead in their blood.

Although the behavior of children improves after they stop snoring, studies suggest they may continue to get poorer grades in school, perhaps because of lasting effects on the brain linked to the snoring. You should have your child evaluated by your doctor if the child snores loudly and frequently—three to four times a week—especially if you note brief pauses in breathing while asleep and if there are signs of hyperactivity or daytime sleepiness, inadequate school achievement, or slower than expected development.

What Treatment Is Available?

Surgery to remove the adenoids and tonsils of children often can cure their snoring and any associated sleep apnea. Such surgery has been linked to a reduction in hyperactivity and improved ability to pay attention, even in children who showed no signs of sleep apnea before surgery.

Snoring in older children may be relieved by less invasive measures, however. These measures include losing weight, refraining from use of tobacco, sleeping on the side rather than on the back, or elevating the head while sleeping. Treating chronic congestion and refraining from alcohol or sedatives before sleeping also may decrease snoring. Although numerous over-the-counter (OTC) nasal strips and sprays claim to relieve snoring, no scientific evidence supports those claims.

Chapter 28

Sleep Apnea

What Is Sleep Apnea?

Sleep apnea is a common disorder that causes your breathing to stop or get very shallow. Breathing pauses can last from a few seconds to minutes. They may occur 30 times or more an hour. You are more at risk for sleep apnea if you are overweight, male, or have a family history or small airways. Children with enlarged tonsils or adenoids may also get it.

Why Is Sleep Apnea Dangerous?

Most people who have sleep apnea don't realize it. That's because this disorder only occurs during sleep. Sleep apnea is when you have pauses in breathing while you're asleep. These pauses can last from seconds to minutes. You may have difficulty breathing a few times or dozens of times an hour.

These breathing pauses can be dangerous if they cause the oxygen level in your body to drop or disturb your sleep. When oxygen drops, your brain does whatever it can to get you to resume breathing. And then you may snore, gasp, snort loudly, or make a choking sound. A family member or bed partner might be the first to notice these disruptions in your sleep.

About This Chapter: Text under the heading "What Is Sleep Apnea?" is excerpted from "Sleep Apnea," MedlinePlus, National Institutes of Health (NIH), February 10, 2016; Text beginning with the heading "Why Is Sleep Apnea Dangerous?" is excerpted from "Struggling To Sleep? Don't Let Apnea Steal Your Sweet Dreams," *NIH News in Health*, National Institutes of Health (NIH), July 2017.

Untreated sleep apnea can lead to changes in energy metabolism (the way your body changes food and oxygen into energy) that increase the risk for developing obesity and diabetes.

(Source: "Your Guide To Healthy Sleep," National Heart, Lung, and Blood Institute (NHLBI).)

Who Is At Risk For Sleep Apnea?

Sleep apnea is a common disorder. Anyone can develop it. "Sleep apnea can occur in both genders, in all races and ethnicities, and in people of all sizes and shapes," says Dr. Michael Twery, a sleep expert at National Institutes of Health (NIH).

What Are The Types Of Sleep Apnea?

Obstructive Sleep Apnea

The most common type of sleep apnea is called obstructive sleep apnea. Any air that squeezes past a blocked airway can cause loud snoring. When you're awake, the muscles in your throat help keep your airway stiff and open. In adults, the throat muscles and tongue can relax during sleep, or fat tissue in the neck can narrow your airway to cause an obstruction. In children, the airway may become blocked if their tonsils are so large they obstruct the airway opening.

Central Sleep Apnea

The other type of sleep apnea is central sleep apnea. In central sleep apnea, the brain doesn't send the correct signals to your breathing muscles, so you stop breathing for brief periods.

What Are The Symptoms Of Sleep Apnea?

Excessive Daytime Sleepiness

One of the most common symptoms is excessive daytime sleepiness. "Anyone who feels so tired on a regular basis that this is a drag on their daytime function—that even if they allow enough time to get enough sleep on a regular basis and they still feel this way—then they need to discuss it with their doctor," Twery says.

Frequent Snoring

Another common symptom is loud, frequent snoring. But not everyone who snores has sleep apnea.

Other Symptoms

Other symptoms of sleep apnea may include feeling irritable or depressed, or having mood swings. You may have memory problems or trouble concentrating. Or, you may wake up with a headache or a dry mouth.

How Is Sleep Apnea Diagnosed?

Your doctor can diagnose sleep apnea based on your symptoms, a physical exam, and a sleep study. For a sleep study, your doctor may send you to a sleep lab or provide a portable sleep monitor. Sleep studies record things like heart rate and oxygen level while you sleep.

A sleep study can show whether apnea is mild or severe. "The largest proportion of the population with sleep apnea has mild sleep apnea," Twery explains. "Mild may or may not be associated with any daytime symptoms." People who are so sleepy that they're at risk of a drowsy driving accident are probably in the moderate to severe range.

How Is Sleep Apnea Treated?

Doctors may prescribe breathing devices that pump air or mouthpieces that adjust the lower jaw or hold the tongue. Other treatments are available and may be considered with advice from a physician familiar with your health.

Everyone deserves a good night's sleep. If you feel extremely sleepy during the daytime or your bed partner says that you stop breathing when you're asleep, go talk with your doctor.

Surgery

Some people who have sleep apnea may benefit from surgery; this depends on the findings of the evaluation by the sleep specialist. Removing tonsils and adenoids that are blocking the airway is done frequently, especially in children.

(Source: "Your Guide To Healthy Sleep," National Heart, Lung, and Blood Institute (NHLBI).)

Tips For Improving Your Breathing

Try these tips for improving your breathing when you're asleep:

- Avoid alcohol before bedtime and don't take medicines that make you sleepy. They make it harder for your throat to stay open when you're asleep.

- Maintain a healthy weight. Extra fat in the walls of your throat can make it narrower.

- Sleep on your side instead of your back. This helps keep your throat open.

- Ask your physician about medicines. Some medications can help open your nasal passages.

Chapter 29

Narcolepsy

What Is Narcolepsy?

Narcolepsy is a chronic neurological disorder that affects the brain's ability to control sleep-wake cycles. People with narcolepsy usually feel rested after waking, but then feel very sleepy throughout much of the day. Many individuals with narcolepsy also experience uneven and interrupted sleep that can involve waking up frequently during the night.

Narcolepsy can greatly affect daily activities. People may unwillingly fall asleep even if they are in the middle of an activity like driving, eating, or talking. Other symptoms may include sudden muscle weakness while awake that makes a person go limp or unable to move (cataplexy), vivid dream-like images or hallucinations, and total paralysis just before falling asleep or just after waking up (sleep paralysis).

In a normal sleep cycle, a person enters rapid eye movement (REM) sleep after about 60–90 minutes. Dreams occur during REM sleep, and the brain keeps muscles limp during this sleep stage, which prevents people from acting out their dreams. People with narcolepsy frequently enter REM sleep rapidly, within 15 minutes of falling asleep. Also, the muscle weakness or dream activity of REM sleep can occur during wakefulness or be absent during sleep. This helps explain some symptoms of narcolepsy.

If left undiagnosed or untreated, narcolepsy can interfere with psychological, social, and cognitive function and development and can inhibit academic, work, and social activities.

About This Chapter: This chapter includes text excerpted from "Your Guide To Healthy Sleep," National Institute of Neurological Disorders and Stroke (NINDS), May 4, 2017.

Who Gets Narcolepsy?

Narcolepsy affects both males and females equally. Symptoms often start in childhood, adolescence, or young adulthood (ages 7–25), but can occur at any time in life. It is estimated that anywhere from 135,000 – 200,000 people in the United States have narcolepsy. However, since this condition often goes undiagnosed, the number may be higher. Since people with narcolepsy are often misdiagnosed with other conditions, such as psychiatric disorders or emotional problems, it can take years for someone to get the proper diagnosis.

What Are The Symptoms?

Narcolepsy is a lifelong problem, but it does not usually worsen as the person ages. Symptoms can partially improve over time, but they will never disappear completely. The most typical symptoms are excessive daytime sleepiness, cataplexy, sleep paralysis, and hallucinations. Though all have excessive daytime sleepiness, only 10–25 percent of affected individuals will experience all of the other symptoms during the course of their illness.

- **Excessive daytime sleepiness (EDS).** All individuals with narcolepsy have EDS, and it is often the most obvious symptom. EDS is characterized by persistent sleepiness, regardless of how much sleep an individual gets at night. However, sleepiness in narcolepsy is more like a "sleep attack," where an overwhelming sense of sleepiness comes on quickly. In between sleep attacks, individuals have normal levels of alertness, particularly if doing activities that keep their attention.

- **Cataplexy.** This sudden loss of muscle tone while a person is awake leads to weakness and a loss of voluntary muscle control. It is often triggered by sudden, strong emotions such as laughter, fear, anger, stress, or excitement. The symptoms of cataplexy may appear weeks or even years after the onset of EDS. Some people may only have one or two attacks in a lifetime, while others may experience many attacks a day. In about 10 percent of cases of narcolepsy, cataplexy is the first symptom to appear and can be misdiagnosed as a seizure disorder. Attacks may be mild and involve only a momentary sense of minor weakness in a limited number of muscles, such as a slight drooping of the eyelids. The most severe attacks result in a total body collapse during which individuals are unable to move, speak, or keep their eyes open. But even during the most severe episodes, people remain fully conscious, a characteristic that distinguishes cataplexy from fainting or seizure disorders. The loss of muscle tone during cataplexy resembles paralysis of muscle activity that naturally occurs during REM sleep. Episodes last a few minutes at most and resolve almost instantly on their own. While scary, the episodes are not dangerous as long as the individual finds a safe place in which to collapse.

- **Sleep paralysis.** The temporary inability to move or speak while falling asleep or waking up usually lasts only a few seconds or minutes and is similar to REM-induced inhibitions of voluntary muscle activity. Sleep paralysis resembles cataplexy except it occurs at the edges of sleep. As with cataplexy, people remain fully conscious. Even when severe, cataplexy and sleep paralysis do not result in permanent dysfunction—after episodes end, people rapidly recover their full capacity to move and speak.

- **Hallucinations.** Very vivid and sometimes frightening images can accompany sleep paralysis and usually occur when people are falling asleep or waking up. Most often the content is primarily visual, but any of the other senses can be involved.

Additional symptoms of narcolepsy include:

- **Fragmented sleep and insomnia.** While individuals with narcolepsy are very sleepy during the day, they usually also experience difficulties staying asleep at night. Sleep may be disrupted by insomnia, vivid dreaming, sleep apnea, acting out while dreaming, and periodic leg movements.

- **Automatic behaviors.** Individuals with narcolepsy may experience temporary sleep episodes that can be very brief, lasting no more than seconds at a time. A person falls asleep during an activity (e.g., eating, talking) and automatically continues the activity for a few seconds or minutes without conscious awareness of what they are doing. This happens most often while people are engaged in habitual activities such as typing or driving. They cannot recall their actions, and their performance is almost always impaired. Their handwriting may, for example, degenerate into an illegible scrawl, or they may store items in bizarre locations and then forget where they placed them. If an episode occurs while driving, individuals may get lost or have an accident. People tend to awaken from these episodes feeling refreshed, finding that their drowsiness and fatigue has temporarily subsided.

What Are The Types Of Narcolepsy?

There are two major types of narcolepsy:

- **Type 1 narcolepsy** (previously termed narcolepsy with cataplexy). This diagnosis is based on the individual either having low levels of a brain hormone (hypocretin) or reporting cataplexy and having excessive daytime sleepiness on a special nap test.

- **Type 2 narcolepsy** (previously termed narcolepsy without cataplexy). People with this condition experience excessive daytime sleepiness but usually do not have muscle weakness triggered by emotions. They usually also have less severe symptoms and have normal levels of the brain hormone hypocretin.

A condition known as **secondary narcolepsy** can result from an injury to the hypothalamus, a region deep in the brain that helps regulate sleep. In addition to experiencing the typical symptoms of narcolepsy, individuals may also have severe neurological problems and sleep for long periods (more than 10 hours) each night.

What Causes Narcolepsy?

Narcolepsy may have several causes. Nearly all people with narcolepsy who have cataplexy have extremely low levels of the naturally occurring chemical hypocretin, which promotes wakefulness and regulates REM sleep. Hypocretin levels are usually normal in people who have narcolepsy without cataplexy.

Although the cause of narcolepsy is not completely understood, current research suggests that narcolepsy may be the result of a combination of factors working together to cause a lack of hypocretin. These factors include:

- **Autoimmune disorders.** When cataplexy is present, the cause is most often the loss of brain cells that produce hypocretin. Although the reason for this cell loss is unknown, it appears to be linked to abnormalities in the immune system. Autoimmune disorders occur when the body's immune system turns against itself and mistakenly attacks healthy cells or tissue. Researchers believe that in individuals with narcolepsy, the body's immune system selectively attacks the hypocretin-containing brain cells because of a combination of genetic and environmental factors.

- **Family history.** Most cases of narcolepsy are sporadic, meaning the disorder occurs in individuals with no known family history. However, clusters in families sometimes occur—up to 10 percent of individuals diagnosed with narcolepsy with cataplexy report having a close relative with similar symptoms.

- **Brain injuries.** Rarely, narcolepsy results from traumatic injury to parts of the brain that regulate wakefulness and REM sleep or from tumors and other diseases in the same regions.

How Is Narcolepsy Diagnosed?

A clinical examination and detailed medical history are essential for diagnosis and treatment of narcolepsy. Individuals may be asked by their doctor to keep a sleep journal noting the times of sleep and symptoms over a one- to two-week period. Although none of the major symptoms are exclusive to narcolepsy, cataplexy is the most specific symptom and occurs in almost no other diseases.

A physical exam can rule out or identify other neurological conditions that may be causing the symptoms. Two specialized tests, which can be performed in a sleep disorders clinic, are required to establish a diagnosis of narcolepsy:

- **Polysomnogram (PSG or sleep study).** The PSG is an overnight recording of brain and muscle activity, breathing, and eye movements. A PSG can help reveal whether REM sleep occurs early in the sleep cycle and if an individual's symptoms result from another condition such as sleep apnea.

- **Multiple sleep latency test (MSLT).** The MSLT assesses daytime sleepiness by measuring how quickly a person falls asleep and whether they enter REM sleep. On the day after the PSG, an individual is asked to take five short naps separated by two hours over the course of a day. If an individual falls asleep in less than 8 minutes on average over the five naps, this indicates excessive daytime sleepiness. However, individuals with narcolepsy also have REM sleep start abnormally quickly. If REM sleep happens within 15 minutes at least two times out of the five naps and the sleep study the night before, this is likely an abnormality caused by narcolepsy. Occasionally, it may be helpful to measure the level of hypocretin in the fluid that surrounds the brain and spinal cord. To perform this test, a doctor will withdraw a sample of the cerebrospinal fluid using a lumbar puncture (also called a spinal tap) and measure the level of hypocretin-1. In the absence of other serious medical conditions, low hypocretin-1 levels almost certainly indicate type 1 narcolepsy.

What Treatments Are Available?

Although there is no cure for narcolepsy, some of the symptoms can be treated with medicines and lifestyle changes. When cataplexy is present, the loss of hypocretin is believed to be irreversible and lifelong. Excessive daytime sleepiness and cataplexy can be controlled in most individuals with medications.

Medications

- **Modafinil.** The initial line of treatment is usually a central nervous system stimulant such as modafinil. Modafinil is usually prescribed first because it is less addictive and has fewer side effects than older stimulants. For most people these drugs are generally effective at reducing daytime drowsiness and improving alertness.

- **Amphetamine-like stimulants.** In cases where modafinil is not effective, doctors may prescribe amphetamine-like stimulants such as methylphenidate to alleviate EDS. However, these medications must be carefully monitored because they can have such side effects as irritability and nervousness, shakiness, disturbances in heart rhythm, and nighttime sleep disruption. In addition, healthcare professionals should be careful when prescribing these drugs and people should be careful using them because the potential for abuse is high with any amphetamine.

- **Antidepressants.** Two classes of antidepressant drugs have proven effective in controlling cataplexy in many individuals: tricyclics (including imipramine, desipramine, clomipramine, and protriptyline) and selective serotonin and noradrenergic reuptake inhibitors (including venlafaxine, fluoxetine, and atomoxetine). In general, antidepressants produce fewer adverse effects than amphetamines. However, troublesome side effects still occur in some individuals, including impotence, high blood pressure, and heart rhythm irregularities.

- **Sodium oxybate.** Sodium oxybate (also known as gamma hydroxybutyrate or GHB) has been approved by the U.S. Food and Drug Administration (FDA) to treat cataplexy and excessive daytime sleepiness in individuals with narcolepsy. It is a strong sedative that must be taken twice a night. Due to safety concerns associated with the use of this drug, the distribution of sodium oxybate is tightly restricted.

Lifestyle Changes

Not everyone with narcolepsy can consistently maintain a fully normal state of alertness using currently available medications. Drug therapy should accompany various lifestyle changes. The following strategies may be helpful:

- **Take short naps.** Many individuals take short, regularly scheduled naps at times when they tend to feel sleepiest.

- **Maintain a regular sleep schedule.** Going to bed and waking up at the same time every day, even on the weekends, can help people sleep better.

- **Avoid caffeine or alcohol before bed.** Individuals should avoid alcohol and caffeine for several hours before bedtime.

- **Avoid smoking,** especially at night.

- **Exercise daily.** Exercising for at least 20 minutes per day at least 4–5 hours before bedtime also improves sleep quality and can help people with narcolepsy avoid gaining excess weight.

- **Avoid large, heavy meals right before bedtime.** Eating very close to bedtime can make it harder to sleep.

- **Relax before bed.** Relaxing activities such as a warm bath before bedtime can help promote sleepiness. Also make sure the sleep space is cool and comfortable.

- Safety precautions, particularly when driving, are important for everyone with narcolepsy. People with untreated symptoms are more likely to be involved in automobile accidents although the risk is lower among individuals who are taking appropriate medication. EDS and cataplexy can lead to serious injury or death if left uncontrolled. Suddenly falling asleep or losing muscle control can transform actions that are ordinarily safe, such as walking down a long flight of stairs, into hazards.

- The Americans with Disabilities Act (ADA) requires employers to provide reasonable accommodations for all employees with disabilities. Adults with narcolepsy can often negotiate with employers to modify their work schedules so they can take naps when necessary and perform their most demanding tasks when they are most alert. Similarly, children and adolescents with narcolepsy may be able to work with school administrators to accommodate special needs, like taking medications during the school day, modifying class schedules to fit in a nap, and other strategies.

Additionally, support groups can be extremely beneficial for people with narcolepsy who want to develop better coping strategies or feel socially isolated due to embarrassment about their symptoms. Support groups also provide individuals with a network of social contacts who can offer practical help and emotional support.

What Is The State Of The Science Involving Narcolepsy?

In the past few decades, scientists have made considerable progress in understanding narcolepsy and identifying genes strongly associated with the disorder.

Groups of neurons in several parts of the brain interact to control sleep, and the activity of these neurons is controlled by a large number of genes. The loss of hypocretin-producing neurons in the hypothalamus is the primary cause of type 1 narcolepsy. These neurons are important for stabilizing sleep and wake states. When these neurons are gone, changes between wake, REM sleep, and non-REM sleep can happen spontaneously. This results in the sleep fragmentation and daytime symptoms that people with narcolepsy experience.

It remains unclear exactly why hypocretin neurons die. However, research increasingly points to immune system abnormalities. HLA—human leukocyte antigen—genes play an important role in regulating the immune system. This gene family provides instructions for making a group of related proteins called the HLA complex, which helps the immune system distinguish between good proteins from an individual's own body and bad ones made by foreign invaders like viruses and bacteria. One of the genes in this family is HLA-DQB1. A variation in this gene, called *HLA-DQB1*06:02*, increases the chance of developing narcolepsy, particularly the type of narcolepsy with cataplexy and a loss of hypocretins (also known as orexins). *HLA-DQB1*06:02* and other *HLA* gene variations may increase susceptibility to an immune attack on hypocretin neurons, causing these cells to die. Most people with narcolepsy have this gene variation and may also have specific versions of closely related *HLA* genes.

However, it is important to note that these gene variations are common in the general population and only a small portion of the people with the *HLA-DQB1*06:02* variation will develop narcolepsy. This indicates that other genetic and environmental factors are important in determining if an individual will develop the disorder.

Narcolepsy follows a seasonal pattern and is more likely to develop in the spring and early summer after the winter season, a time when people are more likely to get sick. By studying people soon after they develop the disorder, scientists have discovered that individuals with narcolepsy have high levels of anti-streptolysin O antibodies, indicating an immune response to a recent bacterial infection such as strep throat. Also, the H1N1 influenza epidemic in 2009 resulted in a large increase in the number of new cases of narcolepsy. Together, this suggests that individuals with the *HLA-DQB1*06:02* variation are at risk for developing narcolepsy after they are exposed to a specific trigger, like certain infections that trick the immune system to attack the body.

Chapter 30

Idiopathic Hypersomnia And Kleine-Levin Syndrome

What Is Idiopathic Hypersomnia (IH)?

Idiopathic hypersomnia (IH) is a rare sleep disorder that can affect many aspects of a person's life. People with IH have a hard time staying awake during the day (chronic excessive daytime sleepiness or EDS) even though they seem to sleep well at night. They need to take long naps, but usually do not feel refreshed upon waking. The immediate need for sleep may come at anytime during the day, including while working, in class, or driving a car. Many people with IH may feel very drowsy and confused when waking up (sleep drunkenness). Other symptoms may include anxiety, feeling irritated, low energy, restlessness, slow thinking or speech, loss of appetite, and memory difficulties. Symptoms often develop during the teen or young adult years.

The cause of IH is unknown. Currently there is no treatment approved by the U.S. Food and Drug Administration (FDA) specifically for IH, but some people may be helped by medications used to treat other disorders.

About This Chapter: Text beginning with the heading "What Is Idiopathic Hypersomnia (IH)?" is excerpted from "Idiopathic Hypersomnia," Genetic and Rare Diseases Information Center (GARD), National Center for Advancing Translational Sciences (NCATS), June 1, 2017; Text beginning with the heading "What Is Kleine-Levin Syndrome?" is excerpted from "Kleine Levin Syndrome," Genetic and Rare Diseases Information Center (GARD), National Center for Advancing Translational Sciences (NCATS), February 10, 2017; Text beginning with the heading "Kleine-Levin Syndrome Treatment" is excerpted from "Kleine-Levin Syndrome Information Page," National Institute of Neurological Disorders and Stroke (NINDS), September 21, 2016.

What Treatment Is There For Idiopathic Hypersomnia?

Treatments for hypersomnia are generally aimed at excessive daytime sleepiness (EDS), rather than at sleep duration or sleep drunkenness (confusion upon waking up). Although there are multiple treatments approved by the FDA for narcolepsy, there are no FDA-approved treatments idiopathic hypersomnia (IH). Therefore, treatment generally involves off-label use of medications approved for narcolepsy. Unfortunately, the use of these medications is inadequate to improve symptoms in many people with IH. These medication options may include:

- Wakefulness-promoting agents (modafinil and armodafinil)

- Traditional psychostimulants (amphetamines, methylphenidate, and their derivatives)

There are also several emerging therapies for cases that do not respond to the above types of medications. These include sodium oxybate, clarithromycin, and flumazenil.

Nonmedical approaches such as behavior modification are not generally effective for people with IH. Unlike in narcolepsy, where scheduled naps can help, daytime naps in people with IH are typically long and nonrestorative.

People with IH should avoid activities that may be dangerous, and should avoid driving or operating dangerous machinery unless sleepiness is well controlled by medication.

Following up with physicians at least annually (preferably more frequently) is recommended to assess for side effects of medication, sleep or mood disturbances, adequate control of symptoms, and any work-related or social issues.

What Is Kleine-Levin Syndrome?

Kleine-Levin syndrome is a rare disorder characterized by recurrent episodes of excessive sleep (hypersomnia) along with cognitive and behavioral changes. Affected individuals may sleep for up to 20 hours per day during an episode. These episodes usually last for a few days to a few weeks. An episode may start abruptly and is sometimes preceded by an upper-respiratory-type infection. During an episode, people with Kleine-Levin syndrome can also display abnormal behavior, such as excessive food intake (hyperphagia), irritability, childishness, disorientation, hallucinations, and an abnormally uninhibited sex drive. Affected individuals are symptom-free between episodes. The time between episodes varies.

Kleine-Levin syndrome primarily affects adolescent males, but it also affects females and individuals of other ages. The underlying cause of this condition is unknown. Episodes tend to decrease with advancing age. There are no consistently effective therapies, although stimulants (modafinil, methylphenidate, amphetamine) and mood stabilizers (lithium) may be prescribed with varying results.

How Long Can A Person Have Kleine-Levin Syndrome?

In most cases, the signs and symptoms of Kleine-Levin syndrome last for about 8–12 years. In a review of 186 cases published in the medical literature, the authors found that the duration of Kleine-Levin syndrome ranged from 6 months to 41 years.

Kleine-Levin Syndrome Treatment

There is no definitive treatment for Kleine-Levin syndrome and watchful waiting at home, rather than pharmacotherapy, is most often advised. Stimulant pills, including amphetamines, methylphenidate, and modafinil, are used to treat sleepiness but may increase irritability and will not improve cognitive abnormalities. Because of similarities between Kleine-Levin syndrome and certain mood disorders, lithium and carbamazepine may be prescribed and, in some cases, have been shown to prevent further episodes. This disorder should be differentiated from cyclic reoccurrence of sleepiness during the premenstrual period in teen-aged girls, which may be controlled with birth control pills. It also should be differentiated from encephalopathy, recurrent depression, or psychosis.

Kleine-Levin Syndrome Prognosis

Episodes eventually decrease in frequency and intensity over the course of 8–12 years.

Chapter 31

Restless Legs Syndrome (RLS)

What Is Restless Legs Syndrome (RLS)?

Restless legs syndrome (RLS), also called Willis-Ekbom Disease (WED), causes unpleasant or uncomfortable sensations in the legs and an irresistible urge to move them. Symptoms commonly occur in the late afternoon or evening hours, and are often most severe at night when a person is resting, such as sitting or lying in bed. They also may occur when someone is inactive and sitting for extended periods (for example, when taking a trip by plane or watching a movie).

Since symptoms can increase in severity during the night, it could become difficult to fall asleep or return to sleep after waking up. Moving the legs or walking typically relieves the discomfort but the sensations often recur once the movement stops. RLS is classified as a sleep disorder since the symptoms are triggered by resting and attempting to sleep, and as a movement disorder, since people are forced to move their legs in order to relieve symptoms. It is, however, best characterized as a neurological sensory disorder with symptoms that are produced from within the brain itself.

RLS is one of several disorders that can cause exhaustion and daytime sleepiness, which can strongly affect mood, concentration, job and school performance, and personal relationships. Many people with RLS report they are often unable to concentrate, have impaired memory, or fail to accomplish daily tasks. Untreated moderate to severe RLS can lead to about a 20-percent decrease in work productivity and can contribute to depression and anxiety. It also can make traveling difficult.

About This Chapter: This chapter includes text excerpted from "Restless Legs Syndrome Fact Sheet," National Institute of Neurological Disorders and Stroke (NINDS), May 2017.

It is estimated that up to 7–10 percent of the U.S. population may have RLS. RLS occurs in both men and women, although women are more likely to have it than men. It may begin at any age. Many individuals who are severely affected are middle-aged or older, and the symptoms typically become more frequent and last longer with age.

More than 80 percent of people with RLS also experience periodic limb movement of sleep (PLMS). PLMS is characterized by involuntary leg (and sometimes arm) twitching or jerking movements during sleep that typically occur every 15–40 seconds, sometimes throughout the night. Although many individuals with RLS also develop PLMS, most people with PLMS do not experience RLS.

Fortunately, most cases of RLS can be treated with nondrug therapies and if necessary, medications.

What Are Common Signs And Symptoms Of RLS?

People with RLS feel the irresistible urge to move, which is accompanied by uncomfortable sensations in their lower limbs that are unlike normal sensations experienced by people without the disorder. The sensations in their legs are often difficult to define but may be described as aching throbbing, pulling, itching, crawling, or creeping. These sensations less commonly affect the arms, and rarely the chest or head. Although the sensations can occur on just one side of the body, they most often affect both sides. They can also alternate between sides. The sensations range in severity from uncomfortable to irritating to painful.

Because moving the legs (or other affected parts of the body) relieves the discomfort, people with RLS often keep their legs in motion to minimize or prevent the sensations. They may pace the floor, constantly move their legs while sitting, and toss and turn in bed.

A classic feature of RLS is that the symptoms are worse at night with a distinct symptom-free period in the early morning, allowing for more refreshing sleep at that time. Some people with RLS have difficulty falling asleep and staying asleep. They may also note a worsening of symptoms if their sleep is further reduced by events or activity.

RLS symptoms may vary from day to day, in severity and frequency, and from person to person. In moderately severe cases, symptoms occur only once or twice a week but often result in significant delay of sleep onset, with some disruption of daytime function. In severe cases of RLS, the symptoms occur more than twice a week and result in burdensome interruption of sleep and impairment of daytime function.

People with RLS can sometimes experience remissions—spontaneous improvement over a period of weeks or months before symptoms reappear—usually during the early stages of the disorder. In general, however, symptoms become more severe over time.

People who have both RLS and an associated medical condition tend to develop more severe symptoms rapidly. In contrast, those who have RLS that is not related to any other condition show a very slow progression of the disorder, particularly if they experience onset at an early age; many years may pass before symptoms occur regularly.

What Causes RLS?

In most cases, the cause of RLS is unknown (called primary RLS). However, RLS has a genetic component and can be found in families where the onset of symptoms is before age 40. Specific gene variants have been associated with RLS. Evidence indicates that low levels of iron in the brain also may be responsible for RLS.

Considerable evidence also suggests that RLS is related to a dysfunction in one of the sections of the brain that control movement (called the basal ganglia) that use the brain chemical dopamine. Dopamine is needed to produce smooth, purposeful muscle activity and movement. Disruption of these pathways frequently results in involuntary movements. Individuals with Parkinson disease, another disorder of the basal ganglia dopamine pathways, have increased chance of developing RLS.

RLS also appears to be related to or accompany the following factors or underlying conditions:

- end-stage renal disease and hemodialysis
- iron deficiency
- certain medications that may aggravate RLS symptoms, such as antinausea drugs (e.g., prochlorperazine or metoclopramide), antipsychotic drugs (e.g., haloperidol or phenothiazine derivatives), antidepressants that increase serotonin (e.g., fluoxetine or sertraline), and some cold and allergy medications that contain older antihistamines (e.g., diphenhydramine)
- use of alcohol, nicotine, and caffeine
- pregnancy, especially in the last trimester; in most cases, symptoms usually disappear within 4 weeks after delivery
- neuropathy (nerve damage)

Sleep deprivation and other sleep conditions like sleep apnea also may aggravate or trigger symptoms in some people. Reducing or completely eliminating these factors may relieve symptoms.

How Is RLS Diagnosed?

Since there is no specific test for RLS, the condition is diagnosed by a doctor's evaluation. The five basic criteria for clinically diagnosing the disorder are:

- A strong and often overwhelming need or urge to move the legs that is often associated with abnormal, unpleasant, or uncomfortable sensations.

- The urge to move the legs starts or gets worse during rest or inactivity.

- The urge to move the legs is at least temporarily and partially or totally relieved by movements.

- The urge to move the legs starts or is aggravated in the evening or night.

- The above four features are not due to any other medical or behavioral condition.

A physician will focus largely on the individual's descriptions of symptoms, their triggers and relieving factors, as well as the presence or absence of symptoms throughout the day. A neurological and physical exam, plus information from the person's medical and family history and list of current medications, may be helpful. Individuals may be asked about frequency, duration, and intensity of symptoms; if movement helps to relieve symptoms; how much time it takes to fall asleep; any pain related to symptoms; and any tendency toward daytime sleep patterns and sleepiness, disturbance of sleep, or daytime function. Laboratory tests may rule out other conditions such as kidney failure, iron deficiency anemia (which is a separate condition related to iron deficiency), or pregnancy that may be causing symptoms of RLS. Blood tests can identify iron deficiencies as well as other medical disorders associated with RLS. In some cases, sleep studies such as polysomnography (a test that records the individual's brain waves, heartbeat, breathing, and leg movements during an entire night) may identify the presence of other causes of sleep disruption (e.g., sleep apnea), which may impact management of the disorder. Periodic limb movement of sleep during a sleep study can support the diagnosis of RLS but, again, is not exclusively seen in individuals with RLS.

Diagnosing RLS in children may be especially difficult, since it may be hard for children to describe what they are experiencing, when and how often the symptoms occur, and how long symptoms last. Pediatric RLS can sometimes be misdiagnosed as "growing pains" or attention deficit disorder.

How Is RLS Treated?

RLS can be treated, with care directed toward relieving symptoms. Moving the affected limb(s) may provide temporary relief. Sometimes RLS symptoms can be controlled by finding and treating an associated medical condition, such as peripheral neuropathy, diabetes, or iron deficiency anemia.

Iron supplementation or medications are usually helpful but no single medication effectively manages RLS for all individuals. Trials of different drugs may be necessary. In addition, medications taken regularly may lose their effect over time or even make the condition worse, making it necessary to change medications.

Treatment options for RLS include:

Lifestyle changes. Certain lifestyle changes and activities may provide some relief in persons with mild to moderate symptoms of RLS. These steps include avoiding or decreasing the use of alcohol and tobacco, changing or maintaining a regular sleep pattern, a program of moderate exercise, and massaging the legs, taking a warm bath, or using a heating pad or ice pack. There are new medical devices that have been cleared by the U.S. Food and Drug Administration (FDA), including a foot wrap that puts pressure underneath the foot and another that is a pad that delivers vibration to the back of the legs. Aerobic and leg-stretching exercises of moderate intensity also may provide some relief from mild symptoms.

Iron. For individuals with low or low-normal blood tests called ferritin and transferrin saturation, a trial of iron supplements is recommended as the first treatment. Iron supplements are available over-the-counter (OTC). A common side effect is upset stomach, which may improve with use of a different type of iron supplement. Because iron is not well-absorbed into the body by the gut, it may cause constipation that can be treated with a stool softeners such as polyethylene glycol. In some people, iron supplementation does not improve a person's iron levels. Others may require iron given through an IV line in order to boost the iron levels and relieve symptoms.

Antiseizure drugs. Antiseizure drugs are becoming the first-line prescription drugs for those with RLS. The FDA has approved gabapentin enacarbil for the treatment of moderate to severe RLS, This drug appears to be as effective as dopaminergic treatment (discussed below) and, at least to date, have been no reports of problems with a progressive worsening of symptoms due to medication (called augmentation). Other medications may be prescribed "off-label" to relieve some of the symptoms of the disorder.

Other antiseizure drugs such as the standard form of gabapentin and pregabalin can decrease such sensory disturbances as creeping and crawling as well as nerve pain. Dizziness,

147

fatigue, and sleepiness are among the possible side effects. Recent studies have shown that pregabalin is as effective for RLS treatment as the dopaminergic drug pramipexole, suggesting this class of drug offers equivalent benefits.

Dopaminergic agents. These drugs, which increase dopamine effect, are largely used to treat Parkinson disease. They have been shown to reduce symptoms of RLS when they are taken at nighttime. The FDA has approved ropinirole, pramipexole, and rotigotine to treat moderate to severe RLS. These drugs are generally well tolerated but can cause nausea, dizziness, or other short-term side effects. Levodopa plus carbidopa may be effective when used intermittently, but not daily.

Although dopamine-related medications are effective in managing RLS symptoms, long-term use can lead to worsening of the symptoms in many individuals. With chronic use, a person may begin to experience symptoms earlier in the evening or even earlier until the symptoms are present around the clock. Over time, the initial evening or bedtime dose can become less effective, the symptoms at night become more intense, and symptoms could begin to affect the arms or trunk. Fortunately, this apparent progression can be reversed by removing the person from all dopamine-related medications.

Another important adverse effect of dopamine medications that occurs in some people is the development of impulsive or obsessive behaviors such as obsessive gambling or shopping. Should they occur, these behaviors can be improved or reversed by stopping the medication.

Opioids. Drugs such as methadone, codeine, hydrocodone, or oxycodone are sometimes prescribed to treat individuals with more severe symptoms of RLS who did not respond well to other medications. Side effects include constipation, dizziness, nausea, exacerbation of sleep apnea, and the risk of addiction; however, very low doses are often effective in controlling symptoms of RLS.

Benzodiazepines. These drugs can help individuals obtain a more restful sleep. However, even if taken only at bedtime they can sometimes cause daytime sleepiness, reduce energy, and affect concentration. Benzodiazepines such as clonazepam and lorazepam are generally prescribed to treat anxiety, muscle spasms, and insomnia. Because these drugs also may induce or aggravate sleep apnea in some cases, they should not be used in people with this condition. These are last-line drugs due to their side effects.

What Is The Prognosis For People With RLS?

RLS is generally a lifelong condition for which there is no cure. However, current therapies can control the disorder, minimize symptoms, and increase periods of restful sleep. Symptoms may gradually worsen with age, although the decline may be somewhat faster for individuals who also suffer from an associated medical condition. A diagnosis of RLS does not indicate the onset of another neurological disease, such as Parkinson disease. In addition, some individuals have remissions—periods in which symptoms decrease or disappear for days, weeks, months, or years—although symptoms often eventually reappear. If RLS symptoms are mild, do not produce significant daytime discomfort, or do not affect an individual's ability to fall asleep, the condition does not have to be treated.

Chapter 32

Periodic Limb Movement Disorder (PLMD)

Periodic limb movement disorder (PLMD) is a type of sleep disorder in which patients experience repetitive, rhythmic jerking or twitching movements in the legs or other limbs during sleep. The movements typically occur in a regular pattern every 20–40 seconds. Episodes most commonly take place in the early part of the night and last for less than an hour. Although the patient is usually not aware of them, the movements often disrupt sleep, resulting in such symptoms as daytime drowsiness and memory or attention problems.

PLMD is often confused with restless legs syndrome. In this condition, patients experience uncomfortable sensations in their legs while awake that create an irresistible urge to move the affected limbs. Although approximately 80 percent of people with restless legs syndrome also have PLMD, PLMD is considered a separate condition and does not appear to increase the risk of restless legs syndrome.

Symptoms

The main symptom of PLMD is tightening or flexing of muscles in the lower legs—including the big toe, foot, ankle, knee, or hip—during sleep. Although PLMD can also affect the arms or occur while awake, this is uncommon. The movements are usually concentrated during nonrapid eye movement (NREM) sleep in the first half of the night. Each movement typically lasts around 2 seconds, and they tend to recur every 20–40 seconds, although the pattern can vary from night to night. The movements can range from slight twitches to strenuous kicks.

About This Chapter: "Periodic Limb Movement Disorder (PLMD)," © 2016 Omnigraphics. Reviewed December 2017.

Most people with PLMD are unaware of the movements and only learn about them from another person who shares the same bed. For some patients, however, the repetitive movements can disrupt sleep and cause such symptoms as not feeling well rested after a good night's sleep, feeling tired or falling asleep during the day, having trouble remembering or paying attention, or becoming depressed.

Causes And Risk Factors

Researchers have not uncovered the cause of primary PLMD, although some believe that it may be linked to abnormalities in the regulation of nerve impulses from the brain to the limbs. PLMD affects males and females equally, and it can affect people of any age. The incidence of PLMD increases with age, however, and affects 34 percent of people over the age of 60.

Secondary PLMD is caused by underlying medical conditions, including the following:

- diabetes

- iron deficiency anemia

- spinal cord injury

- restless legs syndrome

- sleep apnea

- narcolepsy

- REM sleep behavior disorder

- sleep-related eating disorder

- multiple-system atrophy

Certain types of medications have also been found to increase the risk or worsen symptoms of PLMD, including antidepressants such as amitriptyline (Elavil) and lithium; dopamine-receptor antagonists like Haldol; and withdrawal from sedatives like Valium.

Diagnosis

Diagnosis of PLMD begins with a visit to a sleep specialist. Patients are typically asked to keep a sleep diary for several weeks, to evaluate their sleep using a rating system such as the Epworth Sleepiness Scale, and to provide a complete medical history, including any medications taken. In most cases, patients will then undergo an overnight sleep study, during which a polysomnogram (PSG) keeps track of brain activity, heartbeat, breathing, and limb movement. In addition to diagnosing PLMD and other sleep disorders, the sleep specialist can help identify other potential causes of sleep problems, such as medical conditions, medications, substance abuse, or mental health disorders.

Other medical tests can be used to detect underlying causes of PLMD, such as diabetes, anemia, or metabolic disorders. Doctors may take blood samples to check hormone levels, organ function, and blood chemistry. They may also look for infections or traces of drugs that can contribute to secondary PLMD. If no underlying cause can be found, the patient may be referred to a neurologist to rule out nervous system disorders and confirm the diagnosis of PLMD.

Treatment

Many people with PLMD do not experience symptoms or require treatment. When sleep disruption makes treatment necessary, however, there are several medications available to help reduce the movements or help the patient sleep through them. Some of the medications commonly prescribed to treat PLMD include:

- Benzodiazepines like clonazepam (Klonopin), which suppress muscle contractions;

- Anticonvulsant agents like gabapentin (Neurontin), which also reduce muscle contractions;

- Dopaminergic agents like levodopa/carbidopa (Sinemet) and pergolide (Permax), which increase the levels of the neurotransmitter dopamine in the brain and are also used to treat restless legs syndrome and Parkinson disease;

- GABA agonists like baclofen (Lioresal), which inhibit the release of neurotransmitters in the brain that stimulate muscle contractions.

References

1. "Periodic Limb Movement Disorder," WebMD, 2016.

2. "Sleep Education: Periodic Limb Movements," American Academy of Sleep Medicine, 2014.

Chapter 33

Parasomnias

Parasomnias are "odd" actions that we do, or unpleasant events that we experience while asleep or while partially asleep.

Almost everyone has a nightmare. A nightmare is considered a parasomnia since it is an unpleasant event that occurs while we are asleep.

A person with a parasomnia disorder has more than just the occasional nightmare. And the term parasomnia is much broader than just nightmares. Other common parasomnia events include:

- REM behavior disorder (RBD)
- Sleep paralysis
- Sleepwalking
- Confusional arousals

What Are Parasomnias?

In some people, the walking, talking, and other body functions normally suppressed during sleep occur during certain sleep stages. Alternatively, the paralysis or vivid images usually experienced during dreaming may persist after awakening. These occurrences are collectively known as parasomnias.

(Source: "Your Guide To Healthy Sleep," National Heart, Lung, and Blood Institute (NHLBI).)

About This Chapter: This chapter includes text excerpted from "Parasomnias," U.S. Department of Veterans Affairs (VA), September 14, 2017.

What Are Common Parasomnias?

Typically parasomnias are classified by whether they occur during the rapid eye movement (REM) sleep or the non-REM sleep. The REM sleep parasomnias tend to present as traits of wakefulness while in REM sleep, or as traits of REM sleep while awake. The non-REM sleep parasomnias tend to present as a middle ground where the patient is doing activities but is not fully awake.

REM Behavior Disorder (RBD)

Most dreaming occurs in REM sleep. Normally in REM sleep, most of our body muscles are paralyzed to prevent us from acting out our dreams. In REM Behavior Disorder (RBD) a person does not have this protective paralysis during REM sleep. A person therefore might "act out" their dream. Since dreams may involve violence and protecting oneself, a person acting out their dream may injure themselves or their bed partner. The person will usually recall the dream, but not realize that they were moving in real life.

Sleep Paralysis And Sleep Hallucinations

REM sleep is usually associated with dreams and the body paralyzing most of the muscles so dreams do not get acted out. Sometimes the REM-related paralysis or dream images can occur when falling asleep or when waking up from sleep. Sleep paralysis and sleep hallucinations can occur together or alone. The person is full aware of what is happening. Events can be very scary. An event will usually last seconds to minutes and fortunately end on its own.

Sleepwalking

In sleepwalking, the person is just awake enough to be active but is still asleep so unaware of the activities. Sometimes disorders like sleepwalking are called "disorders of arousal" since the person is in a mixed state of awareness (not fully asleep or awake). Sleepwalking disorders can range from sitting up in bed to complex behaviors such as driving a car. Sleepwalkers are unaware of their surroundings and can fall down or put themselves in danger. Despite the myths, it is not dangerous to wake up a sleepwalker. However the person will not typically recall the sleepwalking event and may be confused or disoriented.

Confusional Arousals

We all have experienced that strange and confused feeling when we first wake up. Confusional arousal is a sleep disorder that causes a person to act that way for a prolonged period. Episodes usually start when someone is abruptly woken up. The person does not wake up completely and so remains in a foggy state of mind. The person with a confusional arousal may have difficulty understanding situations around them, react slowly to commands or react aggressively as a first response to others.

What Can I Do For Parasomnias?

Many people with parasomnias see an improvement by improving their sleep habits. Some sleep healthy sleep tips include:

- Ensure you are getting enough sleep
- Keep a regular schedule of going to bed and waking up
- Avoid alcohol or other sedatives at night that might make it hard for you to completely wake up
- Avoid caffeine or smoking
- Keep the bedroom quiet to avoid getting disturbed

We need to make sure that persons suffering from parasomnias remain safe. Some tips for bedroom safety with a parasomnia include:

- Avoiding large objects that can fall by the bedside
- Make sure there are no objects on the floor that can be tripped over
- Close and lock bedroom doors and windows to ensure a person cannot go outside
- Consider an alarm or bell on the door
- Close shades over windows in case they are hit to protect a person from glass
- Remove potentially dangerous objects and weapons in the bedroom
- Avoid significant elevation. No bunk beds. Consider mattresses on the ground, and ground floor bedrooms.

If you or a family member has persistent episodes of sleep paralysis, sleep walking, or acting out of dreams, talk with your doctor.

(Source: "Your Guide To Healthy Sleep," National Heart, Lung, and Blood Institute (NHLBI).)

Chapter 34

Nightmares

It is not unusual to have nightmares during times of stress. If you have frequent and distressing nightmares, please talk to your medical or mental health provider. Frequent nightmares may be a sign of a more serious problem.

What Are Nightmares?

Nightmares are dreams that are threatening and scary. Nearly everyone has had a nightmare from time to time. Among the general public, about 5 percent of people complain of nightmares. Those who have gone through a trauma, though, are more likely to have distressing nightmares after the event.

(Source: "Nightmares And PTSD," U.S. Department of Veterans Affairs (VA).)

Sleep Problems And Nightmares

- Ongoing sleep problems can harm relationships and the ability to work and concentrate

- Nightmares interfere with sleep and can be a sign of other problems

- There are treatments that can help with sleep problems and nightmares

---

About This Chapter: Text in this chapter begins with excerpts from "Sleep Problems And Nightmares," U.S. Department of Veterans Affairs (VA), August 15, 2011. Reviewed December 2017; Text beginning with the heading "Nightmares And Posttraumatic Stress Disorder (PTSD)" is excerpted from "Nightmares And PTSD," U.S. Department of Veterans Affairs (VA), August 13, 2015.

Tips For Coping With Nightmares

- The morning after a nightmare, spend some time thinking about what might be causing increased stress in your life. Even positive stress (such as getting married, a new job, moving) can cause anxiety that may result in nightmares.

- Practice some form of relaxation every night before bed. Try imagining yourself in a calming or relaxing place, practice deep slow breathing, or listen to soothing music or sounds.

- Make your bedroom as soothing and comfortable as possible. Think about leaving a dim light or nightlight on to help you recognize your surroundings more quickly if you wake up from a nightmare.

Nightmares And Posttraumatic Stress Disorder (PTSD)

Nightmares are dreams that are threatening and scary. Nearly everyone has had a nightmare from time to time.

For trauma survivors, though, nightmares are a common problem. Along with flashbacks and unwanted memories, nightmares are one of the ways in which a trauma survivor may relive the trauma for months or years after the event.

How Common Are Nightmares After Trauma?

Among the general public, about 5 percent of people complain of nightmares. Those who have gone through a trauma, though, are more likely to have distressing nightmares after the event. This is true no matter what type of trauma it is.

Those trauma survivors who get posttraumatic stress disorder (PTSD) are even more likely to complain of nightmares. Nightmares are one of the 17 symptoms of PTSD. For example, a study comparing Vietnam Veterans to civilians showed that 52 percent of combat Veterans with PTSD had nightmares fairly often. Only 3 percent of the civilians in the study reported that same level of nightmares.

Other research has found even higher rates of nightmares. Of those with PTSD, 71 percent to 96 percent may have nightmares. People who have other mental health problems, such as panic disorder, as well as PTSD are more likely to have nightmares than those with PTSD alone.

Not only are trauma survivors more likely to have nightmares, those who do may have them quite often. Some survivors may have nightmares several times a week.

What Do Nightmares That Follow Trauma Look Like?

Nightmares that follow trauma often involve the same scary elements that were in the trauma. For example, someone who went through Hurricane Katrina may have dreams about high winds or floods. They may dream about trying to escape the waters or being in a shelter that does not feel safe. A survivor of a hold up might have nightmares about the robber or about being held at gunpoint.

Not all nightmares that occur after trauma are a direct replay of the event. About half of those who have nightmares after trauma have dreams that replay the trauma. People with PTSD are more likely to have dreams that are exact replays of the event than are survivors without PTSD.

Lab research has shown that nightmares after trauma are different in some ways from nightmares in general. Nightmares after trauma may occur earlier in the night and during different stages of sleep. They are more likely to have body movements along with them.

Nightmares And Cultural Differences

Nightmares may be viewed differently in different cultures. For example, in some cultures, nightmares are thought to mean that the dreamer is open to physical or spiritual harm. In other cultures, it is believed that the dreams may contain messages from spirits or may forecast the future. These beliefs may lead those with nightmares to use certain practices in an effort to protect themselves.

Are There Any Effective Treatments For Posttraumatic Nightmares?

Nightmare symptoms often get better with standard PTSD treatment. If nightmares persist, there are treatments that can reduce how often they occur.

One treatment is Imagery Rehearsal Therapy (IRT). In IRT, the person who is having nightmares, while awake, changes how the nightmare ends so that it no longer upsets them. Then the person replays over and over in their minds the new dream with the nonscary ending. Research shows that this type of treatment can reduce how often nightmares occur.

Also, treatment for breathing problems that occur during sleep may reduce the nightmares that follow trauma. High levels of sleep-disordered breathing have been seen in trauma survivors. In one study, patients given a treatment to improve their breathing during sleep no longer had violent, scary dreams.

Little research exists on the use of medicines to treat nightmares from trauma. The medicine with the most promise is prazosin.

Chapter 35

Bladder Control Problems And Bedwetting

What Are Bladder Control Problems In Children?

Children may have a bladder control problem—also called urinary incontinence (UI)—if they leak urine by accident and are past the age of toilet training. A child may not stay dry during the day, called daytime wetting; or through the night, called bedwetting.

Children normally gain control over their bladders somewhere between ages 2 and 4—each in their own time. Occasional wetting is common even in 4- to 6-year-old children.

By age 4, when most children stay dry during the day, daytime wetting can be very upsetting and embarrassing. By ages 5 or 6, children might have a bedwetting problem if the bed is wet once or twice a week over a few months.

Most bladder control problems disappear naturally as children grow older. When needed, a healthcare professional can check for conditions that may lead to wetting.

Loss of urine is almost never due to laziness, a strong will, emotional problems, or poor toilet training. Parents and caregivers should always approach this problem with understanding and patience.

Do Bladder Control Problems Have Another Name?

Bladder control problems are also called urinary incontinence or enuresis.

About This Chapter: This chapter includes text excerpted from "Bladder Control Problems And Bedwetting In Children," National Institute of Diabetes and Digestive and Kidney Diseases (NIDDK), September 2017.

- Primary enuresis is wetting in a child who has never regularly stayed dry.

- Secondary enuresis is wetting that begins after at least 6 months of staying dry.

What Are The Types Of Bladder Control Problems In Children?

Children usually have one of two main bladder control problems:

- daytime wetting, also called diurnal enuresis

- bedwetting, also called nocturnal enuresis

Some children may have trouble controlling their bladders both day and night.

Daytime Wetting

For infants and toddlers, wetting is a normal part of development. Children gradually learn to control their bladders as they grow older. Problems that can occur during this process and lead to daytime wetting include:

- **Holding urine too long.** Your child's bladder can overfill and leak urine.

- **Overactive bladder.** Your child's bladder squeezes without warning, causing frequent runs for the toilet and wet clothes.

- **Underactive bladder.** Your child uses the toilet only a few times a day, with little urge to do so. Children may have a weak or interrupted stream of urine.

- **Disordered urination.** Your child's bladder muscles and nerves do not work together smoothly. Certain muscles cut off urine flow too soon. Urine left in the bladder may leak.

Bedwetting

Children who wet the bed fall into two groups: those who have never been dry at night, and children who started wetting the bed again after staying dry for 6 months.

How Common Are Bladder Control Problems In Children?

Bladder control problems are common in children. About 1 in 10 children has trouble with daytime wetting at age 5. Nighttime wetting is more common than daytime wetting.

Table 35.1. Bedwetting Numbers

Age	Bedwetting Numbers
Age 5	About 1 in 6 children
Age 6	About 1 in 8 children
Age 7	1 in 10 children
Age 15	1–2 in 100 children

Who Is More Likely To Have Bladder Control Problems?

Daytime wetting is more common in girls than boys.

Bedwetting is more common in boys—and in all children whose parents wet the bed when they were young. Your child's chances of wetting the bed are about 1 in 3 when one parent was affected as a child. If both parents were affected, the chances that your child will wet the bed are 7 in 10.

Most children with bladder control problems are physically and emotionally normal. Certain health conditions can make a child more likely to experience wetting, including:

- a bladder or kidney infection (urinary tract infection)
- constipation—fewer than two bowel movements a week, or bowel movements in which stool is painful or hard to pass
- nerve problems, such those seen with spina bifida, a birth defect
- vesicouretal reflux (VUR), backward flow of urine from the bladder to the kidneys
- diabetes, a condition in which blood glucose, also called blood sugar, is too high
- problems with the structure of the urinary tract, such as a blockage or a narrowed urethra
- obstructive sleep apnea (OSA), a condition in which breathing is interrupted during sleep, often because of inflamed or enlarged tonsils
- ADHD, or attention deficit hyperactivity disorder

What Are The Complications Of Bladder Control Problems?

Children can manage or outgrow most bladder control problems with no lasting health effects. However, accidental wetting can cause emotional distress and poor self-esteem for a child as well as frustration for families.

Bladder control problems can sometimes lead to bladder or kidney infections (UTIs). Bedwetting that is never treated during childhood can last into the teen years and adulthood, causing emotional distress.

What Are The Signs And Symptoms Of Bladder Control Problems In Children?

Losing urine by accident is the main sign of a bladder control problem. Your child may often have wet or stained underwear—or a wet bed.

Daytime Wetting

Signs that your child may have a condition that causes daytime wetting include:

- the urgent need to urinate, often with urine leaks
- urinating 8 or more times a day, called frequency
- infrequent urination—emptying the bladder only 2 to 3 times a day, rather the usual 4–7 times a day
- incomplete urination—not fully emptying the bladder during bathroom visits
- squatting, squirming, leg crossing, or heel sitting to avoid leaking urine

Bedwetting

Nighttime wetting is normal for many children—and is often not considered a health problem at all—especially when it runs in the family.

At ages 5 and older, signs that your child may have a nighttime bladder control problem— whether due to slow physical development, an illness, or any cause—can include:

- never being dry at night
- wetting the bed 2 to 3 times a week over 3 months or more
- wetting the bed again after 6 months of dry nights

When Should My Child See A Doctor About Bladder Control Problems?

If you or your child are worried about accidental wetting, talk with a healthcare professional. He or she can check for medical problems and offer treatment, or reassure you that your child is developing normally.

Take your child to a healthcare professional if there are signs of a medical problem, including:

- symptoms of bladder infection such as:
  - pain or burning when urinating
  - cloudy, dark, bloody, or foul-smelling urine
  - urinating more often than usual
  - strong urges to urinate, but passing only a small amount of urine
  - pain in the lower belly area or back
  - crying while urinating
  - fever
  - restlessness
- your child dribbles urine or has a weak urine stream, which can be signs of a birth defect in the urinary tract
- your child was dry, but started wetting again

Although each child is unique, providers often use a child's age to decide when to look for a bladder control problem. In general,

- by age 4, most children are dry during the day
- by ages 5 or 6, most children are dry at night

Seek Care Right Away

If your child has symptoms of a bladder or kidney infection, or has a fever without a clear cause, see a healthcare professional within 24 hours. Quick treatment is important to prevent a urinary tract infection from causing more serious health problems.

What Causes Bladder Control Problems In Children?

Bathroom habits, such as holding urine too long, and slow physical development cause many of the bladder control problems seen in children. Less often, a medical condition can cause wetting.

167

What Causes Daytime Wetting In Children?

Daytime wetting in children is commonly caused by holding urine too long, constipation, or bladder systems that don't work together smoothly. Health problems can sometimes cause daytime wetting, too, such as bladder or kidney infections (UTIs), structural problems in the urinary tract, or nerve problems.

When children hold their urine too long, it can trigger problems in how the bladder works or make existing problems worse. These bladder problems include:

Overactive Bladder Or Urge Incontinence

Bladder muscles squeeze at the wrong time, without warning, causing a loss of urine. Your child may have strong, sudden urges to urinate. She may urinate frequently—eight or more times a day.

Underactive Bladder

Children only empty the bladder a few times a day, with little urge to urinate. Bladder contractions can be weak, and your child may strain when urinating, have a weak stream, or stop-and-go urine flow.

Disordered Urination

Muscles and nerves of the bladder may not work together smoothly. As the bladder empties, sphincter or pelvic floor muscles may cut off urine flow too soon, before the bladder empties all the way. Urine left in the bladder may leak.

What Causes Bedwetting In Children?

Nighttime wetting is often related to slow physical development, a family history of bedwetting, or making too much urine at night. In many cases, there is more than one cause. Children almost never wet the bed on purpose—and most children who wet the bed are physically and emotionally normal.

Sometimes a health condition can lead to bedwetting, such as diabetes or constipation.

Slow Physical Development

Between ages 5–10, slow physical development can cause your child to wet the bed. Your child may have a small bladder, deep sleep cycles, or a nervous system that's still growing and developing. The nervous system handles the body's alarms—sending signals about a full or emptying bladder—and the need to wake up.

Family History

Bedwetting often runs in families. Researchers have found genes that are linked to bedwetting. Genes are parts of the master code that children inherit from each parent for hair color and many other features and traits.

Making Too Much Urine

Your child's kidneys may make too much urine overnight, leading to an overfull bladder. If your child doesn't wake up in time, a wet bed is likely. Often this excess urine at night is due to low levels of a natural substance called antidiuretic hormone (ADH). ADH tells the kidneys to release less water at night.

Sleep Disorders

Sleepwalking and obstructive sleep apnea (OSA) can lead to bedwetting. With OSA, children breathe poorly and get less oxygen, which triggers the kidneys to make extra urine at night. Bedwetting can be a sign that your child has OSA. Other symptoms include snoring, mouth breathing, ear and sinus infections, a dry mouth in the morning, and daytime sleepiness.

Stress

Stress can sometimes lead to bedwetting, and worry about daytime or nighttime wetting can make the problem worse. Stresses that may affect your child include a new baby in the family, sleeping alone, moving or starting a new school, abuse, or a family crisis.

How Do Doctors Diagnose Bladder Control Problems In Children?

To diagnose a bladder control problem, doctors use a child's:

- medical history

- physical exam

- lab tests

- imaging tests, if needed

In addition, doctors will ask questions about:

- symptoms

- when and how often the wetting happens

- dry periods

- family history of bedwetting

Bladder And Liquids Diary

Before an office visit, it's helpful to use a bladder diary to keep track your child's bathroom habits and how much liquid your child drinks. Write down when your child uses the toilet, the amount of urine passed, and when your child leaks urine. Record the timing and amount of liquid your child drinks, too, including whether your child drinks fluids before bedtime.

Because constipation can cause wetting or make it worse, your child's doctor may ask you to record how often your child passes stool and whether it's hard or soft.

What Tests Do Doctors Use To Diagnose Bladder Control Problems In Children?

Lab Tests

Healthcare professionals often test a urine sample, which is called urinalysis, to help diagnose bladder control problems in children. The lab may also perform a urine culture, if requested. White blood cells and bacteria in the urine can be signs of a urinary tract infection.

Other Tests

In a few cases, healthcare professionals may order imaging tests or tests of how the urinary tract works. These tests can show a birth defect or a blockage in the urinary tract that may lead to wetting. Special tests can find nerve or spine problems. Testing can also help show a small bladder, weak muscles, or muscles that don't work together well.

Ultrasound. An ultrasound uses sound waves to look at structures inside the body without exposing your child to radiation. During this painless test, your child lies on a padded table. A technician gently moves a wand called a transducer over your child's belly and back. No anesthesia is needed.

Voiding cystourethrogram (VCUG). A voiding cystourethrogram uses X-rays of the bladder and urethra to show how urine flows. A technician uses a catheter to fill your child's bladder with a special dye. The technician then takes X-rays before, during and after your child urinates. A VCUG uses only a small amount of radiation. Anesthesia is not needed, but the doctor may offer your child a calming medicine, called a sedative.

Magnetic resonance imaging (MRI). Magnetic resonance imaging (MRI) uses magnets and radio waves to make pictures of the urinary tract and spine. During this test, your child lies on a table inside a tunnel-like machine. MRI scans do not expose your child to radiation. No anesthesia is needed, but the doctor may offer your child a calming medicine or suggest watching a children's program during the test.

Urodynamic testing. Urodynamic testing is a group of tests that look at how well the bladder, sphincters, and urethra are storing and releasing urine. These studies are not used often, but they may be helpful when simple bladder management methods are not as successful as expected.

How Can My Child's Doctor And I Treat A Bladder Control Problem?

When a health condition causes the wetting—such as diabetes or a birth defect in the urinary tract—doctors will treat the health problem, and the wetting is likely to stop.

Other common treatments for wetting include bladder training, moisture alarms, medicines, and home care. Teamwork is important among you, your child, and your child's doctor. You should reward your child for following a program, rather than for staying dry—because a child often cannot control wetting.

If your child wets both day and night, the doctor is likely to treat daytime wetting first. Children usually stay dry during the day before they gain bladder control at night.

Daytime Wetting

Treatments for daytime wetting depend on what's causing the wetting, and will often start with changes in bladder and bowel habits. Your child's doctor will treat any constipation, so that hard stools don't press against the bladder and lead to wetting.

Bladder Training

Bladder training helps your child get to the bathroom sooner and may help reset bladder systems that don't work together smoothly. Programs can include:

- urinating on schedule every 2–3 hours, called timed voiding.

- urinating twice during one visit, called double voiding. This method may help the bladder empty completely in children who have an underactive or "lazy" bladder or vesicoureteral reflux (VUR).

- relaxing the pelvic floor muscles so children can empty the bladder fully. A few sessions of biofeedback can retrain muscles that don't work together in the right order.

In extremely rare cases, doctors may suggest using a thin, flexible tube, called a catheter, to empty the bladder. Occasional use of a catheter may help develop better bladder control in children with a weak, underactive bladder.

Medicine

Your child's doctor may suggest medicine to limit daytime wetting or prevent a urinary tract infection (UTI).

Oxybutynin (Ditropan) is often the first choice of medicine to calm an overactive bladder until a child matures and outgrows the problem naturally.

If your child often has bladder infections, the doctor may prescribe an antibiotic, which is a medicine that kills the bacteria that cause infections. Your child's doctor may suggest taking a low-dose antibiotic for several months to prevent repeated bladder infections.

Home Care And Support

Changes in your child's routines and behavior may greatly improve daytime wetting, even without other treatments. Encourage your child to:

- use the bathroom whenever the urge occurs.

- drink more liquid, mainly water, if the doctor suggests doing so. Drinking more liquid produces more urine and more trips to the bathroom.

- take extra time in the bathroom to relax and empty the bladder completely.

- avoid drinks with caffeine or bubbles, citrus juices, and sports drinks. These drinks may irritate the bladder or produce extra urine.

Children need plenty of support from parents and caregivers to overcome daytime wetting, not blame or punishment. Calming your child's stresses may help—stresses about a new baby or new school, for example. A counselor or psychologist can help treat anxiety.

Bedwetting

If your child's provider suggests treatment, it's likely to start with ways to motivate your child and change his or her behavior. The next steps include moisture alarms or medicine.

For a bedwetting treatment program to work, both the parent and child must be motivated. Treatment doesn't always completely stop bedwetting—and there are likely to be some setbacks. However, treatment can greatly reduce how often your child wets the bed.

Motivational Therapy

For motivational therapy, you and your child agree on ways to manage bedwetting and rewards for following the program. Keep a record of your child's tasks and progress, such as a calendar with stickers. You can give rewards to your child for remembering to use the bathroom before bed, helping to change and clean wet bedding, and having a dry night.

Motivational therapy helps children gain a sense of control over bedwetting. Many children learn to stay dry with this approach, and many others have fewer wet nights. Taking back rewards, shaming, penalties, and punishments don't work; your child is not wetting the bed on purpose. If there's no change in your child's wetting after 3–6 months, talk with a healthcare professional about other treatments.

Moisture Alarms

Moisture alarms detect the first drops of urine in a child's underwear and sound an alarm to wake the child. A sensor clips to your child's clothes or bedding. At first you may need to wake your child, get him or her to the bathroom, and clean up wet clothes and bedding. Eventually, your child learns to wake up when his or her bladder is full and get to the bathroom in time.

Moisture alarms work well for many children and can end bedwetting for good. Families need to use the alarm regularly for 3–4 months as the child learns to sense his or her signals and control the bladder. Signs of progress usually appear in the first few weeks—smaller wet spots, fewer alarms each night, and your child waking on his or her own.

Medicine

Your child's doctor may suggest medicine when other treatments haven't worked well.

Desmopressin (DDAVP) is often the first choice of medicine for bedwetting. This medicine slows the amount of urine your child's body makes overnight, so the bladder doesn't overfill and leak. Desmopressin can work well, but bedwetting often returns when a child stops taking the medicine. You can use desmopressin for sleepovers, camp, and other short periods of time. You can also keep a child on desmopressin safely for long periods of time.

Home Care

Changes in your child's routines may improve bedwetting, when used alone or with other treatments. Encourage your child to:

- drink most of his or her liquids during the morning and early afternoon.

- urinate regularly during the day—every 2 to 3 hours—and just before bed, which is a total of about 4–7 times a day.

- urinate twice before bedtime (about a half hour apart) to fully empty the bladder and allow room for new urine made overnight.

- avoid drinks with caffeine or bubbles, citrus juices, and sports drinks. These drinks may irritate the bladder or produce extra urine.

How Can I Help My Child Cope With Bladder Control Problems?

Your patience, understanding, and encouragement are vital to help your child cope with a bladder control problem. If you think a health problem may be causing your child's wetting, make an appointment with your child's healthcare provider.

Clothing, Bedding, And Wearable Products

For children with daytime wetting, clothes that come on and off easily may help prevent accidents. A wristwatch alarm set to vibrate can privately remind your child to visit the toilet, without help from a teacher or parent.

For children who wet the bed, the following practices can make life easier and may boost your child's confidence:

- Leave out dry pajamas and towels so your child can clean up easily.

- Layer waterproof pads and fitted sheets on the bed. Your child can quickly pull off wet bedding and put it in a hamper. Fewer signs of wetting may help your child feel less embarrassed.

- Have your child help with the clean-up and laundry the next day. However, don't make it a punishment.

- Be sure your child showers or bathes every day to wash away the smell of urine.

- Plan to stop using diapers, training pants, or disposable training pants, except when sleeping away from home. These items may discourage your child from getting out of bed to use the toilet.

Don't make a habit of waking your child during the night to use the bathroom. Researchers don't think it helps children overcome bedwetting.

Emotional Support

Let your child know that bedwetting is very common and most children outgrow it. If your child is age 4 or older, ask him or her for ideas on how to stop or manage the wetting. Involving your child in finding solutions may provide a sense of control.

Calming your child's stresses may help—stresses about a new baby or new school, for example. A counselor or psychologist can help treat anxiety.

How Can I Help My Child Prevent Bladder Control Problems?

Often, you can't prevent a bladder control problem, especially bedwetting, which is a common pattern of normal child development. However, good habits may help your child have more dry days and nights, including:

- avoid or treat constipation.

- urinate every 2 to 3 hours during the day—4 to 7 times total in a day.

- drink the right amount of liquid, with most liquids consumed between morning and about 5 p.m. Ask your child's healthcare provider how much liquid is healthy, based on age, weather, and activities.

- avoid drinks with caffeine or bubbles, citrus juices, and sports drinks. These drinks may irritate the bladder or produce extra urine.

Chapter 36

Bruxism And Sleep

Bruxism is a type of movement disorder characterized by the grinding, gnashing, and clenching of the teeth. Many people may unconsciously grind or clench their teeth, but whether or not it qualifies as a case of bruxism depends largely on such factors as frequency, physical damage, and discomfort. The marked absence of clinical symptoms makes it difficult to estimate the prevalence of bruxism. Most cases go unreported, since the majority of "bruxers" remain unaware of their problem until a diagnosis can be made on the basis of visible signs of teeth wear.

Bruxism is thought to affect an estimated 30–40 million people in the United States and tends to occur episodically during certain periods of a person's life. Bruxism can be either diurnal (daytime) or nocturnal (night). When people unconsciously clench their jaws during the day, it is called awake bruxism, and when they grind or clench their teeth while they are asleep, it is called sleep bruxism.

Prevalence Of Sleep Bruxism

Since sleep bruxism (SB) is a type of parasomnia disorder that takes place during the night, it is consequently harder to control. While many people who grind their teeth during the night are not even aware of it, severe cases of sleep bruxism can have serious health consequences. According to reports, SB is more common in children than in adults. In most cases, the onset of SB is around one year of age, soon after the appearance of the primary incisors. The prevalence among adults is nearly 12 percent, dropping to 3 percent in older individuals. Although, awake bruxism is more common among females, there does not appear to be any gender difference in SB prevalence.

About This Chapter: "Bruxism And Sleep," © 2016 Omnigraphics. Reviewed December 2017.

Risk Factors

SB has been shown to have a wide range of causes. But long-term studies linking bruxism to its causal factors are still ongoing. Among the peripheral factors studied, the most important one is dental occlusion, which refers to the misalignment of the teeth in the upper and lower jaws. Certain pathophysiological factors have also been linked to SB, the most significant one being sleep arousal disorder. This condition is characterized by a sudden shift in the brain wave pattern during the transition from REM (rapid eye movement) sleep to non-REM sleep, or wakefulness, and is accompanied by an increase in respiratory rate and muscle activity. Bruxism has been shown to be a part of this arousal response.

Among all the factors that may contribute to sleep bruxism, the ones most extensively studied have been the psychosocial factors, which include stress and anxiety. Bruxing in children may often be traced to their emotional and psychological state. For instance, anxiety in children stemming from such causes as school exams, bullying, scolding from parents, or moving to a new neighborhood, may be a significant risk factor for SB. Some small children may grind their teeth as part of the teething process or due to frequent earaches. Among children, SB may tend to disappear on its own at puberty.

Certain personality types tend to be more vulnerable to stress-related bruxism, including those who are highly aggressive, competitive, or hyperactive. The risk of developing bruxism can be increased by certain lifestyle factors, such as smoking, alcohol consumption, and drug use. Bruxism may also develop as a side effect of certain medications or as a symptom of neurological disorders like Huntington disease and Parkinson disease. Studies have also shown that bruxism is often related to other sleep disorders, such as excessive snoring, pauses in breathing, or obstructive sleep apnea.

Symptoms And Diagnosis

The most common symptom of SB is rhythmic masticatory muscle activity (RMMA), or repetitive jaw muscle contractions. While mild to moderate muscle activity in bruxers may not cause any issues, severe cases could lead to dental problems, such as premature wearing of the teeth and dental implants, as well as temporomandibular dysfunction, which is pain and atrophy of the muscles and joints associated with chewing.

Bruxism is usually diagnosed through a visit to a dentist. During a regular checkup, the dentist will look for and inquire about the following symptoms:

- Damaged teeth

- Unusual teeth sensitivity

- Swelling and pain in the jaw or facial muscles around the mouth
- Tongue indentations
- Headaches or earaches
- Frequent awakening or poor quality of sleep

Treatment For Sleep Bruxism

Treatments for bruxism should be selected to best fit the individual patient and the underlying cause of the disorder. When a dental problem is determined to be the cause of bruxism, a dental appliance, like a splint or mouth guard, might alleviate the condition. These devices help prevent the teeth from grinding together and also protect the tooth enamel from further damage. Various dental procedures can also be performed to correct misalignment of the teeth and jaw or address damage to the teeth from clenching and grinding.

Cognitive behavioral therapy (CBT) can also help patients deal with improper mouth and jaw alignment. Correcting the position and placement of the tongue, teeth, and lips can bring about a significant improvement in the condition. Biofeedback is another treatment method used to assess and alter the movement of the muscles around the mouth and jaw. The doctor may use monitoring equipment to help guide the patient toward overcoming the habit of clenching the jaw or grinding the teeth.

If the primary cause of bruxism is determined to be psychological in nature, a number of behavioral and related therapies may help alleviate the condition. Stress management is the foremost issue to be addressed in people with bruxism. Counseling sessions with experts can help patients develop coping strategies. Other common means of reducing stress include meditation, relaxation, exercise, and music. Hypnosis has also proven to be an effective treatment for people who grind their teeth at night. Most patients with bruxism tend to respond well with proper treatment prescribed by the appropriate professional.

References

1. "Causes Of Bruxism," The Bruxism Association, n.d.

2. "Bruxism," The Nemours Foundation/KidsHealth, n.d.

3. Shilpa Shetty et al. "Bruxism: A Literature Review," The *Journal of Indian Prosthodontic Society*, Volume 10 (3): 141–148, National Center for Biotechnology Information (NCBI), U.S. National Library of Medicine (NLM), January 22, 2011.

Chapter 37

Night-Time (Nocturnal) Asthma

Night-time or nocturnal asthma is a common type of the disease characterized by symptoms that worsen at night. People with nocturnal asthma may be awakened from sleep by wheezing, shortness of breath, coughing, and a feeling of tightness in the chest. When experienced at night, these symptoms are potentially dangerous. In fact, studies have shown that a majority of asthma-related deaths occur at night. People with nocturnal asthma also tend to have more severe daytime asthma symptoms.

Night-time asthma sufferers may also experience health problems stemming from sleep disturbances. People who are unable to get adequate, quality sleep often feel tired and irritable during the day. They may also have trouble concentrating at work or at school. In fact, sleep disturbances due to asthma are one of the leading causes of children missing school. Studies have shown that children with nocturnal asthma may experience decreased mental function that affects their performance in school. When nocturnal asthma is treated effectively, however, sleep disturbance is reduced and mental function improves.

Causes Of Nocturnal Asthma

Researchers have identified a number of factors that may contribute to the worsening of asthma symptoms at night.

Sleep-Related Airway Changes

Airways tend to narrow during sleep, which increases airflow resistance. As a result, airway function decreases gradually through the night. Although healthy people may not notice this

About This Chapter: "Night-Time (Nocturnal) Asthma," © 2016 Omnigraphics. Reviewed December 2017.

effect, it can trigger symptoms in people with asthma. In fact, research has shown that people with asthma are more likely to experience breathing problems during sleep no matter when the sleep period occurs. Lung function test results tend to be worst around five hours after falling asleep, even for people who sleep during the daytime hours.

Sleep-Related Hormone Changes

The levels of certain hormones in the bloodstream tend to fluctuate according to a general pattern throughout the day and night. The changing hormone levels create the natural sleep-wake cycle, or circadian rhythms, and can also exert a powerful effect on asthma symptoms. The hormone epinephrine, for instance, reaches its lowest level in most people around 4 a.m. This hormone helps keep airways open by relaxing muscles surrounding the bronchial tubes. In addition, epinephrine suppresses histamines and other substances that cause the body to produce mucus.

Mucus Drainage Or Sinusitis

The increased production of mucus in the sinuses at night, combined with the narrowing of airways during sleep, can cause coughing and breathing problems in people with asthma. Sinusitis due to a viral or bacterial infection can also irritate sensitive airways and increase nocturnal asthma symptoms.

Reclining Position

Lying down may also contribute to night-time asthma symptoms. Reclining allows mucus secretions to drain from the sinuses and accumulate in the airways. In addition, it increases the volume of blood and decreases the volume of air in the lungs, which contributes to airway resistance.

Exposure To Allergens

About half of people who have an asthma attack immediately following exposure to an allergen will experience a second airway obstruction 3–8 hours later. Known as a late phase response, this second episode can be more severe and prolonged than the initial one. Research indicates that exposure to allergens in the evening increases a patient's susceptibility to a late phase response at night.

Cooling Of The Airways

Whether from sleeping in an air-conditioned bedroom in summer or turning the thermostat down in winter, breathing cold, dry air can result in the loss of heat from the airways. The cooling of the airways at night is considered a contributing factor to nocturnal asthma.

Heartburn

Gastroesophageal reflux disease (GERD), commonly known as acid reflux or heartburn, occurs when stomach acid flows back into the esophagus and larynx. In people with frequent heartburn, stomach acid can irritate the lower esophagus and lead to bronchial spasm and airway constriction. Stomach acid that reaches the throat can also drip down into the lungs, causing airway irritation and increased mucus production. Since lying down often makes heartburn worse, it can be related to nocturnal asthma.

Treatment Of Nocturnal Asthma

Night-time asthma can interfere with sleep and create serious health risks. The keys to managing asthma symptoms that worsen at night include finding the right asthma medications and determining when to use them to ensure quality sleep. Daily medications, such as inhaled corticosteroids, can help reduce inflammation of the airways and thus prevent night-time symptoms. But some short-term medications cannot cover a long enough time period to allow patients to sleep through the night. In such cases, a long-acting inhaled corticosteroid or bronchodilator may help alleviate symptoms.

For people whose nocturnal asthma may be triggered by allergens, it is important to avoid exposure to common allergens like dust mites or animal dander, especially in the evening hours. Regulating the temperature and humidity of the bedroom and elevating the head of the bed may also be helpful. Finally, people with GERD can often get relief from nocturnal asthma symptoms by taking medication that reduces acid production in the stomach.

Chapter 38

Nocturia: When The Need To Urinate Interrupts Sleep

Nocturia

Nocturia, also known as nocturnal polyuria or frequent nighttime urination, is a problem that affects an estimated 33 percent of adults. Normally, hormones signal the bladder to produce less urine at night, so most people can sleep for 6–8 hours without needing to get up to use the bathroom. Waking up once per night to empty the bladder is considered normal as well. People with nocturia, on the other hand, produce excessive amounts of urine and are regularly awakened several times per night by the need to urinate.

Waking up multiple times each night to use the bathroom can lead to chronic sleep deprivation. Since the incidence of nocturia increases with age, the majority of people affected are over the age of 60. Nocturia often appears as a symptom of underlying medical conditions, such as an enlarged prostate, diabetes, heart failure, or bladder problems. Nocturia should not be confused with enuresis—also known as bed-wetting—a condition in which urine is passed unintentionally during sleep. Nocturia also differs from urinary incontinence, in which patients experience a lack of voluntary control over urination in the daytime.

Causes Of Nocturia

The main causes of nocturia are excessive urine production and reduced bladder capacity. Many different factors and conditions can contribute to nocturia, including the following:

About This Chapter: "Nocturia: When The Need To Urinate Interrupts Sleep," © 2016 Omnigraphics. Reviewed December 2017.

- Diabetes

  Poorly controlled diabetes leads to sugar in the urine, which stimulates the production of additional urine.

- Congestive heart failure and other circulatory problems

  When the heart cannot adequately pump blood through the body, fluid tends to buildup in the legs (edema). Lying down at night reduces the burden on the heart and improves circulation, causing the fluid to fill the bladder.

- Pregnancy

  The growing fetus takes up space usually occupied by the bladder and restricts its capacity to hold fluids.

- Lower urinary tract conditions

  Infections of the urinary tract or kidneys can cause nocturia by irritating the bladder and decreasing its capacity to hold urine. Conditions like cystitis can result in an overactive bladder. Bladder obstructions can prevent the full elimination of urine, which may increase the frequency of urination at night.

- Constipation

  Excessive waste in the bowels or intestines can put pressure on the bladder.

- Medications

  Certain drugs, such as diuretics, increase the production of urine. Other examples include cardiac glycosides, demeclocycline, lithium, methoxyflurane, phenytoin, and propoxyphene. It is important to consult a doctor before stopping any prescribed medication, however, even if it causes nocturia as a side effect.

- Diet

  Consuming excessive fluids before bedtime can contribute to nocturia. Alcohol and caffeinated beverages, in particular, act as diuretics to increase urine production.

- Sleep disorders

  Obstructive sleep apnea and other sleep disorders can disrupt the normal reduction in urine output at night.

- Neurological disorders

  Conditions that affect the transmission of signals and hormones from the brain to the bladder—such as multiple sclerosis, Parkinson disease, or spinal cord injury—can result in nocturia.

Symptoms And Diagnosis

Many experts consider nocturia to be a symptom rather than a health condition. As a result, doctors usually place an emphasis on diagnosing the underlying medical causes of frequent and excessive nighttime urination that disrupts sleep. To evaluate a patient with nocturia, medical practitioners generally collect detailed information about the problem as well as the patient's overall health. The patient may be asked to keep a record of their bladder activity for several days, including the amount of fluid consumed, the frequency of urination during the day and at night, the amount of urine output, and any leaking of urine or wetting the bed. The patient will also be asked about any medications they take regularly, how much alcohol and caffeine they consume each day, and any discomfort they may experience during urination. The doctor may order a urinalysis to evaluate kidney function and check for a urinary tract infection.

Prevention And Treatment

Since nocturia is usually a symptom, most methods of treatment address the underlying medical conditions that contribute to frequent nighttime urination. Several of these conditions—such as enlarged prostate or overactive bladder—can be managed with the help of medications. A number of lifestyle modifications can also help reduce urine production at night and prevent people from needing to get up to use the bathroom. Some of the recommended methods of prevention and treatment for nocturia include the following:

- Avoid consuming fluids in the evening (but be sure that total fluid intake is adequate during the day)

- Eliminate or reduce consumption of caffeinated beverages and alcohol

- Take an afternoon nap to improve circulatory function and drain fluids from the extremities consistently throughout the day

- Wear compression stockings or elevate the legs to reduce fluid accumulation

- Perform Kegel exercises to strengthen the pelvic muscles and improve bladder control (these exercises are particularly helpful for pregnant women and for men with an enlarged prostate)

- Take diuretic medications in the late afternoon—six hours before bedtime—so that their therapeutic effects are completed before nighttime

- Eliminate urinary tract infections with antibiotic medications

- Treat enlarged prostate with medications such as tamsulosin (Flomax), finasteride, or dutasteride

- Control an unstable or overactive bladder with anticholinergic medications such as oxybutynin, tolterodine, or solifenacin

- Reduce urine production at night with medications such as desmopressin (DDAVP)

References

1. Marchione, Victor. "Nocturia: Frequent Urination At Night," Doctors Health Press, 2016.

2. "Nocturia," Cleveland Clinic, 2016.

3. "Nocturia (Night-Time Urination)," NetDoctor, October 4, 2012.

Chapter 39

Pain And Sleep: An Overview

Pain is the leading cause of insomnia. People who experience chronic pain—which includes about 15 percent of the overall U.S. population and half of all elderly people—often have trouble falling asleep and staying asleep. In fact, about 65 percent of people with chronic pain report having disrupted sleep or nonrestorative sleep, resulting in an average deficit of 42 minutes between the amount of sleep they need and the amount they actually get. Shorter sleep duration and poorer sleep quality, in turn, exacerbate chronic pain and interfere with activities, work, mood, relationships, and other aspects of daily life.

How Pain Impacts Sleep

People who experience chronic pain often have trouble falling asleep. Most people prepare for sleep by eliminating distractions and trying to relax. This process may include preparing the covers and pillows, turning off the lights, quieting noises in the bedroom, and making themselves comfortable. For people with chronic pain, however, distractions may serve as a pain management tool. As long as they are able to focus on working, socializing, preparing meals, performing household tasks, reading, watching television, or engaging in recreational activities, their perception of pain tends to decrease. When they eliminate distractions and try to fall asleep, however, their brain tends to focus on the pain. Their level of stress and experience of pain may increase with the amount of time it takes them to fall asleep.

People dealing with pain also tend to have trouble sleeping through the night. Research has shown, for instance, that people with chronic back pain experience a number of

About This Chapter: "Pain And Sleep: An Overview," © 2016 Omnigraphics. Reviewed December 2017.

microarousals—or changes from a deeper to a lighter stage of sleep—per hour each night. Such disruptions to the normal stages of sleep lead to frequent awakenings during the night and less restorative sleep. The poor quality of sleep means that people with chronic pain do not feel rested and refreshed in the morning. As a result, they often experience drowsiness, diminished energy, depressed mood, and increased pain throughout the day.

In some cases, people with pain also have other medical problems that disrupt sleep, such as restless legs syndrome or nocturnal leg cramps. People with restless legs syndrome experience an uncomfortable tingling or tickling sensation in their legs at night. This sensation creates an uncontrollable urge to move the legs, which can result in involuntary kicking or jerking motions during sleep. The symptoms of restless legs syndrome can contribute to problems falling asleep or staying asleep. They are sometimes relieved through massage, hot baths before bedtime, daily exercise, or eliminating caffeine or nicotine. They can also be treated with prescription medications.

Nocturnal leg cramps are sudden, painful muscle spasms that tend to occur during sleep or during the process of falling asleep. They may affect the feet, calves, or thighs and last between a few seconds and several minutes. Dehydration is the most common cause of muscle cramps, so staying well hydrated during the day can help prevent them from occurring. Overuse of the leg muscles is another factor that sometimes contributes to nocturnal cramping. Stretching before bedtime often helps with this problem. Deficiencies in calcium, magnesium, or potassium may also cause muscle cramps, so supplementing intake of these minerals in the diet may also prove helpful.

Improving Pain And Sleep

When pain impacts sleep, it is important to treat both problems together with a multidisciplinary approach. Since chronic pain and insomnia reinforce each other in a vicious cycle, treatments aimed at improving pain may also help improve sleep, while treatments aimed at improving sleep may also help improve pain. Many behavioral and psychological approaches are available to treat both pain and sleep issues.

Practices and habits that can lead to better quality sleep are known as "sleep hygiene." In many cases, people who experience chronic pain develop bad habits and poor sleep hygiene over time. Some of the practices that have proven safe and effective in improving sleep include the following:

- Develop a regular routine to help the body get into a consistent, healthy sleep-wake cycle. Try to go to bed at the same time every night and wake up at the same time each morning. Chronic pain sufferers sometimes try to compensate for having trouble falling asleep by sleeping late the next morning, but this practice disrupts the sleep-wake pattern.

- Avoid taking naps during the day, which can make insomnia worse in the long run by disrupting the sleep-wake cycle.

- Do not go to bed unless sleepy. Instead, spend some time engaging in relaxing activities like listening to music, reading a book, or meditating.

- Get out of bed if sleep does not come within 30 minutes. Trying to fall asleep for hours on end only increases anxiety levels and turns the bedroom into a stressful place. Instead, get up and return to a relaxing activity until a feeling of drowsiness occurs.

- Develop bedtime rituals to aid in relaxation and train the body to fall asleep. Suggestions include taking a warm bath or shower, listening to music, reading a book, or having a light snack.

- Avoid caffeine, nicotine, and alcohol before bedtime. Research has shown that these substances can be disruptive to a good night's sleep.

- Exercise at least 4–6 hours before bedtime. Although regular exercise can help ease chronic pain and promote good sleep, vigorous exercise within a few hours of bedtime can disrupt sleep.

- Create a comfortable, pleasant, relaxing sleep environment. People with chronic pain tend to be highly sensitive to environmental factors, such as light, noise, temperature, mattresses, and bedding. As a result, choosing comfortable bedding, making sure the temperature is neither too hot nor too cold, and eliminating sources of distracting noise or light can make a big difference in helping them get a good night's sleep.

- Try alternative techniques such as meditation, yoga, deep breathing, deep muscle relaxation, or hypnosis to aid in chronic pain management and relaxation. These techniques can help people reduce stress, decrease the perception of pain, and improve sleep.

If these approaches are not effective in improving sleep, chronic pain sufferers should consult a doctor. A variety of medications are available to help address sleep problems. Before taking any sleep medication, however, patients must be sure to tell the doctor about any other medications they may be taking for chronic pain or other medical conditions.

References

1. "Chronic Pain And Insomnia: Breaking The Cycle," Drugs and Usage, December 23, 2015.

2. "Pain And Sleep," National Sleep Foundation, 2016.

3. Silberman, Stephanie. "What's Really Causing Your Sleepless Nights?" Huffington Post, July 21, 2011.

Chapter 40

Alcohol And Sleep

Alcohol And The Body

Alcohol In

After alcohol enters the stomach, it is absorbed quickly into the bloodstream through the stomach wall. The rest enters the blood stream through the small intestine. How fast alcohol is absorbed you're your bloodstream depends on several things. Higher concentrations of alcohol like shots are absorbed faster than lower concentrations like light beer. Absorption is faster for a person who weighs less. If you've eaten recently, the absorption of alcohol will be slower than if you drink on an empty stomach.

Alcohol Out

Alcohol leaves your body in several ways. First, 90 percent is removed from the blood by the liver. Alcohol is then broken down into several chemicals, including carbon dioxide and water. The carbon dioxide and water come out in your urine. The final 10 percent is not removed by the liver and is expelled through sweat and breath. The reason why it is difficult to sober someone up is because the liver can only process about one drink per hour (this is slow considering the body absorbs alcohol through the stomach lining in about 10 minutes). There's not much that can influence how fast your liver processes alcohol. That's why cold showers, hot coffee or vomiting don't help.

About This Chapter: This chapter includes text excerpted from "Alcohol Effects And Safer Drinking Habits," U.S. Department of Veterans Affairs (VA), June 2013. Reviewed December 2017.

Tolerance

Over time, a person who drinks regularly has to drink more and more to feel the same effect as they did when they first began drinking. People develop tolerance because they have adapted, both physically and psychologically, to having alcohol in their system. Low tolerance is like a built-in warning system when alcohol levels get too high in our body. Tolerance may seem like a good thing because it allows heavy drinkers to function when they have high levels of alcohol in their bodies, but it is not a good thing. People with high alcohol tolerance short circuit this internal warning system. They don't experience negative reactions to the alcohol and continue drinking. Tolerant individuals are able to keep high levels of toxins in their bodies for long periods of time, which increases stress on sensitive internal organs and increases the chances of developing long-term health problems.

The good news about tolerance is you can decrease it (and the associated health risks) fairly easily. Tolerance can be reversed gradually through either moderating the quantity and frequency of your drinking, or taking a break from the alcohol for a few weeks.

A standard drink of alcohol:

- 1–12 oz beer
- 1–shot of liquor
- 1–wine cooler
- 1–cocktail
- 1–5 oz glass of wine

Alcohol Intoxication And Performance

Sleep

Bottom line is alcohol is bad for your sleep. Poor sleep can limit your ability to think, act quickly and perform well. Alcohol intoxication shortens the time necessary to fall asleep, but sleep is usually disturbed and fragmented after just a few hours. Restful, restorative sleep decreases during the second half of the night. So, heavy drinking compromises your sleep throughout the night. Poor sleep decreases the body's ability to function optimally. Poor sleep also decreases your physical endurance. If you want peak performance (at work, sports, or other engagements), either plan to abstain from alcohol use altogether or drink in moderation.

Up And Down Response To Alcohol In Your Body

The up and down response refers to two different effects that alcohol produces. The up response is feeling stimulated or excited. This is followed by the down response of feeling depressed and tired. The initial up response is associated with low but rising blood alcohol levels (BAL). The BAL is the ratio of alcohol to blood in your bloodstream. The down response is associated more with falling BALs. The up and down response is important because it allows you to test whether "more" alcohol means "better" is really true. It also helps you understand how tolerance affects you physiologically when it comes to drinking alcohol. Over time, as blood alcohol levels begin to fall, people experience the down effects of alcohol. This is the time when people begin to drink more in an attempt to get back their initial stimulated or excited state. However, the more alcohol that is consumed, the greater both the arousal and the depressant effects will be. At some point, the stimulating effects of a rising BAL will not amount to euphoria. The point at which an increase in BAL will not result in elevated mood or energy is known as the point of diminishing returns. For most people, that point is a BAL of 0.05%.

Table 40.1. Effects Of Alcohol On The Body

BAL	Effects Of Alcohol On The Body
0.02%	Light to moderate drinkers begin to feel some effect
0.04%	Most people begin to feel relaxed
0.06%	Judgment is somewhat impaired; people are less able to make rational decisions about their capabilities (e.g., driving)
0.08%	Definite impairment of muscle coordination and driving skills. Increased risk of nausea and slurred speech. Legal intoxication.
0.10%	Clear deterioration of reaction time and control.
0.15%	Balance and movement are impaired. Risk of blackouts and accidents.
0.30%	Many people lose consciousness. Risk of death.
0.45%	Breathing stops, death occurs.

Moderating Your Drinking

Decide what you want from drinking alcohol: Think about the pros and cons (short and long-term) for moderating your use versus maintaining your usual drinking behavior. Also consider what you absolutely want to avoid when you drink.

Set drinking limits:

- What's your upper limit on the number of drinks you consume per week?

- At what point do you decide you've had enough (consider a BAL limit)?

- What's the maximum number of days for drinking you will choose to give yourself?

- Use standard guidelines to determine what constitutes one drink: (1.25 oz of 80-proof liquor; 4 oz of wine; 10 oz of beer with 5 percent alcohol (microbrews and "ice" beer); 12 oz of beer with 4 percent alcohol (standard beer)

Count your drinks and monitor your drinking behavior:

Try it! Most people are surprised by what they learn when they actually count how much they drink. Simply observe your behavior—this is like standing outside yourself and watching how you are acting when you are drinking. Some people put the bottle caps in their pockets while drinking to monitor how many beers they have had. You can also make tick marks with a pen on a napkin to monitor the number of drinks.

Alter how and what you drink:

- Switch to drinks that contain less alcohol (e.g., light beers)

- Slow down your pace of drinking

- Space drinks further apart

- Alternate drinking nonalcoholic beverages with alcoholic drinks

Manage your drinking in the moment:

- Stay awake and on top of how you drink and what you're drinking when you're at a party

- Choose what's right for you and ask a close friend to help you monitor (preferably the friend that doesn't think being drunk is cool and cooler with company)

Safe drinking guidelines:

- For women, no more than 3 drinks/day; no more than 9 drinks/week.

- For men, no more than 4 drinks/day; no more than 14 drinks/week.

Part Four
The Consequences Of Sleep Deprivation

Chapter 41

Sleep Deprivation And Deficiency

What Are Sleep Deprivation And Deficiency?

Sleep deprivation is a condition that occurs if you don't get enough sleep. Sleep deficiency is a broader concept. It occurs if you have one or more of the following:

- You don't get enough sleep (sleep deprivation)
- You sleep at the wrong time of day (that is, you're out of sync with your body's natural clock)
- You don't sleep well or get all of the different types of sleep that your body needs
- You have a sleep disorder that prevents you from getting enough sleep or causes poor quality sleep

Sleeping is a basic human need, like eating, drinking, and breathing. Like these other needs, sleeping is a vital part of the foundation for good health and well-being throughout your lifetime.

Sleep deficiency can lead to physical and mental health problems, injuries, loss of productivity, and even a greater risk of death.

Who Is At Risk For Sleep Deprivation And Deficiency?

Sleep deficiency, which includes sleep deprivation, affects people of all ages, races, and ethnicities. Certain groups of people may be more likely to be sleep deficient.

About This Chapter: This chapter includes text excerpted from "What Are Sleep Deprivation And Deficiency?" National Heart, Lung, and Blood Institute (NHLBI), June 7, 2017.

Examples include people who:

- Have limited time available for sleep, such as caregivers or people working long hours or more than one job

- Have schedules that conflict with their internal body clocks, such as shift workers, first responders, teens who have early school schedules, or people who must travel for work

- Make lifestyle choices that prevent them from getting enough sleep, such as taking medicine to stay awake, abusing alcohol or drugs, or not leaving enough time for sleep

- Have undiagnosed or untreated medical problems, such as stress, anxiety, or sleep disorders

- Have medical conditions or take medicines that interfere with sleep

Certain medical conditions have been linked to sleep disorders. These conditions include heart failure, heart disease, obesity, diabetes, high blood pressure, stroke or transient ischemic attack (mini-stroke), depression, and attention deficit hyperactivity disorder (ADHD). If you have or have had one of these conditions, ask your doctor whether you might benefit from a sleep study.

A sleep study allows your doctor to measure how much and how well you sleep. It also helps show whether you have sleep problems and how severe they are. If you have a child who is overweight, talk with the doctor about your child's sleep habits.

What Are The Signs And Symptoms Of Problem Sleepiness?

Sleep deficiency can cause you to feel very tired during the day. You may not feel refreshed and alert when you wake up. Sleep deficiency also can interfere with work, school, driving, and social functioning.

How sleepy you feel during the day can help you figure out whether you're having symptoms of problem sleepiness. You might be sleep deficient if you often feel like you could doze off while:

- Sitting and reading or watching TV

- Sitting still in a public place, such as a movie theater, meeting, or classroom

- Riding in a car for an hour without stopping

- Sitting and talking to someone

- Sitting quietly after lunch

- Sitting in traffic for a few minutes

Sleep deficiency can cause problems with learning, focusing, and reacting. You may have trouble making decisions, solving problems, remembering things, controlling your emotions and behavior, and coping with change. You may take longer to finish tasks, have a slower reaction time, and make more mistakes.

The signs and symptoms of sleep deficiency may differ between children and adults. Children who are sleep deficient might be overly active and have problems paying attention. They also might misbehave, and their school performance can suffer.

Sleep-deficient children may feel angry and impulsive, have mood swings, feel sad or depressed, or lack motivation.

You may not notice how sleep deficiency affects your daily routine. A common myth is that people can learn to get by on little sleep with no negative effects. However, research shows that getting enough quality sleep at the right times is vital for mental health, physical health, quality of life, and safety.

To find out whether you're sleep deficient, try keeping a sleep diary for a couple of weeks. Write down how much you sleep each night, how alert and rested you feel in the morning, and how sleepy you feel during the day.

Strategies For Getting Enough Sleep

You can take steps to improve your sleep habits. First, make sure that you allow yourself enough time to sleep. With enough sleep each night, you may find that you're happier and more productive during the day.

Sleep often is the first thing that busy people squeeze out of their schedules. Making time to sleep will help you protect your health and well-being now and in the future.

To improve your sleep habits, it also may help to:

- Go to bed and wake up at the same time every day. For children, have a set bedtime and a bedtime routine. Don't use the child's bedroom for timeouts or punishment.

- Try to keep the same sleep schedule on weeknights and weekends. Limit the difference to no more than about an hour. Staying up late and sleeping in late on weekends can disrupt your body clock's sleep—wake rhythm.

- Use the hour before bed for quiet time. Avoid strenuous exercise and bright artificial light, such as from a TV or computer screen. The light may signal the brain that it's time to be awake.

- Avoid heavy and/or large meals within a couple hours of bedtime. (Having a light snack is okay.) Also, avoid alcoholic drinks before bed.

- Avoid nicotine (for example, cigarettes) and caffeine (including caffeinated soda, coffee, tea, and chocolate). Nicotine and caffeine are stimulants, and both substances can interfere with sleep. The effects of caffeine can last as long as 8 hours. So, a cup of coffee in the late afternoon can make it hard for you to fall asleep at night.

- Spend time outside every day (when possible) and be physically active.

- Keep your bedroom quiet, cool, and dark (a dim night light is fine, if needed).

- Take a hot bath or use relaxation techniques before bed.

Napping during the day may provide a boost in alertness and performance. However, if you have trouble falling asleep at night, limit naps or take them earlier in the afternoon.

Napping in preschool-aged children is normal and promotes healthy growth and development.

Strategies For Special Groups

Some people have schedules that conflict with their internal body clocks. For example, shift workers and teens who have early school schedules may have trouble getting enough sleep. This can affect how they feel mentally, physically, and emotionally.

If you're a shift worker, you may find it helpful to:

- Take naps and increase the amount of time available for sleep

- Keep the lights bright at work

- Limit shift changes so your body clock can adjust

- Limit caffeine use to the first part of your shift

- Remove sound and light distractions in your bedroom during daytime sleep (for example, use light-blocking curtains)

What To Do If Sleep Problem Persists

If your sleep problems persist or if they interfere with how you feel or function during the day, you should seek the assistance of a physician or other health professional. Before visiting your physician, consider keeping a diary of your sleep habits for about ten days to discuss at the visit.

(Source: "Teen Sleep Habits—What Should You Do?" Centers for Disease Control and Prevention (CDC).)

Chapter 42

Sleep Deprivation And Chronic Diseases

As chronic diseases have assumed an increasingly common role in premature death and illness, interest in the role of sleep health in the development and management of chronic diseases has grown. Notably, insufficient sleep has been linked to the development and management of a number of chronic diseases and conditions, including diabetes, cardiovascular disease (CVD), obesity, and depression.

Diabetes

Research has found that insufficient sleep is linked to an increased risk for the development of type 2 diabetes. Specifically, sleep duration and quality have emerged as predictors of levels of *Hemoglobin A1c*, an important marker of blood sugar control. Recent research suggests that optimizing sleep duration and quality may be important means of improving blood sugar control in persons with type 2 diabetes.

Cardiovascular Disease

Persons with sleep apnea have been found to be at increased risk for a number of cardiovascular diseases. Notably, hypertension, stroke, coronary heart disease (CHD), and irregular heartbeats (*cardiac arrhythmias*) have been found to be more common among those with disordered sleep than their peers without sleep abnormalities. Likewise, sleep apnea and hardening

About This Chapter: This chapter includes text excerpted from "Sleep And Sleep Disorders—Sleep And Chronic Disease," Centers for Disease Control and Prevention (CDC), July 1, 2013. Reviewed December 2017.

of the arteries (*atherosclerosis*) appear to share some common physiological characteristics, further suggesting that sleep apnea may be an important predictor of cardiovascular disease.

Obesity

Laboratory research has found that short sleep duration results in metabolic changes that may be linked to obesity. Epidemiologic studies conducted in the community have also revealed an association between short sleep duration and excess body weight. This association has been reported in all age groups—but has been particularly pronounced in children. It is believed that sleep in childhood and adolescence is particularly important for brain development and that insufficient sleep in youngsters may adversely affect the function of a region of the brain known as the *hypothalamus*, which regulates appetite and the expenditure of energy.

Depression

The relationship between sleep and depression is complex. While sleep disturbance has long been held to be an important symptom of depression, recent research has indicated that depressive symptoms may decrease once sleep apnea has been effectively treated and sufficient sleep restored. The interrelatedness of sleep and depression suggests it is important that the sleep sufficiency of persons with depression be assessed and that symptoms of depression be monitored among persons with a sleep disorder.

Chapter 43

Attention Deficit Hyperactivity Disorder (ADHD) And Sleep Deprivation

Do you find it hard to pay attention? Do you feel the need to move constantly during times when you shouldn't? Do you find yourself constantly interrupting others? If these issues are ongoing and you feel that they are negatively impacting your daily life, it could be a sign of attention deficit hyperactivity disorder (ADHD).

What Is ADHD?

ADHD is a disorder that makes it difficult for a person to pay attention and control impulsive behaviors. He or she may also be restless and almost constantly active. ADHD is not just a childhood disorder. Although the symptoms of ADHD begin in childhood, ADHD can continue through adolescence and adulthood. Even though hyperactivity tends to improve as a child becomes a teen, problems with inattention, disorganization, and poor impulse control often continue through the teen years and into adulthood.

What Causes ADHD?

Current research suggests ADHD may be caused by interactions between genes and environmental or nongenetic factors. Like many other illnesses, a number of factors may contribute to ADHD such as:

• Genes

About This Chapter: Text in this chapter begins with excerpts from "Attention Deficit Hyperactivity Disorder (ADHD): The Basics," National Institute Of Mental Health (NIMH), March 7, 2016; Text under the heading "ADHD And Sleep Deprivation" is © 2017 Omnigraphics. Reviewed December 2017.

- Cigarette smoking, alcohol use, or drug use

- Exposure to environmental toxins, such as high levels of lead, at a young age

- Low birth weight

- Brain injuries

Warning Signs

Teens with ADHD show an ongoing pattern of three different types of symptoms:

- Difficulty paying attention (inattention)

- Being overactive (hyperactivity)

- Acting without thinking (impulsivity)

These symptoms get in the way of functioning or development. People who have ADHD have combinations of these symptoms:

- Overlook or miss details, make careless mistakes in schoolwork, at work, or during other activities

- Have problems sustaining attention in tasks or play, including conversations, lectures, or lengthy reading

- Seem to not listen when spoken to directly

- Fail to not follow through on instructions, fail to finish schoolwork, chores, or duties in the workplace, or start tasks but quickly lose focus and get easily sidetracked

- Have problems organizing tasks and activities, such as doing tasks in sequence, keeping materials and belongings in order, keeping work organized, managing time, and meeting deadlines

- Avoid or dislike tasks that require sustained mental effort, such as schoolwork or homework, or for teens and older adults, preparing reports, completing forms, or reviewing lengthy papers

- Lose things necessary for tasks or activities, such as school supplies, pencils, books, tools, wallets, keys, paperwork, eyeglasses, and cell phones

- Become easily distracted by unrelated thoughts or stimuli

- Forgetful in daily activities, such as chores, errands, returning calls, and keeping appointments

ADHD And Sleep Deprivation

Sleep deprivation among adolescents is a common problem in the United States, and researchers have found substantial links between attention deficit hyperactivity disorder (ADHD) and sleep issues. Adolescents who are diagnosed with ADHD tend to experience such problems as trouble falling asleep, staying asleep, and disrupted sleep. National Sleep Foundation studies have found that 50 percent of children and teens with ADHD suffer from sleep-disordered breathing and have more daytime sleepiness compared to just 22 percent of other children and teens. Sleep issues can aggravate ADHD symptoms, and a few studies have even suggested that regular sleep patterns can help eliminate hyperactivity among some young people. Interestingly, lack of sleep affects children and teens quite differently than it does adults. While adults who get very little sleep generally become lethargic, young people tend to get high-strung, inattentive, and often display disruptive behavior. As a result, sleep disorders in children and teens can lead to more serious issues in school, at home, and in social situations. Here are some tips to help teens with ADHD get better sleep:

- Caffeine is a major stimulant; therefore, avoiding caffeinated beverages and foods can help ensure proper sleep

- Consistent habits such as specific bedtimes, waking times, and a healthy diet can be helpful

- A dark, quiet, and cozy room helps promote undisturbed sleep

- Avoid sleep medication, which can result in daytime grogginess and lead to dependency

- Daily exercise can help teens sleep better

- Take a warm bath before bedtime to encourage relaxation

References

1. "ADHD And Sleep," Sleep Foundation, n.d.

2. Bhandari, Smitha, MD. "ADHD And Sleep Disorders," WebMD, November 18, 2014.

3. "Diagnosing ADHD In Adolescence," CHADD The National Resource on ADHD, n.d.

4. Spruyt, Karen, PhD, and David Gozal, MD. "Sleep Disturbances In Children With Attention-Deficit/Hyperactivity Disorder," SleepMed, December 10, 2009.

Chapter 44

Sleep Deprivation And Learning

The Learning Process And Sleep

Learning, sleep, and memory are interconnected processes that are not yet fully understood. The main function of sleep has generally been thought to be related to learning and memory, and research on humans and animals indicates that both the quality and quantity of sleep can impact those functions. Adequate sleep is required for the body and mind to repair and replenish energy. Sleep deprivation can therefore have a negative impact on the cognitive capacity of the brain. It can hinder spatial learning, along with other functions, such as memory, attention span, and reaction time. It can also take a toll on general health and the immune system, and in extreme cases may even result in hallucinations.

Learning and memory are characterized by three phases: acquisition, consolidation, and recall. During acquisition, the brain is fully alert and gathering new information. Consolidation occurs when a person is at rest, and the brain solidifies the freshly acquired information. The last phase, recall, is the process of retrieving stored information when the person is awake.

Though it is only during waking hours that acquisition and recall take place, research shows that memory consolidation, through the strengthening of neural connections, occurs during sleep. It is still not clear how this process takes place, but it is hypothesized by many researchers that certain characteristics of brainwaves at different sleep stages aid in the formation of memory.

Sleep researchers take two approaches when studying the effect of sleep on learning and memory. The first explores the various stages of sleep and changes in duration as they affect learning new tasks, and the second analyzes the impact of sleep deprivation on learning.

About This Chapter: "Sleep Deprivation And Learning," © 2016 Omnigraphics. Reviewed December 2017.

211

What Is Memory?

Every day, you have different experiences and you learn new things. Your brain cannot store all of that information, so it has to decide what is worth remembering. Memory is the process of storing and then remembering this information. There are different types of memory. Short-term memory stores information for a few seconds or minutes. Long-term memory stores it for a longer period of time.

(Source: "Memory," MedlinePlus, National Institutes of Health (NIH).)

Sleep Stages And Types Of Memory

Every learning situation provides different types of memories to be consolidated into the brain. Scientists, through various studies, are investigating the relationship between the consolidation of these types of memories and the stages of sleep. There is, however, speculation that it is most efficient for the brain to form strong neural connections and pathways during sleep, when there is little new information or external stimuli to process.

Lack of adequate sleep can impact attention and short-term (working) memory, thereby affecting retention of long-term (episodic) memories and also higher cognitive functions, such as reasoning and decision-making. Numerous studies have demonstrated how sleep promotes long-term memory processing, which includes both consolidation of short-term memory into long-term memory, and also reconsolidation of existing long-term memories.

Long-term memory can be classified into two main types: procedural memory (the unconscious storage of skills and the way we accomplish tasks) and declarative memory (the storage of facts and events). Other aspects that play an important role include motor learning, which seems to be dependent on lighter stages of non-REM (rapid eye movement) sleep, and a few types of visual learning that seem to rely on timing and duration of both slow wave sleep (SWS) and REM sleep. REM sleep has also been shown to aid in the retention of emotionally charged declarative memory.

Impact Of Sleep Deprivation On Learning

Scientists are also examining the impact that sleep deprivation has on learning and the formation of new memories. Lack of adequate sleep can be partial (deprivation of either early or late sleep), total (no sleep at all) or selective (deprivation of specific stages of sleep).

Sleep deprivation can lead to poor focus, which makes it difficult to grasp information. It also causes the neurons to overwork, which in turn impairs the brain's ability to coordinate information. As a result, one's ability to recall previously stored information is affected. Furthermore, the interpretation of events and the capacity to make logical decisions may also be impeded.

Without proper rest, the body can feel tired to the extreme point of exhaustion. At such a stage, the muscles can weaken from lack of sleep, the body's organs are not synchronized, and neurons do not function optimally. Poor sleep can also have a negative impact on mood, which may affect the ability to acquire and retain new pieces of information. Although the effects of chronic sleep deprivation are not the same in each individual, it is evident that resting well has a profound impact on learning and memory.

Students who have trouble grasping new information or learning new skills are often advised to "sleep on it," and that advice seems well founded. Studies reveal that people can learn a task better if they are well rested. They also can better remember what they learned if they get a good night's sleep after learning the task than if they are sleep deprived.

(Source: "Your Guide To Healthy Sleep," National Heart, Lung, and Blood Institute (NHLBI).)

References

1. "Sleep, Learning, And Memory," Division of Sleep Medicine, Harvard Medical School, December 18, 2007.

2. Mastin, Luke. "Why Do We Sleep? Memory Processing And Learning," n.d.

3. Renee. "The Surprising Relationship Between Sleep And Learning," Udemy, Inc., January 26, 2012.

Chapter 45

Teens, Sleep Deprivation, And Depression

Feeling Low? You May Have Depression

If you have been feeling sad, hopeless, or irritable for what seems like a long time, you might have depression.

- Depression is a real, treatable brain illness, or health problem.

- Depression can be caused by big transitions in life, stress, or changes in your body's chemicals that affect your thoughts and moods.

- Even if you feel hopeless, depression gets better with treatment.

- There are lots of people who understand and want to help you.

- Ask for help as early as you can so you can get back to being yourself.

Relationship Between Sleep And Depression

The relationship between sleep and depression is complex. While sleep disturbance has long been held to be an important symptom of depression, recent research has indicated that depressive symptoms may decrease once sleep apnea has been effectively treated and sufficient sleep restored. The interrelatedness of sleep and depression suggests it is important that the sleep sufficiency of persons with depression be assessed and that symptoms of depression be monitored among persons with a sleep disorder.

(Source: "Sleep And Sleep Disorders—Sleep And Chronic Disease," Centers of Diseases Control and Prevention (CDC).)

About This Chapter: This chapter includes text excerpted from "Teen Depression," National Institute of Mental Health (NIMH), June 11, 2015.

Regular Sadness And Depression Are Not The Same

Regular Sadness

Feeling moody, sad, or grouchy? Who doesn't once in a while? It's easy to have a couple of bad days. Your schoolwork, activities, and family and friend drama, all mixed with not enough sleep, can leave you feeling overwhelmed. On top of that, teen hormones can be all over the place and also make you moody or cry about the smallest thing. Regular moodiness and sadness usually go away quickly though, within a couple of days.

Depression

Untreated depression is a more intense feeling of sadness, hopelessness, and anger or frustration that lasts much longer, such as for weeks, months, or longer. These feelings make it hard for you to function as you normally would or participate in your usual activities. You may also have trouble focusing and feel like you have little to no motivation or energy. You may not even feel like seeing your best friends. Depression can make you feel like it is hard to enjoy life or even get through the day.

If You Think You Are Depressed, Ask For Help As Early As You Can

If you have symptoms of depression for more than 2 weeks, ask for help. Depression can get better with care and treatment. Don't wait for depression to go away by itself. If you don't ask for help, depression may get worse.

1. **Talk to:**
    - Your parents or guardian
    - Your teacher or counselor
    - Your doctor
    - A helpline, such as 800-273-TALK (800-273-8255), free 24-hour help
    - Or call 911 if you are in a crisis or want to hurt yourself

2. **Ask your parent or guardian to make an appointment with your doctor for a checkup.** Your doctor can make sure that you do not have another health problem

that is causing your depression. If your doctor finds that you do not have another health problem, he or she can treat your depression or refer you to a mental health professional. A mental health professional can give you a thorough evaluation and also treat your depression.

3. **Talk to a mental health professional, such as a psychiatrist, counselor, psychologist, or other therapist.** These mental health professionals can diagnose and treat depression and other mental health problems.

Know The Signs And Symptoms Of Depression

Most of the day or nearly every day you may feel one or all of the following:

- Sad
- Empty
- Hopeless
- Angry, cranky, or frustrated, even at minor things

You also may:

- Not care about things or activities you used to enjoy.
- Have weight loss when you are not dieting or weight gain from eating too much.
- Have trouble falling asleep or staying asleep, or sleep much more than usual.
- Move or talk more slowly.
- Feel restless or have trouble sitting still.
- Feel very tired or like you have no energy.
- Feel worthless or very guilty.
- Have trouble concentrating, remembering information, or making decisions.
- Think about dying or suicide or try suicide.

Not everyone experiences depression the same way. And depression can occur at the same time as other mental health problems, such as anxiety, an eating disorder, or substance abuse.

There Are Ways You Can Feel Better

Effective treatments for depression include talk therapy or a combination of talk therapy and medicine.

Talk Therapy

A therapist, such as a psychiatrist, a psychologist, a social worker, or counselor can help you understand and manage your moods and feelings. You can talk out your emotions to someone who understands and supports you. You can also learn how to stop thinking negatively and start to look at the positives in life. This will help you build confidence and feel better about yourself. Research has shown that certain types of talk therapy or psychotherapy can help teens deal with depression. These include cognitive behavioral therapy, which focuses on thoughts, behaviors, and feelings related to depression, and interpersonal psychotherapy, which focuses on working on relationships.

Medicines

If your doctor thinks you need medicine to help your depression, he or she can prescribe an antidepressant. There are a few antidepressants that have been widely studied and proven to help teens. If your doctor recommends medicine, it is important to see your doctor regularly and tell your parents or guardian about your feelings, especially if you start feeling worse or have thoughts of hurting yourself.

Chapter 46

Sleep Deprivation Affects Sports Performance

According to the National Institutes of Health (NIH), although there is still much that is not known about sleep, we do know that sleep is crucial to human physiology and cognition. Lack of sleep may cause autonomic nervous system imbalance, increase stress levels, and decrease glycogen and carbohydrate production. In athletes, reduced sleep can lead to lack of energy, poor focus, fatigue, and slow recovery after a game. Sports place a lot of demand on the muscles and tissues, depleting energy and fluids and breaking down muscle. Sleep helps the body recover quicker, repairs memory, and releases essential hormones. In sports, a split-second decision can make the difference between a win and a loss. And research indicates that poor sleep results in a decline in quick decision-making, while the proper amount of sleep shows an increase in this ability.

Effects Of Sleep Deprivation

Reduced sleep can cause a decline in athletic performance, cognition, and immune function and an increase in weight. The amount of sleep required for any given athlete depends on genetic factors, conditioning, and the level of physical activity demanded by the sport. Adolescence is a period of growth in which sleep is vital. However, it has become increasingly clear from research that most teens do not get the proper amount of sleep. Studies suggest that an average of 10 hours of sleep per night can boost athletic performance. Athletes tend to focus on training and practice to achieve success; however, sleep has too often been an overlooked factor.

About This Chapter: "Sleep Deprivation Affects Sports Performance," © 2017 Omnigraphics. Reviewed December 2017.

Listed below are a few effects of lack of sleep:

- **Lower attention span.** Inability to stay focused on the game.

- **Decreased reaction time.** Overall reaction time is vital to athletic performance.

- **Longer recovery.** Some physical activities demand more energy; recovery and healing are slower when sleep is lost.

- **Higher cortisol levels.** High levels of the stress hormone cortisol can hinder tissue repair and growth. Over time, this may prevent an athlete from responding well to heavy training and may also lead to over-training.

- **Lack of endurance.** Glycogen (stored glucose) is the main source of energy that is needed for endurance. Sleep deprivation causes slower storage of glycogen, preventing athletes from performing well in endurance events.

How Sleep Can Improve Sports Performance

Studies suggest that increased sleep enables better sports performance. Some benefits of proper sleep are noted below.

- In a study, basketball players who got an extra two hours of sleep per night tended to increase their speed by 5 percent and accuracy by 9 percent.

- Athletes who sleep an average of 8–9 hours nightly are better able to perform high-intensity workouts, such as weight-lifting, running, or biking.

- Mental strain is a part of any sport. Sleep will help athletes improve their mood, memory, and alertness.

- Players have better reaction time and reflexes.

- Training and practice can cause physical exhaustion. The proper amount of sleep helps the body restore muscle and other tissue.

- Sleep promotes better coordination. While sleeping, the body recalls and consolidates memories linked to the motor skills that were practiced.

Sleep Tips For Athletes

Athletes have tight schedules when it comes to training and practice. However, experts say that as much as an athlete needs practice, so does he or she need sleep. Since the body is pushed on a regular basis, in order to recover, it needs rest and time. Below are a few tips that can help an athlete get better sleep.

- Establish a regular schedule for going to bed and waking up at the same time every day.

- Since traveling can upset sleep, it's best to get to the place of the competition two or three days early in order to allow the body adjust.

- Sleep medication should be avoided, unless prescribed by a doctor, since it can disturb the quality of sleep and hinder performance.

- It's best to avoid caffeine and alcohol, because they can disrupt healthful sleep patterns.

- Natural relaxation techniques, such as deep breathing or listening to soft music, can help promote sleep.

References

1. Fullagar, HH, S. Skorski, R. Duffield, D. Hammes, A.J. Coutts, And T. Meyer. "Sleep And Athletic Performance: The Effects Of Sleep Loss On Exercise Performance, And Physiological And Cognitive Responses To Exercise," U.S. National Library of Medicine (NLM), February, 2015.

2. Griffin, R. Morgan. "Can Sleep Improve Your Athletic Performance?" WebMD, August 13, 2014.

3. "How Sleep Affects Athletes' Performance," Sleep.org, n.d.

4. Quinn, Elizabeth. "Sleep Deprivation And Athletes," Verywell.com, October 5, 2017.

5. Sherwood, Chris. "Does A Lack Of Sleep Affect An Athlete's Performance?" Livestrong.com, August 14, 2017.

6. "Sleep And Athletes," Gatorade Sports Science Institute," n.d.

7. "Sleep, Athletic Performance, And Recovery," National Sleep Foundation, n.d.

Chapter 47

Does Sleep Deprivation Lead To Weight Gain?

A poor night's sleep can leave you feeling foggy and drowsy throughout the day. Sleep deprivation has also been associated with higher risks of weight gain and obesity.

Obesity

Laboratory research has found that short sleep duration results in metabolic changes that may be linked to obesity. Epidemiologic studies conducted in the community have also revealed an association between short sleep duration and excess body weight. This association has been reported in all age groups—but has been particularly pronounced in children. It is believed that sleep in childhood and adolescence is particularly important for brain development and that insufficient sleep in youngsters may adversely affect the function of a region of the brain known as the hypothalamus, which regulates appetite and the expenditure of energy.

(Source: "Sleep And Chronic Disease," Centers for Disease Control and Prevention (CDC).)

Research Findings

A group led by Drs. Erin Hanlon and Eve Van Cauter at the University of Chicago wanted to better understand how sleep and weight gain interact biologically. They noticed that sleep deprivation has effects in the body similar to activation of the endocannabinoid (eCB) system, a key player in the brain's regulation of appetite and energy levels. Perhaps most well known

---

About This Chapter: Text in this chapter begins with excerpts from "Molecular Ties Between Lack Of Sleep And Weight Gain," National Institutes of Health (NIH), March 22, 2016; Text beginning with the heading "Sleep And Obesity Risk" is excerpted from "How Does Inadequate Sleep Affect Health?" *Eunice Kennedy Shriver* National Institute of Child Health and Human Development (NICHD), December 5, 2012. Reviewed December 2017.

for being activated by chemicals found in marijuana, the eCB system affects the brain's motivation and reward circuits and can spark a desire for tasty foods.

The researchers enrolled 14 healthy, nonobese people—11 men and 3 women—who were 18–30 years old. The participants were placed on a fixed diet and allowed either a normal 8.5 hours of sleep or a restricted 4.5 hours of sleep for 4 consecutive days. All participants underwent both sleep conditions in a controlled clinical setting, with at least 4 weeks in between testing. For both conditions, the researchers collected blood samples from the participants beginning the afternoon following the second night. The study was supported in part by National Institutes of Health's (NIH) National Center for Research Resources (NCRR) and National Heart, Lung, and Blood Institute (NHLBI). Results were published in the March 2016 issue of *Sleep*.

When sleep deprived, participants had eCB levels in the afternoons that were both higher and lasted longer than when they'd had a full night's rest. This occurred around the same time that they reported increases in hunger and appetite.

After dinner on the fourth night, the participants fasted until the next afternoon. They were then allowed to choose their own meals and snacks for the rest of the day. All food was prepared and served in the clinical setting. Under both sleep conditions, people consumed about 90 percent of their daily calories at their first meal. But when sleep deprived, they consumed more and unhealthier snacks in between meals. This is when eCB levels were at their highest, suggesting that eCBs were driving hedonic, or pleasurable, eating.

Hanlon explains that if you see junk food and you've had enough sleep, you may be able to control some aspects of your natural response. "But if you're sleep deprived, your hedonic drive for certain foods gets stronger, and your ability to resist them may be impaired. So you are more likely to eat it. Do that again and again, and you pack on the pounds."

The authors noted that though the results are based on a small sample size, they are consistent with evidence from other research. Additional studies are needed to look at how changes in eCB levels and timing are affected by other cues, such as the body's internal clock or meal schedules.

Sleep And Obesity Risk

Clinical research funded by the NIH shows that a short duration of sleep is associated with excess body weight. All age groups, including children, seem to be affected in the same manner. In addition, analysis of blood samples from people with inadequate sleep has shown metabolic changes that are similar to those seen in obese people. Researchers think that inadequate sleep could lead to changes in the brain's hypothalamus, which regulates appetite and energy expenditure. These changes in the brain may explain how inadequate sleep contributes to weight gain.

Chapter 48

Drowsy Driving: A Potentially Deadly Result Of Sleep Deprivation

Drowsy driving is a major problem in the United States. The risk, danger, and sometimes tragic results of drowsy driving are alarming.

> Most people are aware of the hazards of drunk driving. But driving while sleepy can be just as dangerous. Indeed, crashes due to sleepy drivers are as deadly as those due to drivers impaired by alcohol. And you don't have to be asleep at the wheel to put yourself and others in danger. Both alcohol and a lack of sleep limit your ability to react quickly to a suddenly braking car, a sharp curve in the road, or other situations that require rapid responses. Just a few seconds' delay in reaction time can be a life-or-death matter when driving. When people who lack sleep are tested on a driving simulator, they perform as badly as or worse than those who are drunk. The combination of alcohol and lack of sleep can be especially dangerous. There is increasing evidence that sleep deprivation and inexperience behind the wheel, both particularly common in adolescents, is a lethal combination.
>
> *(Source: "Your Guide To Healthy Sleep," National Heart, Lung, and Blood Institute (NHLBI).)*

What Is Drowsy Driving?

Operating a motor vehicle while fatigued or sleepy is commonly referred to as "drowsy driving."

It is the dangerous combination of driving and sleepiness or fatigue. This usually happens when a driver has not slept enough, but it can also happen due to untreated sleep disorders, medications, drinking alcohol, and shift work.

About This Chapter: This chapter includes text excerpted from "Sleep And Sleep Disorders—Drowsy Driving," Centers for Disease Control and Prevention (CDC), February 18, 2016.

The Impact Of Drowsy Driving

Drowsy driving poses a serious risk not only for one's own health and safety, but also for the other people on the road. The National Highway Traffic Safety Administration (NHTSA) estimates that between 2005 and 2009 drowsy driving was responsible for an annual average of:

- 83,000 crashes

- 37,000 injury crashes

- 886 fatal crashes (846 fatalities in 2014)

These estimates are conservative, though, and up to 6,000 fatal crashes each year may be caused by drowsy drivers.

How Often Do Americans Fall Asleep While Driving?

- Approximately 1 out of 25 adults aged 18 years and older surveyed reported that they had fallen asleep while driving in the past 30 days.

- Individuals who snored or slept 6 hours or less per day were more likely to fall asleep while driving.

> Young drivers are at high risk for drowsy driving, which causes thousands of crashes every year. Teens are most tired and at risk when driving in the early morning or late at night.
>
> *(Source: "Eight Danger Zones For Teens Behind The Wheel," Centers for Disease Control and Prevention (CDC).)*

How Does Sleepiness Affect Driving?

Falling asleep at the wheel is very dangerous, but being sleepy affects your ability to drive safely even if you don't fall asleep. Drowsiness—

- Makes drivers less attentive.

- Slows reaction time.

- Affects a driver's ability to make decisions.

The Warning Signs Of Drowsy Driving

- Yawning or blinking frequently.

- Difficulty remembering the past few miles driven.

- Missing your exit.

- Drifting from your lane.

- Hitting a rumble strip.

How To Prevent Drowsy Driving

There are four things you should do before taking the wheel to prevent driving while drowsy:

- Get enough sleep! Most adults need at least 7 hours of sleep a day, while adolescents need at least 8 hours.

- Develop good sleeping habits such as sticking to a sleep schedule.

- If you have a sleep disorder or have symptoms of a sleep disorder such as snoring or feeling sleepy during the day, talk to your physician about treatment options.

- Avoid drinking alcohol or taking medications that make you sleepy. Be sure to check the label on any medications or talk to your pharmacist.

Drowsy Driving Is Similar To Drunk Driving

Your body needs adequate sleep on a daily basis. The more hours of sleep you miss, the harder it is for you to think and perform as well as you would like. Lack of sleep can make you less alert and affect your coordination, judgement, and reaction time while driving. This is known as cognitive impairment (CI).

Studies have shown that going too long without sleep can impair your ability to drive the same way as drinking too much alcohol.

- Being awake for at least 18 hours is the same as someone having a blood content blood alcohol concentration (BAC) of 0.05 percent.

- Being awake for at least 24 hours is equal to having a blood alcohol content of 0.10 percent. This is higher than the legal limit (0.08% BAC) in all states.

Additionally, drowsiness increases the effect of even low amounts of alcohol.

Opening a window or turning up the radio won't help you stay awake while driving. The bottom line is that there is no substitute for sleep. Be aware of these warning signs that you are too sleepy to drive safely: trouble keeping your eyes open or focused, continual yawning, or being unable to recall driving the past few miles. Remember, if you are short on sleep, stay out of the driver's seat!

(Source: "Your Guide To Healthy Sleep," National Heart, Lung, and Blood Institute (NHLBI).)

Chapter 49

Ways To Avoid Sleep Deprivation

Humans require 6–8 hours of sleep every 24 hours to restore memory and concentration, physical and emotional function. People have individual needs for amount of sleep and their own circadian sleep phase (the timing of their sleep rhythms).

Humans are also diurnal mammals, which means they prefer to be awake in the day and asleep at night. Day sleep has been clearly shown to be shorter and less efficient than night sleep. One's resistance to sleep deprivation is a function of age, environmental distraction, and internal or external stimulation. As we age (usually as we enter the mid-40s), we become less able to tolerate the effects of acute and chronic sleep deprivation.

Substantial research from National Aeronautics and Space Administration (NASA) and the U.S. military in both acute and chronic sleep deprivation protocols has established that there is a significant impairment in cognitive function following 15–17 hours of sustained wakefulness.

Sleep Deprivation: What Research Says

A large body of medical research has shown that sleep deprivation adversely affects outcomes ranging from cognitive function to pain sensitivity and cardiovascular function.

(Source: "Chronic Sleep Deprivation Among The Poor: A Lab-In-The-Field Approach," ClinicalTrials. gov, National Institutes of Health (NIH).)

About This Chapter: This chapter includes text from "Ways To Avoid Sleep Deprivation," National Institute of Justice (NIJ), March 27, 2009. Reviewed December 2017.

How To Protect Your Sleep

1. **Determine how much sleep you need** to feel well rested on a daily basis. Multiply that number by 7. The resulting number is the amount of sleep you need per week.

2. **Determine how much sleep you get.** Add up the total amount of sleep you get on day/afternoon/evening shifts per week and night shift per week. Then determine your sleep debt in each situation by subtracting those numbers from your sleep need.

3. **Focus on minimizing your total sleep debt by taking the following actions:**

    *   Improve your day sleep environment.

    *   Catch up on your sleep on your days off.

    *   Learn to catnap.

    *   Sleep longer during the day when you have a night rotation or tour of duty.

4. **Give yourself a quiet, completely dark, comfortable day-sleep environment** with no distractions.

5. **Try to get two three- to four-hour blocks of sleep** during the day when you work the night shift.

6. **Learn to catnap.** Take a short 20–30 minutes of time with eyes closed, situated in a comfortable and resting position. You do not have to sleep to get the benefit of a catnap.

Some people nap as a way to deal with sleepiness. Naps may provide a short-term boost in alertness and performance. However, napping doesn't provide all of the other benefits of nighttime sleep.

(Source: "Sleep Deprivation And Deficiency," National Heart, Lung, and Blood Institute (NHLBI).)

Part Five
Sleep Research And Clinical Trials

Chapter 50

Research And Studies About Sleep

Research has uncovered many of the nuts and bolts that link the need for sleep to the chemistry of life in the brain and virtually every part of our body. Insufficient sleep damages areas of the brain involved in managing stress, learning, and memory. Individuals who experience excessive sleepiness are often unable to perform at school or in the workplace. Sleep problems also contribute to the risk of serious medical conditions and the management of mental health illnesses.

The brain lives in a fluid that is important for its continued health across the lifespan. Researchers have discovered that during sleep the flow of this fluid is redirected deeper into the cortex, the thinking part of the brain, where it helps flush out waste products that contribute to the risk of Alzheimer and other neurological disorders.

Evidence indicates that sleep is also important to maternal and fetal health during pregnancy. Untreated sleep disorders during pregnancy may threaten the health of approximately 500,000 pregnant women and their unborn babies each year.

Studies are now underway to determine how poor sleep and difficulty breathing during sleep contribute to the risk of gestational medical conditions such as diabetes, hypertension, and preterm delivery. A landmark National Institutes of Health (NIH)-supported study called nuMoM2b found that pregnant women with difficulty breathing during sleep (sleep apnea) are more likely to develop hypertension and preeclampsia—a pregnancy complication that includes high blood pressure and organ damage, often to the kidneys. These women are also

About This Chapter: Text in this chapter begins with excerpts from "Advances In Sleep Studies," MedlinePlus, National Institutes of Health (NIH), 2015; Text under the heading "What Is The Purpose Of Sleep Studies?" is excerpted from "Sleep Studies," National Heart, Lung, and Blood Institute (NHLBI), December 9, 2016; Text beginning with the heading "What Is A Clinical Study?" is excerpted from "Learn About Clinical Studies," ClinicalTrials.gov, National Institutes of Health (NIH), January 2017.

three times more likely to develop gestational diabetes compared with pregnant women who do not have difficulty breathing during sleep.

Mounting evidence indicates that irregular sleep and untreated sleep disorders may contribute to health disparities. A landmark study funded by the National Heart, Lung, and Blood Institute (NHLBI) on Hispanic community health—The Hispanic Community Health Study (HCHS)/Study of Latinos (SOL)—has revealed that sleep apnea, which is characterized by difficulty breathing during sleep, is common and rarely diagnosed and treated. Approximately 26 percent of the more than 1400 study participants had sleep disordered breathing which is associated with increased risk for developing high blood pressure, heart disease, diabetes, and stroke. The study also found that sleep apnea was associated with peripheral arterial disease, a condition in which narrowed arteries reduce blood flow to the arms and legs.

You may have a sleep disorder and should see your doctor if your sleep diary reveals any of the following:

- You consistently take more than 30 minutes each night to fall asleep.
- You consistently awaken more than a few times or for long periods of time each night.
- You take frequent naps.
- You often feel sleepy during the day—or you fall asleep at inappropriate times during the day.

(Source: "Your Guide To Healthy Sleep," National Heart, Lung, and Blood Institute (NHLBI).)

What Are Sleep Studies?

Sleep studies are tests that measure how well you sleep and how your body responds to sleep problems. These tests can help your healthcare provider find out whether you have a sleep disorder and how severe it is. Sleep studies are important because untreated sleep disorders can raise your risk for heart disease, high blood pressure, stroke, and other medical conditions. Sleep disorders also have been linked to an increased risk of injury, such as falling, particularly among the elderly, and car accidents.

Research is helping to improve our understanding of the connection between sleep disorders and our physical, mental, and behavioral health. NIH supports a range of sleep-related research that focuses on:

- Better understanding of how a lack of sleep increases the risk for obesity, diabetes, heart disease, and stroke.

- Genetic, environmental, and social factors that lead to sleep disorders.

- The adverse effects from a lack of sleep on body and brain.

Polysomnography

Sleep recording in a sleep laboratory (polysomnogram). A sleep recording or polysomnogram (PSG) is usually done while you stay overnight at a sleep center or sleep laboratory. Electrodes and other monitors are placed on your scalp, face, chest, limbs, and finger. While you sleep, these devices measure your brain activity, eye movements, muscle activity, heart rate and rhythm, blood pressure, and how much air moves in and out of your lungs. This test also checks the amount of oxygen in your blood. A PSG test is painless. In certain circumstances, the PSG can be done at home. A home monitor can be used to record heart rate, how air moves in and out of your lungs, the amount of oxygen in your blood, and your breathing effort.

(Source: "Your Guide To Healthy Sleep," National Heart, Lung, and Blood Institute (NHLBI).)

What Is The Purpose Of Sleep Studies?

Sleep studies can help your doctor diagnose sleep-related breathing disorders (SRBD) such as sleep apnea, sleep-related seizure disorders, sleep-related movement disorders (SRMD), and sleep disorders that cause extreme daytime tiredness such as narcolepsy. Doctors also may use sleep studies to help diagnose or rule out restless legs syndrome.

Sleep Studies For Diagnosing Narcolepsy

If your doctor thinks you have narcolepsy, he or she will likely suggest that you see a sleep specialist.

Sleep studies usually are done at a sleep center. Doctors use the results from two tests to diagnose narcolepsy. These tests are a polysomnogram (PSG) and a multiple sleep latency test (MSLT).

(Source: "How Is Narcolepsy Diagnosed?" National Heart, Lung, and Blood Institute (NHLBI).)

Your doctor will determine whether you must have your sleep study at a sleep center or if you can do it at home with a portable diagnostic device. If your sleep study will be done at a sleep center, you will sleep in a bed at the sleep center for the duration of the study.

Removable sensors will be placed on your scalp, face, eyelids, chest, limbs, and a finger. These sensors record your brain waves, heart rate, breathing effort and rate, oxygen levels, and muscle movements before, during, and after sleep. There is a small risk of irritation from the sensors, but this will go away after they are removed.

Your doctor will review your sleep study test results and develop a treatment plan for any diagnosed sleep disorder.

What Is A Clinical Study?

A clinical study involves research using human volunteers (also called participants) that is intended to add to medical knowledge. There are two main types of clinical studies: clinical trials (also called interventional studies) and observational studies. ClinicalTrials.gov includes both interventional and observational studies.

Clinical Trials

In a clinical trial, participants receive specific interventions according to the research plan or protocol created by the investigators. These interventions may be medical products, such as drugs or devices; procedures; or changes to participants' behavior, such as diet. Clinical trials may compare a new medical approach to a standard one that is already available, to a placebo that contains no active ingredients, or to no intervention. Some clinical trials compare interventions that are already available to each other. When a new product or approach is being studied, it is not usually known whether it will be helpful, harmful, or no different than available alternatives (including no intervention). The investigators try to determine the safety and efficacy of the intervention by measuring certain outcomes in the participants. For example, investigators may give a drug or treatment to participants who have high blood pressure to see whether their blood pressure decreases.

Clinical trials used in drug development are sometimes described by phase. These phases are defined by the U.S. Food and Drug Administration (FDA).

Some people who are not eligible to participate in a clinical trial may be able to get experimental drugs or devices outside of a clinical trial through expanded access.

Observational Studies

In an observational study, investigators assess health outcomes in groups of participants according to a research plan or protocol. Participants may receive interventions (which can include medical products such as drugs or devices) or procedures as part of their routine medical care, but participants are not assigned to specific interventions by the investigator (as in a clinical trial). For example, investigators may observe a group of older adults to learn more about the effects of different lifestyles on cardiac health.

Every clinical study is led by a principal investigator, who is often a medical doctor. Clinical studies also have a research team that may include doctors, nurses, social workers, and other healthcare professionals.

Clinical studies can be sponsored, or funded, by pharmaceutical companies, academic medical centers, voluntary groups, and other organizations, in addition to Federal agencies such as the National Institutes of Health, the U.S. Department of Defense (DOD), and the U.S. Department of Veterans Affairs (VA). Doctors, other healthcare providers, and other individuals can also sponsor clinical research.

Reasons For Conducting Clinical Studies

Clinical studies can take place in many locations, including hospitals, universities, doctors' offices, and community clinics. The location depends on who is conducting the study. The length of a clinical study varies, depending on what is being studied. Participants are told how long the study will last before they enroll.

In general, clinical studies are designed to add to medical knowledge related to the treatment, diagnosis, and prevention of diseases or conditions. Some common reasons for conducting clinical studies include:

- Evaluating one or more interventions (for example, drugs, medical devices, approaches to surgery or radiation therapy) for treating a disease, syndrome, or condition.

- Finding ways to prevent the initial development or recurrence of a disease or condition. These can include medicines, vaccines, or lifestyle changes, among other approaches.

How To Find A Sleep Center And Sleep Specialist

If your doctor refers you to a sleep center or sleep specialist, make sure that center or specialist is qualified to diagnose and treat your sleep problem. To find sleep centers accredited by the American Academy of Sleep Medicine, go to www.aasmnet.org and click on "Find a Sleep Center" (under the Patients & Public menu), or call 708-492-0930. To find sleep specialists certified by the American Board of Sleep Medicine (ABSM), go to www.absm.org and click on "Verification of Diplomates of the ABSM."

(Source: "Your Guide To Healthy Sleep," National Heart, Lung, and Blood Institute (NHLBI).)

- Evaluating one or more interventions aimed at identifying or diagnosing a particular disease or condition.

- Examining methods for identifying a condition or the risk factors for that condition.

- Exploring and measuring ways to improve the comfort and quality of life through supportive care for people with a chronic illness.

Chapter 51

Schools Start Too Early

Health Risk Due To Less Sleep Duration

Adolescents need 8–10 hours of sleep per night. But, more than two-thirds of U.S. high school students report getting less than 8 hours of sleep on school nights. Female students are more likely to report not getting enough sleep than male students. Short sleep duration (<8 hours) is lowest among 9th graders and highest among 12th graders. Prevalence of short sleep duration also varies by race/ethnicity, with the lowest prevalence among American Indian/Alaska Native students and the highest among Asian students.

Starting School Later Can Help Adolescents Get Enough Sleep

Starting school later can help adolescents get enough sleep and improve their health, academic performance, and quality of life. Not getting enough sleep is common among high school students and is associated with several health risks including being overweight, drinking alcohol, smoking tobacco, and using drugs, as well as poor academic performance. One of the reasons adolescents do not get enough sleep is early school start times. The American Academy of Pediatrics (AAP) has recommended that middle and high schools start at 8:30 a.m. or later to give students the opportunity to get the amount of sleep they need, but most American adolescents start school too early.

About This Chapter: Text under the heading "Health Risk Due To Less Sleep Duration" is excerpted from "Sleep And Sleep Disorders—Data And Statistics," Centers for Disease Control and Prevention (CDC), May 2, 2017; Text beginning with the heading "Starting School Later Can Help Adolescents Get Enough Sleep" is excerpted from "Schools Start Too Early," Centers for Disease Control and Prevention (CDC), August 10, 2017.

241

According to the 2014 School Health Policies and Practices Study (SHPPS), 93 percent of high schools and 83 percent of middle schools in the United States started before 8:30 a.m.

According to an earlier Centers for Disease Control and Prevention (CDC) study that analyzed U.S. Department of Education (ED) data from the 2011–2012 school year:

- 42 states reported that most (75%–100%) public middle and high schools started before 8:30 a.m.

- The percentage of schools starting at 8:30 a.m. or later varied greatly by state. For example,

  - No schools in Hawaii, Mississippi, and Wyoming started after 8:30 a.m.

  - Most schools in North Dakota (78%) and Alaska (76%) started after 8:30 a.m.

Adolescents And Sleep

The American Academy of Sleep Medicine (AASM) recommends that teenagers aged 13–18 years should regularly sleep 8–10 hours per day for good health. Adolescents who do not get enough sleep are more likely to:

- Be overweight.

- Not engage in daily physical activity.

- Suffer from symptoms of depression.

- Engage in unhealthy risk behaviors such as drinking, smoking tobacco, and using illicit drugs.

- Perform poorly in school.

During puberty, adolescents become sleepy later at night and need to sleep later in the morning as a result in shifts in biological rhythms. These biological changes are often combined

What Is Puberty?

Puberty is the time in life when a boy or girl becomes sexually mature. It is a process that usually happens between ages 10–14 for girls and ages 12–16 for boys. It causes physical changes, and affects boys and girls differently.

(Source: "Puberty," MedlinePlus, National Institutes of Health (NIH).)

with poor sleep habits (including irregular bedtimes and the presence of electronics in the bedroom).

During the school week, school start times are the main reason students wake up when they do. The combination of late bedtimes and early school start times results in most adolescents not getting enough sleep.

Everyone Can Play An Important Role

Parents

- Model and encourage habits that help promote good sleep:

  - **Regular bedtiming.** Setting a regular bedtime and rise time, including on weekends, is recommended for everyone—children, adolescents, and adults alike. Adolescents with parent-set bedtimes usually get more sleep than those whose parents do not set bedtimes.

  - **Dim lighting.** Adolescents who are exposed to more light (such as room lighting or from electronics) in the evening are less likely to get enough sleep.

  - **Implement a "media curfew."** Technology use (computers, video gaming, or mobile phones) may also contribute to late bedtimes. Parents should consider banning technology use after a certain time or removing these technologies from the bedroom.

- Consider contacting local school officials about later school start times. Some commonly mentioned barriers to keep in mind are potential increases in transportation costs and scheduling difficulties.

Healthcare Professionals

- Educate adolescent patients and their parents about the importance of adequate sleep and factors that contribute to insufficient sleep among adolescents.

School Officials

- Learn more about the research connecting sleep and school start times. Good sleep hygiene in combination with later school times will enable adolescents to be healthier and better academic achievers.

Chapter 52

Sleep Duration And Injury-Related Risk Behaviors Among High School Students

Insufficient Sleep Is Common Among High School Students

Insufficient sleep is common among high school students and has been associated with an increased risk for motor vehicle crashes, sports injuries, and occupational injuries. To evaluate the association between self-reported sleep duration on an average school night and several injury-related risk behaviors (infrequent bicycle helmet use, infrequent seatbelt use, riding with a driver who had been drinking, drinking and driving, and texting while driving) among U.S. high school students, Centers for Disease Control and Prevention (CDC) analyzed data from 50,370 high school students (grades 9–12) who participated in the national Youth Risk Behavior Surveys (YRBSs) in 2007, 2009, 2011, or 2013. The likelihood of each of the five risk behaviors was significantly higher for students who reported sleeping ≤7 hours on an average school night; infrequent seatbelt use, riding with a drinking driver, and drinking and driving were also more likely for students who reported sleeping ≥10 hours compared with 9 hours on an average school night. Although insufficient sleep directly contributes to injury risk, some of the increased risk associated with insufficient sleep might be caused by engaging in injury-related risk behaviors. Intervention efforts aimed at these behaviors might help reduce injuries resulting from sleepiness, as well as provide opportunities for increasing awareness of the importance of sleep.

About This Chapter: This chapter includes text excerpted from "Sleep Duration And Injury-Related Risk Behaviors Among High School Students—United States, 2007–2013," Centers for Disease Control and Prevention (CDC), August 25, 2017.

Analysis Of YRBS Results

The national YRBS monitors health-risk behaviors among students in public and private high schools and is conducted by CDC in the spring of odd-numbered years. Each national YRBS uses an independent, three-stage cluster sample design to obtain a nationally representative sample of students in grades 9–12. The overall response rates were 68 percent in 2007, 71 percent in 2009, 71 percent in 2011, and 68 percent in 2013, and sample sizes ranged from 13,583 (2013) to 16,410 (2009). Students completed the anonymous, self-administered questionnaires during a single class period.

The combined analytic sample was composed of 50,370 high school students who responded to questions about sleep duration on an average school night (≤4 hours, 5 hours, 6 hours, 7 hours, 8 hours, 9 hours, ≥10 hours); demographic characteristics (sex, grade, and race/ethnicity); and how frequently they used a bicycle helmet (among students who had ridden a bicycle during the past 12 months; responses = never or rarely versus sometimes, most of the time, or always); wore a seatbelt when riding in a car driven by someone else (never or rarely versus sometimes, most of the time, or always); rode in a car or other vehicle with a driver who had been drinking alcohol (i.e., rode with a drinking driver; at least one time during the past 30 days versus 0 times); drove a car or other vehicle when they had been drinking alcohol (i.e., drinking and driving; at least one time during the past 30 days versus 0 times); or texted or emailed while driving a car or other vehicle (i.e., texting while driving; at least 1 day during the past 30 days versus 0 days). The percentage reporting insufficient sleep duration (≤7 hours according to the Healthy People 2020 sleep objective for adolescents) and distribution of hours of sleep were calculated by survey year, sex, grade, and race/ethnicity; pairwise t-tests and Analysis of variance (ANOVA) (i.e., linear trend) were used to assess crude significant differences.

Because no differences were found in mean sleep duration or prevalence of insufficient sleep duration by survey year, data from all four survey years were aggregated for subsequent analyses. Aggregating the data from four survey years provided adequate sample size for the calculation of low prevalence risk behaviors among students reporting each category of sleep duration. Unadjusted prevalence of each risk behavior was calculated by sleep duration. Pairwise t-tests were used to assess significant differences compared with 9 hours, the median of the sleep duration recommendation for teens by the National Sleep Foundation (NSF). Logistic regression analyses were used to calculate adjusted prevalence ratios (APRs) and 95 percent confidence intervals (CIs) for the likelihood of each injury-related behavior with a referent sleep duration of 9 hours and were adjusted for sex, grade, and race/ethnicity. All analyses accounted for the sampling weights and complex survey design. P-values of <0.05 were defined to be statistically significant.

Reported sleep duration during an average school night was ≤4 hours for 6.3 percent of respondents, 5 hours (10.5%), 6 hours (21.9%), 7 hours (30.1%), 8 hours (23.5%), 9 hours (5.8%), and ≥10 hours (1.8%). Sleep duration varied by sex, grade, and race/ethnicity. Female students reported a higher prevalence of insufficient sleep (≤7 hours) than did male students (71.3% versus 66.4%, p<0.001). The percentage reporting insufficient sleep ranged from 59.7 percent of students in 9th grade to 76.6 percent of students in 12th grade (p<0.001 for linear trend). Among racial/ethnic groups, the prevalence of insufficient sleep was lowest for American Indian/Alaska Native students (60.3%) and highest for Asian students (75.7%).

Overall, 86.1 percent of students reported infrequent bicycle helmet use and 8.7 percent reported infrequent seatbelt use. Twenty-six percent of students reported riding with a drinking driver at least one time during the past 30 days; 8.9 percent of students reported drinking and driving; and 30.3 percent reported texting while driving during the past 30 days. Unadjusted prevalence of all five injury-related risk behaviors varied by sleep duration. The likelihood of each of the five risk behaviors was significantly higher (APR >1.0) among students with sleep durations ≤7 hours; infrequent seatbelt use, riding with drinking driver, and drinking and driving were also more likely among students reporting sleeping ≥10 hours compared with 9 hours. The likelihood of drinking and driving was also significantly higher among students sleeping 8 hours compared with 9 hours.

Chapter 53

New Genes For Body's Internal Clock

Circadian Rhythms—The Body's Internal Clock

If you feel energized or tired around the same time each day, or routinely get up early or stay up late—the familiar 'early riser' or 'night owl' syndrome—you are witnessing, in real time, your circadian rhythm at work. That's the 24-hour internal body clock which controls your sleep/wake cycle.

Circadian rhythms have long fascinated researchers—decades ago three of them marked a critical milestone when they discovered the molecular components behind that mysterious timing cycle. For this game-changing finding, the trio was awarded the 2017 Nobel Prize in Physiology or Medicine. Since their discovery researchers have come to know that the circadian clock affects not just sleep, but hormone production, eating habits, body temperature, heart rate, and other biological functions.

> The 2017 Nobel Prize in Physiology or Medicine has been awarded to National Institutes of Health grantees Jeffrey C. Hall, Ph.D., of the University of Maine, Orono; Michael Rosbash, Ph.D., of Brandeis University, Waltham, Massachusetts; and Michael W. Young, Ph.D., of Rockefeller University, New York City, for their discoveries (link is external) of molecular mechanisms controlling the circadian rhythm.
>
> *(Source: "NIH Grantees Win 2017 Nobel Prize In Physiology Or Medicine," National Institutes of Health (NIH).)*

About This Chapter: This chapter includes text excerpted from "Dancing To The Circadian Rhythm: NHLBI Researcher Finds New Genes For Body's Internal Clock," National Heart, Lung, and Blood Institute (NHLBI), November 6, 2017.

What The Research Says About Circadian Rhythms

Yet, for all these advances, scientists still know relatively little about the clock's genetic underpinnings. A team of National Heart, Lung, and Blood Institute (NHLBI) researchers is working to change that with the discovery of scores of new genes they say have a profound impact on the circadian rhythm. These researchers say these genes could hold the key to a new understanding of a wide range of health conditions, from insomnia to heart disease, and perhaps pave the way for new treatments for them.

"We all 'dance' to the circadian rhythm," said Susan Harbison, Ph.D., an investigator in the NHLBI's Laboratory of Systems Genetics, who is among an elite cadre of scientists studying the complex genetics of the biological clock. "Quietly, this clock influences our body and our health in ways that are just now being understood."

For sure, the studies are slowly unfolding. For example, long-term night shift work has been associated with an increased risk of high blood pressure, obesity, and heart disease. Some studies have shown a link between circadian rhythm changes and cancer. And a study by researchers in France found that heart surgery is safer in the afternoon than in the morning, a phenomenon they attribute to the body's circadian clock having a better repair mechanism in the afternoon than in the morning.

Now, thanks to Harbison and her research team, new insights into why some people experience longer or shorter periods of wakefulness or sleepiness than others—and what it might mean for a host of health conditions—could be on the horizon.

To explore this line of research more deeply, Harbison is working with a favorite laboratory model of sleep researchers: Drosophila melanogaster, the common fruit fly. While this little fly may seem like an unlikely choice, it turns out to be an appropriate stand-in for humans.

"The clock mechanisms regulating circadian rhythm in humans and fruit flies are remarkably similar," Harbison said. "They both have biological rhythms of about 24 hours. In fact, the genes involved in mammalian circadian rhythms were first identified in flies."

Previous studies by other researchers had identified approximately 126 genes for circadian rhythms in fruit flies. In recent studies using a natural population of flies, Harbison's group estimates that there are more than 250 new genes associated with the circadian clock, among the largest number identified to date. Many of the genes appear to be associated with nerve cell development—not surprising, she said, given the wide-ranging impact of circadian rhythms on biological processes.

In addition to finding this treasure trove of clock-related genes, Harbison's group also found that the circadian patterns among the flies were highly variable, and that some of the genes code for variability in the circadian clock. Some flies had unusually long circadian periods—up to 31 hours—while others had extremely short circadian periods of 15 hours. In other words: Just like people, there were 'early risers' and 'night owls' and long sleepers and short sleepers among the fruit flies.

"Before we did our studies, there was little attention paid to the genes responsible for variability in the circadian period," noted Harbison, who is also looking at environmental factors that might influence these genes, such as drugs like alcohol and caffeine. "We now have new details about this variability, and that opens up a whole new avenue of research in understanding what these genes do and how they influence the circadian clock."

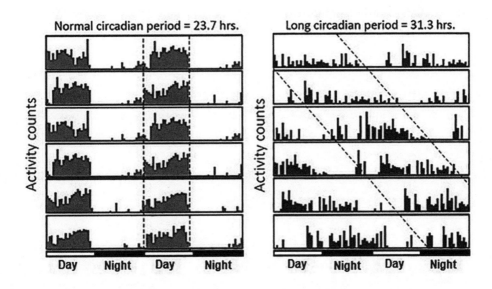

Figure 53.1. *Rest And Activity Patterns Of Two Different Fruit Flies*

This graph shows rest and activity patterns for two different fruit flies. The graph on the left shows the rest and activity of a fly with a normal circadian period (about 24 hours). Vertical blue bars show the fly's activity during the day (yellow horizontal bars) and night (black horizontal bars). The graph on the right shows the rest and activity of a fly with an abnormal circadian period (about 31 hours). The abnormal pattern is similar to an individual with a circadian rhythm disorder. Graphic courtesy of Susan Harbison, NHLBI.

Harbison says that for most people, disruptions to the circadian clock have a temporary effect, as occurs with daylight saving time or jet lag from overseas travel, when a person may experience short-term fatigue as they adjust to a time change or new time zone. But for some, disruptions to the clock are associated with chronic health effects, as occurs with night shift workers. Others who suffer from certain circadian rhythm disorders—such as delayed sleep phase disorder—may find it extremely difficult to fall asleep at a desired time.

"The clock architecture is not set in stone and is not a 'one size fits all' device," she noted. "What we're finding is that the effect of disrupting the circadian clock differs depending on the genetic makeup of the individual. Just as human height and other traits are variable, the same is true of circadian traits among different individuals."

In the future, Harbison hopes that these newly identified genes might ultimately be linked to specific disease processes in humans. Her findings could lead to the discovery of new bio-markers for diagnosing circadian disorders and lay the groundwork for new treatments for sleep and circadian disorders in humans.

Chapter 54

Increased Communication Between Key Brain Areas During Sleep

Using an innovative "NeuroGrid" technology, scientists showed that sleep boosts communication between two brain regions whose connection is critical for the formation of memories. The work, published in Science, was partially funded by the Brain Research through Advancing Innovative Neurotechnologies (BRAIN) Initiative, a project of the National Institutes of Health (NIH) devoted to accelerating the development of new approaches to probing the workings of the brain.

"Using new technologies advanced by the BRAIN Initiative, these researchers made a fundamental discovery about how the brain creates and stores new memories," said Nick Langhals, Ph.D., program director at NIH's National Institute of Neurological Disorders and Stroke (NINDS).

A brain structure called the hippocampus is widely thought to turn new information into permanent memories while we sleep. Previous work by the new study's senior author, New York University School of Medicine professor György Buzsáki, M.D., Ph.D., revealed high-frequency bursts of neural firing called ripples in the hippocampus during sleep and suggested they play a role in memory storage. The current study confirmed the presence of ripples in the hippocampus during sleep and found them in certain parts of association neocortex, an area on the brain's surface involved in processing complex sensory information.

About This Chapter: This chapter includes text excerpted from "Study Shows How Memories Ripple Through The Brain," National Institutes of Health (NIH), October 31, 2017.

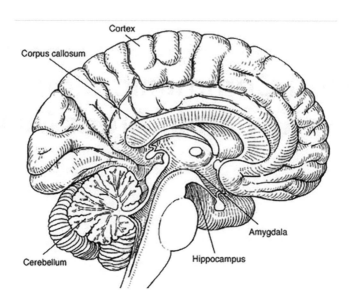

Figure 54.1. Structure Of Brain

(Source: "Alcohol And The Adolescent Brain—Human Studies," National Institute on Alcohol Abuse and Alcoholism (NIAAA).)

"When we first observed this, we thought it was incorrect because it had never been observed before," said Dion Khodagholy, Ph.D., the study's co-first author and assistant professor at Columbia University in New York.

Using a cutting-edge NeuroGrid system they invented, along with recording electrodes placed deeper into the brain, the researchers examined activity in several parts of rats' brains during non-rapid eye movement (NREM) sleep, the longest stage of sleep. Their NeuroGrid consists of a collection of tiny electrodes linked together like the threads of a blanket, which is then laid across an area of the brain so that each electrode can continuously monitor the activity of a different set of neurons.

"This particular device allows us to look at multiple areas of the brain at the same time," said Jennifer Gelinas, M.D., Ph.D., the study's co-first author and assistant professor at Columbia University.

The team was also surprised to find that the ripples in the association neocortex and hippocampus occurred at the same time, suggesting the two regions were communicating as the rats slept. Because the association neocortex is thought to be a storage location for memories, the researchers theorized that this neural dialogue could help the brain retain information.

To test that idea, they examined brain activity during NREM sleep in rats trained to locate rewards in a maze and in rats that explored the maze in a random fashion. In the latter group of animals, the ripples in the hippocampus and cortex were no more synchronized before exploring the maze than afterwards. In the trained rats, the learning task increased the cross-talk between those areas, and a second training session boosted it even more, further suggesting that such communication is important for the creation and storage of memories.

The group hopes to use the NeuroGrid in people undergoing brain surgery for other reasons to determine if the same ripples occur in the human brain. The researchers also plan to investigate if manipulating that neural firing in animals can boost or suppress memory formation in order to confirm that ripples are important for that process.

"Identifying the specific neural patterns that go along with memory formation provides a way to better understand memory and potentially even address disorders of memory," said Dr. Gelinas.

Chapter 55

Cognitive Behavioral Treatment For Improving Sleep In Overweight And Obese Youth

Purpose

The purpose of this study is to conduct a randomized controlled trial (RCT) to evaluate the efficacy of brief cognitive behavioral treatment for child sleep (CBTcs) to improve sleep in an important high-risk population, overweight/obese (OV/OB) youth with behavioral sleep disorders. OV/OB youth with behavioral sleep disorders and their parent(s) will be randomly assigned to 8 sessions of either CBTcs or an Educational Control (EC). CBTcs will address behavioral sleep issues in children; EC will address sleep and dietary education and general coping strategies. Child sleep (total wake time, total sleep time, bed/wake times), height, weight, physical activity, dietary intake, quality of life (QOL), fatigue, and daytime sleepiness will be assessed at baseline, posttreatment, and 3-month followup. It is hypothesized the children in the CBTcs will experience greater improvement in sleep than children in the EC.

Detailed Description

Assessment Procedures: Subjects will participate in 8 treatment sessions and 3 full assessment meetings over the course of 7 months. All meetings will be held at the Magnolia Park Sleep Disorders Center. The following procedures will be performed:

Stage 1. Phone screening

About This Chapter: This chapter includes text excerpted from "Cognitive Behavioral Treatment For Improving Sleep In Overweight And Obese Youth," ClinicalTrials.gov, National Institutes of Health (NIH), April 5, 2017.

Stage 2. Screening and baseline measures

Stage 3. Overnight sleep monitoring

Stage 4. Two weeks wrist actigraphy, sleep diaries, dietary recalls

Stage 5. Intervention

Stage 6. Posttreatment measures

Stage 7. 3-Month followup

Eligibility

Ages eligible for study: 6 Years to 12 Years (child)

Sexes eligible for study: All

Accepts healthy volunteers: No

Criteria

Inclusion Criteria

- 6–12 years of age

- Prepubescent

- Have a body mass index ≥85th percentile for age and gender norms as published by the Centers of Disease Control and Prevention (CDC), and

- Accompanied by a parent or legal guardian that lives in the same home as the child. The parent must be able to read and understand English at the 5th grade level.

Exclusion Criteria

- **Sleep apnea:** previous diagnosis or an apnea/hypopnea index (AHI) >10 according to PSG.

- **Periodic limb movement disorder (PLMD):** previous diagnosis or myoclonus arousals per hour >5 according to PSG.

- **Circadian rhythm sleep disorder, delayed sleep phase type**

- **Medication exclusions:** Prescribed or OTC sleep medication within the last 1 month (unless stabilized on medication for 6+ months); Currently taking **psychostimulants;** antipsychotic agents; monoamine oxidase inhibitors; systemic corticosteroids; antibiotics for human immunodeficiency virus (HIV) or tuberculosis (TB); chemotherapeutic drugs; or use of prescription weight-loss drugs within six months.

- **Conditions or behaviors likely to affect trial conduct:** unwilling to accept random assignment; participation in another randomized research project; parent unable to read and understand English at the 5th grade level; presence of bipolar or seizure disorder (potential sleep restriction); restless legs syndrome, major psychiatric disorder other than anxiety or depression; child with major cognitive or developmental delay; unable to complete forms, implement treatment procedures, etc. due to cognitive impairment; psychotropic or other medications (beta blockers) known to alter sleep; participation in other CBT treatment or nonpharmacological sleep treatment; or any other condition/situation which would adversely affect trial participation.

Chapter 56

The Cognitive And Metabolic Effects Of Sleep Restriction In Adolescents (NFS4)

Purpose

The aim of this study is to examine the neurobehavioral and glucose metabolic responses to two successive cycles of sleep restriction and recovery in adolescents, and to determine the benefits of napping on cognitive performance, alertness, mood and glucose metabolism. Using a split-sleep design, 60 participants, aged 15–19 years old, are divided into a nap and a no-nap group. Both groups undergo two cycles of sleep restriction and recovery over a period of 15 days. The no-nap group receives a 6.5-hour sleep opportunity on sleep restriction nights, with no daytime nap opportunity. The nap group receives a 5-hour sleep opportunity on sleep restriction nights, and has a 1.5-hour nap opportunity the following afternoon.

Detailed Description

The present study investigates whether a continuous stretch of night time sleep (6.5 hours) will lead to better neurobehavioral outcomes relative to nocturnal sleep restriction (5 hours) and daytime nap (1.5 hours) of the same total duration, and how sleep restriction affects glucose metabolism. The 15-day protocol is conducted in a dormitory on 60 high school students, aged 15–19 years old. Participants are assigned to a nap or no-nap group. Both groups start with two 9-hour adaptation and baseline nights, followed by two successive cycles of sleep

About This Chapter: This chapter includes text excerpted from "The Cognitive And Metabolic Effects Of Sleep Restriction In Adolescents (NFS4)," ClinicalTrials.gov, National Institutes of Health (NIH), November 7, 2017.

restriction (5-h time in bed (TIB); 01:00-06:00 or 6.5-h TIB; 00:15–06:45) and recovery (9-h TIB; 23:00-08:00). Following each sleep-restricted night, the nap group receives a 1.5-h nap opportunity, while participants in the no-nap group watch a documentary. Throughout the protocol, sleep-wake patterns are assessed with actigraphy and polysomnography. Sleepiness levels, mood, vigilance, working memory/executive functions, and speed of processing are assessed 3 times daily (10:00, 16:15, and 20:00). Other cognitive functions such as memory and mindfulness levels are investigated through computer-based tasks. Glucose metabolism is measured using oral glucose tolerance tests in the mornings after the second baseline night, the third night of sleep restriction and second recovery night in the first cycle, as well as the last sleep restriction night in the second cycle.

All participants stay in air-conditioned, twin-share bedrooms with en-suite bathrooms. Bedroom windows are fitted with blackout panels to ensure participants are not woken up prematurely by sunlight. Earplugs are provided, and participants are allowed to adjust the temperature of their bedrooms to their personal comfort. Three main meals are served each day, with snacks being provided for upon request. Caffeinated drinks, unscheduled sleep, and strenuous physical activities are prohibited.

Outside of scheduled sleep, meal, and cognitive testing times, participants spend the majority of their free time in a common room that is illuminated by natural and artificial lighting. They are allowed to read, play nonphysically exerting games, watch videos, and interact with research staff and other participants. Participants are under constant supervision by the research staff.

Eligibility

Ages eligible for study: 15 Years to 19 Years (child, adult)

Sexes eligible for study: All

Accepts healthy volunteers: Yes

Criteria

Inclusion Criteria

- healthy
- no sleep disorder
- body mass index not greater than 30

Exclusion Criteria

- smoker

- habitual short sleeper (time in bed during term time of less than 6 hours and no sign of sleep extension of greater than 1 hour on weekends)

- consumption of more than 5 cups of caffeinated beverages a day

- travelling across more than 2-time zones in the month prior to the study protocol

- diagnosed with any psychiatric conditions

The Efficacy Of A Depression Intervention For Adolescents With Depression And Sleep Disturbances

Purpose

The focus of this study is on identifying how Interpersonal Psychotherapy for Adolescents (IPT-A) with depression works to change sleep and related biological markers found in saliva, namely cortisol and pro-inflammatory cytokine levels. The long-term goal of this project is to understand the biological mechanisms of recovery from depression in order to assist in selecting and guiding personalized psychotherapeutic interventions with the highest likelihood of success for individual adolescents with depression.

Detailed Description

The primary aim of this project is to examine whether adolescent depression and the associated symptoms of sleep disturbance are best treated using an empirically supported psychotherapy that is augmented with a sleep improvement module. Twenty adolescents (ages 12–17) who meet criteria for major depressive disorder, dysthymic disorder, depressive disorder not otherwise specified, or adjustment disorder with depressed mood and also report elevated levels of sleep disturbance will receive Interpersonal Psychotherapy for Depressed Adolescents (IPT-A) with an adjunctive sleep module that is integrated throughout the treatment. Identifying the best approach to treating both the adolescent's depression and the commonly

About This Chapter: This chapter includes text excerpted from "The Efficacy Of A Depression Intervention For Adolescents With Depression And Sleep Disturbances," ClinicalTrials.gov, National Institutes of Health (NIH), July 18, 2017.

associated symptom of sleep disturbance will have significant implications for the long-term outcomes of depressed adolescents. Moreover, identifying unique symptom and biological profiles at the outset of treatment may enable doctors to predict treatment outcome.

Eligibility

Ages eligible for study: 12 Years to 17 Years (child)

Sexes eligible for study: All

Accepts healthy volunteers: No

Criteria

Inclusion Criteria

- outpatient participant

- parent or legally authorized representative must provide consent and assent by the participant

- *Diagnostic and Statistical Manual of Mental Disorders Fifth Edition* (DSM-V) criteria for a depressive disorder

- Clinical Global Assessment Scale (C-GAS) <65

- Quick Inventory of Depression Symptoms—Self Report 16 (QIDS-SR16) over 8 and less than 24.

- English speaking

- significant sleep complaints

Exclusion Criteria

- comorbid psychiatric diagnosis of bipolar disorder, psychosis, autism spectrum disorder, intellectual development disorder, conduct disorder or substance abuse disorder

- any condition or illness such as uncontrolled seizure disorder, uncontrolled diabetes, or any other conditions that represent as an inappropriate risk to the participant and/or could confound the interpretation of the study

- currently in active evidence-based psychotherapy for the same condition

- currently taking medication for a psychiatric diagnosis that is not a stable dose.

- currently considered at risk for suicide in the opinion of the study doctor, has made a suicide attempt in the past 4 months, or is currently reporting active suicidal ideation.

- history of alcohol or other substance abuse as defined by DSM-V within the last 6 months.

- evidence from clinical diagnosis or report by youth or parent of sleep apnea, restless legs or periodic limb movements during sleep

- sleep treatment that might confound the interpretation of sleep outcomes.

Chapter 58

Sleep Apnea In Asthmatic Children And Teenagers

Purpose

Asthma and sleep apnea are both respiratory diseases and one can worsen the other. Those who suffer from asthma have a higher risk of sleep apnea and sleep apnea can make the asthma more difficult to control.

As girls usually have a more severe asthma than boys, the investigators believe that girls have a higher risk of sleep apnea.

To test if asthmatic girls have more sleep apnea than boys, the investigators are going to ask them questions regarding asthma and sleep symptoms (such as snore) and the investigators are going test the lung function and how many times they stop breathing during the sleep. The sleep test is going to be performed in children's home.

In children, having sleep apnea can make the asthmatic stay in the hospital 30 percent more when they have an asthma attack. It will also be looked if sleep apnea increases the number of hospitalizations and asthma attacks in the past 12 months.

Detailed Description

Obstructive sleep apnea (OSA) and asthma are both inflammatory airway diseases. A systematic review regarding sleep-disordered breathing (SDB) in asthmatic children analyzed 17 studies but only two of them had objective OSA measurement. In total, 45,115

About This Chapter: This chapter includes text excerpted from "Sleep Apnea In Asthmatic Children And Teenagers," ClinicalTrials.gov, National Institutes of Health (NIH), January 30, 2017.

children were included, 53 percent boys, mean age 8.6 ± 2.5 years. SDB was present in 23.8 percent of asthmatic children and in 16.7 percent of nonasthmatic (p < 0.001, or 1.9, 95%CI 1.7–2.2).

An American study found that OSA in asthmatic children increases hospital length of stay (OR 2.3; 95% CI = 1.8–2.9). Brazilian database of the year 2015 showed that, among children 5–19 years, asthma was the 5th cause of hospitalization: a total of 2.4 percent of the hospitalization in this age group, after birth and its complication (31%), limb fractures (5.7%), pneumonia (3.8%), and appendicitis (3.2%).

The relationship among asthma severity (mild, moderate, and severe) and OSA has been described previously, but not in every study. Poor asthma control has also been linked to a higher OSA risk in adults and children.

OSA and asthma share many risk factors: rhinitis, increased collapsibility of the upper airway, local and systemic inflammation, gastroesophageal reflux, and obesity.

A higher risk of SDB in asthmatic girls has recently been described (OR 2.55 for girls and 0.70 for boys). Among nonasthmatic children OSA is usually equal among boys and girls until adolescence. A possible explanation is asthma severity in children: younger boys are more severe but after puberty, girls are.

Since OSA and asthma are linked diseases and that little is known about them in the pediatric field, specially differences related to sex, the investigators hypothesize that:

1. Asthmatic girls have a higher OSA risk;

2. OSA will be higher in asthmatic children compared to the pediatric literature;

3. Asthma severity, asthma control, and rhinitis will be related to a higher OSA risk.

The investigators also aim to analyze factors associated with a higher risk of hospitalizations and asthma attacks.

Eligibility

Estimated enrollment: 80

Study start date: December 2016

Estimated study completion date: November 2017

Estimated primary completion date: November 2017 (Final data collection date for primary outcome measure)

Criteria

Inclusion Criteria

- Persistent asthma

Exclusion Criteria

- Craniofacial malformation
- Thoracic malformation
- Genetic syndromes
- Bronchopulmonary dysplasia
- Bronchiolitis obliterans
- Neuromuscular diseases
- Sickle cell anemia
- Cystic fibrosis

Chapter 59

Brain Maturation And Sleep (BMS)

Purpose

In this study, the investigator evaluates whether there are age-specific diurnal changes in markers of cortical plasticity in children, adolescents and adults. The question will be investigated by the quantification of brain metabolites and structural brain volumes using magnet resonance imaging (MRI) and electrophysiological markers using sleep encephalography (sleep EEG). In a second step, it will be tested how these markers of cortical plasticity change depending on a modulation of sleep by applying tones during deep sleep.

Detailed Description

Given that children and adolescents undergo entirely different maturational processes (children show an increase, adolescents a decrease in synapse density) larger diurnal changes in children are expected compared to adolescents concerning brain metabolites and structural markers. These cortical changes in synapse density are thought to be reflected in electrophysiological markers in the sleep EEG (children show a higher slow wave activity, adolescents a reduced slow wave activity). With the modulation of the deep (slow wave) sleep by playing short, low volume tones, the investigators want to test if there is a causal relationship between slow wave sleep and markers of cortical plasticity.

Eligibility

Ages eligible for study: 8 Years to 30 Years (Child, Adult)

About This Chapter: This chapter includes text excerpted from "Brain Maturation And Sleep (BMS)," ClinicalTrials. gov, National Institutes of Health (NIH), October 11, 2016.

Sexes eligible for study: All

Accepts healthy volunteers: Yes

Criteria

Inclusion Criteria

- Male and female subjects 8–30 years of age

- good general health status

- right-handedness

- Written informed consent after participants'information

Exclusion Criteria

- sleep disorders (insomnia, sleep disordered breathing, restless legs syndrome)

- sleep complaints in general

- irregular sleep-wake rhythm

- daytime sleep

- travelling across a time zone within the last month

- diseases or lesions of the central nervous system

- psychiatric diseases

- learning disability

- skin allergy or very sensitive skin

- acute pediatric disease

- pregnancy

- drug and medication use and abuse

- nicotine use

- high caffeine consumption (>2 servings/day (>160 mg caffeine); including coffee, tea, white and dark chocolate, coca cola, energy drink)

- Alcohol consumption in children and adolescents under 16 years

- high alcohol consumption in adults (>1 standard serving/day (>14 mg Alcohol))

- high alcohol consumption in adolescents aged 16 years and above (>3–4 Standard servings per week)

Chapter 60

Sleep Timing And Insulin Resistance In Adolescents With Obesity

Purpose

This study examines the relationship between sleep timing and insulin resistance in adolescents with obesity. The investigators also aim to develop a physiologically-based mathematical model of adolescent sleep/wake and circadian interactions.

Eligibility

Ages eligible for study: 15 Years to 19 Years (child, adult)

Sexes eligible for study: All

Accepts healthy volunteers: Yes

Sampling method: Nonprobability sample

Criteria

Inclusion Criteria

- High school students between the ages of 15–19

- BMI > 90th percentile

- Tanner stage 2 or greater

About This Chapter: This chapter includes text excerpted from "Sleep Timing And Insulin Resistance In Adolescents With Obesity," ClinicalTrials.gov, National Institutes of Health (NIH), June 8, 2017.

Exclusion Criteria

- Any medications that affect insulin resistance or sleep (e.g., metformin, hormonal contraception, stimulants, atypical antipsychotics)

- Regular use of melatonin or sleep aids

- A prior diagnosis of obstructive sleep apnea, diabetes (HbA1c > 6.5), liver disease other than nonalcoholic fatty liver disease, pregnancy or breastfeeding

- IQ < 70 or severe mental illness that may impact sleep (e.g., schizophrenia, psychotic episodes)

- Not enrolled in a traditional high school academic program (e.g., home school students)

- Night shift employment

- Travel across more than 2 time zones in the month prior to the study

Part Six
If You Need More Information

Chapter 61

Resources For Additional Information About Sleep And Sleep Disorders

Government Agencies That Provide Information About Sleep And Sleep Disorders

Centers for Disease Control and Prevention (CDC)
1600 Clifton Rd.
Atlanta, GA 30333
Toll-Free: 800-CDC-INFO (800-232-4636)
Phone: 404-639-3311
Toll-Free TTY: 888-232-6348
Website: www.cdc.gov

The Cool Spot
National Institute on Alcohol Abuse and Alcoholism (NIAAA)
5635 Fishers Ln.
Rm. 3098 MSC 9304
Bethesda, MD 20892-9304
Website: www.thecoolspot.gov

About This Chapter: Resources in this chapter were compiled from several sources deemed reliable; all contact information was verified and updated in December 2017.

Eunice Kennedy Shriver *National Institute of Child Health and Human Development*

P.O. Box 3006
Rockville, MD 20847
Toll-Free: 800-370-2943
Toll-Free Fax: 866-760-5947
Website: www.nichd.nih.gov
E-mail: NICHDInformationResourceCenter@mail.nih.gov

girlshealth.gov

Office on Women's Health (OWH)
200 Independence Ave. S.W.
Rm. 712E
Washington, DC 20201
Toll-Free: 800-994-9662
Website: www.girlshealth.gov

healthfinder.gov

U.S. Department of Health and Human Services (HHS)
P.O. Box 1133
Washington, DC 20013-1133
Phone: 240-453-8280
Fax: 301-984-4256
Website: www.healthfinder.gov
E-mail: info@nhic.org

National Cancer Institute (NCI)

9609 Medical Center Dr.
BG 9609 MSC 9760
Bethesda, MD 20892-9760
Toll-Free: 800-4-CANCER (800-422-6237)
Website: www.cancer.gov
E-mail: cancergovstaff@mail.nih.gov

National Center for Complementary and Integrative Health (NCCIH)

9000 Rockville Pike
Bethesda, MD 20892
Toll-Free: 888-644-6226
Toll-Free TTY: 866-464-3615
Toll-Free Fax: 866-464-3616
Website: www.nccih.nih.gov
E-mail: info@nccih.nih.gov

National Center on Sleep Disorders Research (NCSDR)

6701 Rockledge Dr.
Bethesda, MD 20892
Phone: 301-435-0199
Fax: 301-480-3451
Website: www.nhlbi.nih.gov/about/org/ncsdr

National Heart, Lung, and Blood Institute (NHLBI)

Center for Health Information
P.O. Box 30105
Bethesda, MD 20824-0105
Phone: 301-592-8573
Website: www.nhlbi.nih.gov/health
E-mail: nhlbiinfo@nhlbi.nih.gov

National Institute of Allergy and Infectious Diseases (NIAID)

Office of Communications and Government Relations
5601 Fishers Ln. MSC 9806
Bethesda, MD 20892-9806
Toll-Free: 866-284-4107
Phone: 301-496-5717
Toll-Free TDD: 800-877-8339
Fax: 301-402-3573
Website: www.niaid.nih.gov
E-mail: ocpostoffice@niaid.nih.gov

National Institute of Arthritis and Musculoskeletal and Skin Diseases (NIAMS)

Office of Science Policy, Planning, and Communications (OSPPC)
31 Center Dr. MSC 2350
Bldg. 31 Rm. 4C02
Bethesda, MD 20892-2350
Toll-Free: 877-22-NIAMS (877-226-4267)
Phone: 301-496-8190
TTY: 301-565-2966
Fax: 301-480-2814
Website: www.niams.nih.gov
E-mail: NIAMSinfo@mail.nih.gov

National Institute of Diabetes and Digestive and Kidney Diseases (NIDDK)

Office of Communications and Public Liaison (OCPL)
31 Center Dr. MSC 2560
Bldg. 31 Rm. 9A06
Bethesda, MD 20892-2560
Phone: 301-496-3583
Website: www.niddk.nih.gov

National Institute of General Medical Sciences (NIGMS)

45 Center Dr. MSC 6200
Bethesda, MD 20892-6200
Phone: 301-496-7301
Website: www.nigms.nih.gov
E-mail: info@nigms.nih.gov

National Institute of Mental Health (NIMH)

6001 Executive Blvd.
Rm. 6200 MSC 9663
Bethesda, MD 20892-9663
Toll-Free: 866-615-6464
TTY: 301-443-8431
Toll-Free TTY: 866-415-8051
Fax: 301-443-4279
Website: www.nimh.nih.gov
E-mail: nimhinfo@nih.gov

National Institute of Neurological Disorders and Stroke (NINDS)

NIH Neurological Institute
P.O. Box 5801
Bethesda, MD 20824
Toll-Free: 800-352-9424
Phone: 301-496-5751
Website: www.ninds.nih.gov

National Institute on Alcohol Abuse and Alcoholism (NIAAA)

5635 Fishers Ln. MSC 9304
Bethesda, MD 20892-9304
Website: www.niaaa.nih.gov
E-mail: niaaaweb-r@exchange.nih.gov

National Institute on Drug Abuse (NIDA)

Office of Science Policy and Communications (OSPC)
6001 Executive Blvd.
Rm. 5213 MSC 9561
Bethesda, MD 20892
Phone: 301-443-1124
Website: www.drugabuse.gov

National Institutes of Health (NIH)

9000 Rockville Pike
Bethesda, MD 20892
Phone: 301-496-4000
TTY: 301-402-9612
Website: www.nih.gov
E-mail: NIHinfo@od.nih.gov

National Library of Medicine (NLM)

8600 Rockville Pike
Bethesda, MD 20894
Toll-Free: 888-FIND-NLM (888-346-3656)
Phone: 301-594-5983
Toll-Free TDD: 800-735-2258
Fax: 301-402-1384
Website: www.nlm.nih.gov
E-mail: publicinfo@nlm.nih.gov

National Science Foundation (NSF)
2415 Eisenhower Ave.
Arlington, VA 22314
Toll-Free: 800-877-8339
Phone: 703-292-5111
TDD: 703-292-5090
Toll-Free TDD: 800-281-8749
Website: www.nsf.gov
E-mail: info@nsf.gov

Office on Women's Health (OWH)
U.S. Department of Health and Human Services (HHS)
200 Independence Ave. S.W.
Rm. 712E
Washington, DC 20201
Toll-Free: 800-994-9662
Phone: 202-690-7650
Fax: 202-205-2631
Website: www.womenshealth.gov
E-mail: womenshealth@hhs.gov

Ready Campaign
U.S. Department of Homeland Security (DHS)
500 C St. S.W.
Washington, DC 20472
Toll-Free: 800-621-FEMA (800-621-3362)
Toll-Free TTY: 800-462-7585
Website: www.ready.gov/kids

StopBullying.gov
U.S. Department of Health and Human Services (HHS)
200 Independence Ave. S.W.
Washington, DC 20201
Website: www.stopbullying.gov

Substance Abuse and Mental Health Services Administration (SAMHSA)

Health Information Network
5600 Fishers Ln.
Rockville, MD 20857
Toll-Free: 877-SAMHSA-7 (877-726-4727)
Toll-Free TTY: 800-487-4889
Fax: 240-221-4292
Website: www.samhsa.gov
E-mail: SAMHSAInfo@samhsa.hhs.gov

U.S. Department of Health and Human Services (HHS)

200 Independence Ave. S.W.
Washington, DC 20201
Toll-Free: 877-696-6775
Website: www.hhs.gov

U.S. Department of Veterans Affairs (VA)

810 Vermont Ave. N.W.
Washington, DC 20420
Toll-Free: 800-827-1000
Toll-Free TDD: 800-829-4833
Website: www.va.gov

Private Agencies That Provide Information About Sleep And Sleep Disorders

American Academy of Allergy, Asthma, and Immunology (AAAAI)

555 E. Wells St.
Ste. 1100
Milwaukee, WI 53202-3823
Phone: 414-272-6071
Website: www.aaaai.org
E-mail: info@aaaai.org

American Academy of Child and Adolescent Psychiatry (AACAP)

3615 Wisconsin Ave. N.W.
Washington, DC 20016-3007
Phone: 202-966-7300
Fax: 202-464-0131
Website: www.aacap.org
E-mail: communications@aacap.org

American Academy of Dermatology (AAD)

930 E. Woodfield Rd.
P.O. Box 4014
Schaumburg, IL 60618-4014
Toll-Free: 866-503-SKIN (866-503-7546)
Phone: 847-240-1280
Fax: 847-240-1859
Website: www.aad.org

American Academy of Experts in Traumatic Stress (AAETS)

127 Echo Ave.
Miller Place, NY 11764
Phone: 631-543-2217
Fax: 631-543-6977
Website: www.aaets.org
E-mail: info@aaets.org

American Academy of Family Physicians (AAFP)

11400 Tomahawk Creek Pkwy
Leawood, KS 66211-2680
Toll-Free: 800-274-2237
Phone: 913-906-6000
Fax: 913-906-6075
Website: www.aafp.org
E-mail: contactcenter@aafp.org

American Academy of Sleep Medicine (AASM)
2510 N. Frontage Rd.
Darien, IL 60561
Phone: 630-737-9700
Fax: 630-737-9790
Website: www.aasm.org
E-mail: publications@aasm.org

American Foundation for Suicide Prevention (AFSP)
120 Wall St.
29th Fl.
New York, NY 10005
Toll-Free: 888-333-AFSP (888-333-2377)
Phone: 212-363-3500
Fax: 212-363-6237
Website: www.afsp.org
E-mail: info@afsp.org

American Heart Association (AHA)
7272 Greenville Ave.
Dallas, TX 75231
Toll-Free: 800-AHA-USA-1 (800-242-8721)
Phone: 214-373-6300
Website: www.heart.org
E-mail: inquiries@heart.org

American Institute of Stress (AIS)
6387 Camp Bowie Blvd. Ste. B #334
Fort Worth, TX 76116
Phone: 682-239-6823
Fax: 817-394-0593
Website: www.stress.org
E-mail: info@stress.org

American Massage Therapy Association (AMTA)
500 Davis St. Ste. 900
Evanston, IL 60201-4695
Toll-Free: 877-905-0577
Fax: 847-864-5196
Website: www.amtamassage.org
E-mail: info@amtamassage.org

American Meditation Institute (AMI)

60 Garner Rd.
Averill Park, NY 12018
Phone: 518-674-8714
Fax: 518-674-8714
Website: www.americanmeditation.org
E-mail: ami@americanmeditation.org

American Psychiatric Association (APA)

1000 Wilson Blvd.
Ste. 1825
Arlington, VA 22209-3901
Toll-Free: 888-35-PSYCH (888-357-7924)
Phone: 703-907-7300
Website: www.psychiatry.org
E-mail: apa@psych.org

American Psychological Association (APA)

750 First St. N.E.
Washington, DC 20002-4242
Toll-Free: 800-374-2721
Phone: 202-336-5500
TDD/TTY: 202-336-6123
Website: www.apa.org
E-mail: public.affairs@apa.org

American Sleep Apnea Association (ASAA)

641 S. St. N.W.
Third Fl.
Washington, DC 20001-5196
Toll-Free: 888-293-3650
Toll-Free Fax: 888-293-3650
Website: www.sleepapnea.org
E-mail: asaa@sleepapnea.org

Anxiety and Depression Association of America (ADAA)
8701 Georgia Ave.
Ste. 412
Silver Spring, MD 20910
Phone: 240-485-1001
Fax: 240-485-1035
Website: www.adaa.org
E-mail: information@adaa.org

Association for Behavioral and Cognitive Therapies (ABCT)
305 Seventh Ave.
16th Fl.
New York, NY 10001
Phone: 212-647-1890
Fax: 212-647-1865
Website: www.abct.org
E-mail: publications@abct.org

Center for Young Women's Health (CYWH)
333 Longwood Ave.
Fifth Fl.
Boston, MA 02115 USA
Phone: 617-355-2994
Fax: 617-730-0186
Website: www.youngwomenshealth.org
E-mail: cywh@childrens.harvard.edu

Cleveland Clinic
9500 Euclid Ave.
Cleveland, OH 44195
Toll-Free: 800-223-CARE (800-223-2273)
TTY: 216-444-0261
Website: www.my.clevelandclinic.org

CopeCareDeal
The Annenberg Public Policy Center (APPC)
202 S. 36th St.
Philadelphia, PA 19104-3806
Phone: 215-898-9400
Fax: 215-573-7116
Website: www.annenbergpublicpolicycenter.org

FamilyDoctor.org

American Academy of Family Physicians (AAFP)
11400 Tomahawk Creek Pkwy
Leawood, KS 66211-2680
Website: www.familydoctor.org

HealthyChildren.org

The American Academy of Pediatrics (AAP)
141 N.W. Pt. Blvd.
Elk Grove Village, IL 60007-1098
Phone: 847-434-4000
Fax: 847-434-8000
Website: www.healthychildren.org
E-mail: info@healthychildren.org

International Society for Traumatic Stress Studies (ISTSS)

One Parkview Plaza
Ste. 800
Oakbrook Terrace, IL 60181
Phone: 847-686-2234
Fax: 847-686-2251
Website: www.istss.org
E-mail: info@istss.org

Maternal and Family Health Services (MFHS)

15 Public Sq.
Ste. 600
Wilkes-Barre, PA 18701
Toll-Free: 800-FOR-MFHS (800-367-6347)
Phone: 570-826-1777
Fax: 570-823-3040
Website: www.mfhs.org
E-mail: info@mfhs.org

Mental Health America (MHA)

500 Montgomery St.
Ste. 820
Alexandria, VA 22314
Toll-Free: 800-969-6642
Phone: 703-684-7722
Website: www.mentalhealthamerica.net

Narcolepsy Network

P.O. Box 2178
Lynnwood, WA 98036
Toll-Free: 888-292-6522
Phone: 401-667-2523
Fax: 401-633-6567
Website: www.narcolepsynetwork.org

National Alliance on Mental Illness (NAMI)

3803 N. Fairfax Dr.
Ste. 100
Arlington, VA 22203
Toll-Free: 800-950-NAMI (800-950-6264)
Phone: 703-524-7600
Fax: 703-524-9094
Website: www.nami.org
E-mail: info@nami.org

National Eczema Society (NES)

11 Murray St.
London, NW1 9RE
Toll-Free: 800-089-1122
Phone: 020-7281-3553
Website: www.eczema.org
E-mail: helpline@eczema.org

National Multiple Sclerosis Society

733 Third Ave.
Third Fl.
New York, NY 10017
Toll-Free: 800-344-4867
Phone: 212-463-7787
Fax: 212-986-7981
Website: www.nationalmssociety.org
E-mail: info@mynyc.org

National Sleep Foundation (NSF)
1010 N. Glebe Rd.
Ste. 420
Arlington, VA 22201
Phone: 703-243-1697
Website: www.sleepfoundation.org
E-mail: nsf@sleepfoundation.org

The Nemours Foundation
10140 Centurion Pkwy N.
Jacksonville, FL 32256
Website: www.kidshealth.org / www.nemours.org

North American Spine Society (NASS)
7075 Veterans Blvd.
Burr Ridge, IL 60527
Toll-Free: 866-960-6277
Phone: 630-230-3600
Fax: 630-230-3700
Website: www.spine.org

Palo Alto Medical Foundation (PAMF)
2025 Soquel Ave.
Santa Cruz, CA 95062
Toll-Free: 888-398-5677
Phone: 831-423-4111
Website: www.pamf.org

Psych Central
55 Pleasant St. Ste. 207
Newburyport, MA 01950
Website: www.psychcentral.com

Restless Legs Syndrome Foundation (RLSF)
3006 Bee Caves Rd.
Ste. D206
Austin, TX 78746
Phone: 512-366-9109
Fax: 512-366-9189
Website: www.rls.org
E-mail: info@rls.org

S.A.F.E. Alternatives®
8000 Bonhomme
Ste. 211
St. Louis, MO 63105
Toll-Free: 800-DONTCUT (800-366-8288)
Phone: 630-819-9505
Toll-Free Fax: 888-296-7988
Website: www.selfinjury.com

Safe Teens
Website: www.safeteens.org
E-mail: info@safeteens.org

Students Against Destructive Decisions (SADD)
201 Boston Post Rd.W.
Ste. 202
Marlborough, MA 01752
Phone: 508-481-3568
Fax: 508-481-5759
Website: www.sadd.org
E-mail: info@sadd.org

United Advocates for Children and Families (UACF)
2035 Hurley Way
Ste. 290
Sacramento, CA 95825
Phone: 916-643-1530
Fax: 916-643-1592
Website: www.uacf4hope.org

Young Men's Health (YMH)
333 Longwood Ave.
Fifth Fl.
Boston, MA 02115
Phone: 617-355-2994
Website: www.youngmenshealthsite.org
E-mail: ymh@childrens.harvard.edu

Chapter 62

Suggestions For Further Reading About Sleep And Sleep Disorders

Web-Based Resources For People With Sleep Problems

Baby Sleep Basics

BabyCenter
BabyCenter provides parents with trusted information, advice from peers, and support that's Remarkably Right® at every stage of their child's development. Products include websites, mobile apps, online communities, e-mail series, social programs, print publications, and public health initiatives.
Website: www.babycenter.com/baby-sleep-basics

Can't Sleep?

Sleep Psychologist and Insomnia Therapy
Stephanie Silberman, Ph.D., FAASM, is a Licensed Psychologist who is a Fellow of the American Academy of Sleep Medicine. She is active in professional organizations and legislative activities affecting psychology and sleep disorders, including two terms as president of the Broward Chapter of the Florida Psychological Association and past co-chair of the Legislative Affairs and Public Policy Board for FPA. She has appeared on television news and in national magazines regarding sleep-related issues.
Website: www.sleeppsychology.com

About This Chapter: Resources in this chapter were compiled from multiple sources deemed reliable. This list is intended as a starting point only, and it is not comprehensive. Inclusion does not constitute endorsement and there is no implication associated with omission. All website information was verified and updated in December 2017.

Delayed Sleep Phase Disorder

Circadian Sleep Disorders Network
Circadian Sleep Disorders Network is an independent nonprofit organization dedicated to improving the lives of people with chronic circadian rhythm disorders.
Website: www.circadiansleepdisorders.org/docs/DSPS-QandA.php

Get Enough Sleep

Healthfinder.gov
The healthfinder.gov has resources on a wide range of health topics selected from approximately 1,400 government and nonprofit organizations to bring the best, most reliable health information on the Internet.
Website: healthfinder.gov/healthtopics/population/men/mental-health-and-relationships/get-enough-sleep

How Depression Affects Your Sleep

Sleep.org
Sleep.org, by the National Sleep Foundation, is dedicated to starting a movement about the positive benefits of sleep health. Sleep health is an emerging field of research focused on how we sleep and the benefits it provides to our minds, bodies and lives.
Website: sleep.org/articles/depression-affects-sleep

How Does Anxiety Affect Sleep?

HealthStatus
HealthStatus, an Internet based health risk assessment, along with several calculators to take a quick snapshot of a person's health. It provides the best interactive health tools on the Internet and millions of visitors have used its health risk assessment, body fat, and calories burned calculators.
Website: www.healthstatus.com/health_blog/sleep-2/anxiety-affect-sleep

How Sleep Works

How Stuff Works
HowStuffWorks Science has explanations and colorful illustrations related to earth science, life science, and other wonders of the physical world.
Website: science.howstuffworks.com/life/inside-the-mind/human-brain/sleep.htm

How To Cope With Sleep Problems

Mind

Mind has worked to improve the lives of all people with experience of mental health problems. Through public campaigns, government lobbying, and more than 1,000 services, local Minds have delivered in communities across England and Wales, and have touched millions of lives.
Website: www.mind.org.uk/information-support/types-of-mental-health-problems/sleep-problems/#.WiFNlVV97IU

How To Get Great Sleep

Psychology Today

Psychology Today gives the view of the latest from the world of psychology, from behavioral research to practical guidance on relationships, mental health, and addiction.
Website: www.psychologytoday.com/collections/201407/how-get-great-sleep

Mental Illness And Sleep Disorders

Tuck

Tuck aims to improve sleep hygiene, health, and wellness through the creation and dissemination of comprehensive, unbiased, free resources. Boasting the largest collection of aggregated data on sleep surfaces on the web (over 95,000 customer experiences from nearly 1,000 individual sources). Tuck aims to power consumers, sleep professionals, and the troubled sleeper looking for answers. Check back often for updates and expanded sleep product information.
Website: www.tuck.com/mental-illness-and-sleep

Sleep

Nova Science Now (PBS)

NOVA is a science series on American television, reaching an average of five million viewers weekly. Now in its fourth decade of production, the series remains committed to producing in-depth science programming in the form of one-hour documentaries and long-form mini-series, from the latest breakthroughs in technology to the deepest mysteries of the natural world.
Website: www.pbs.org/wgbh/nova/body/sleep.html

HealthyWomen

HealthyWomen is an independent, nonprofit health information source for women and to educate and empower women to make informed health choices for themselves and their families.
Website: www.healthywomen.org/content/article/4-most-common-sleep-disorders

Basics Of Sleep Problems In Children

American Sleep Association (ASA)

The American Sleep Association (ASA) is a group of sleep professionals seeking to improve public health by increasing awareness of the importance of sleep in ensuring a high quality of life, as well as the dangers of sleep disorders.
Website: faculty.washington.edu/chudler/sleep.html

Sleep Apnea

MedlinePlus

MedlinePlus is the National Institutes of Health's website for patients and their families and friends. Produced by the National Library of Medicine brings you information about diseases, conditions, and wellness issues in language you can understand. MedlinePlus offers reliable, up-to-date health information, anytime, anywhere, for free.
Website: medlineplus.gov/sleepapnea.html

Sleep Disorders

American Psychiatric Association (APA)

APA has more than 37,000 members involved in psychiatric practice, research, and academia representing the diversity of the patients for whom they care. APA encompasses members practicing in more than 100 countries.
Website: www.psychiatry.org/patients-families/sleep-disorders/what-are-sleep-disorders

Infinity Sleep Solutions

Infinity Sleep Solutions provides patients with comprehensive sleep diagnostic testing and specializes in personalized care led by a board certified sleep physician and also will work hand-in-hand to diagnose and treat even the most complicated sleep disorders.
Website: www.infinitysleep.com/education-1.html

MedicineNet

MedicineNet is an online, healthcare media publishing company, which provides easy-to-read, in-depth, authoritative medical information for consumers via its robust, user-friendly, interactive website.
Website: www.medicinenet.com/sleep/article.htm

Sleep Disorders And Problems

Helpguide.org

Helpguideorg International is dedicated to charitable and educational purposes and is also a trusted nonprofit with over 200 science-based articles and other resources to help you overcome mental and emotional challenges, improve all your relationship and much more.
Website: www.helpguide.org/articles/sleep/sleep-disorders-and-problems.htm

Suggestions For Further Reading About Sleep And Sleep Disorders

Sleep Disorders: Categories

American Academy of Sleep Medicine (AASM)
The American Academy of Sleep Medicine (AASM) improves sleep health and promotes high quality, patient-centered care through advocacy, education, strategic research, and practice standards.
Website: www.sleepeducation.org/sleep-disorders-by-category

Sleep Disorders Center

Mayo Clinic
Mayo Clinic is a nonprofit organization that provides the best care to all patients, through the integration of clinical practice, education, and research in order to instill hope and contribute to health and well-being.
Website: www.mayoclinic.org/es-es/departments-centers/neurology/sleep-disorders-center-florida/overview

Sleep Disorders Health Center

WebMD
WebMD provides valuable health information, tools for managing your health, and support to those who seek information.
Website: www.webmd.com/sleep-disorders

Sleep Disorders: Information, Diagnosis, And Treatment

Disabled World
Disabled-World.Com is an independent Health and Disability news source that offers subject areas covering seniors and disability news, assistive device reviews, and articles on everything from helpful tips to disability sports articles.
Website: www.disabled-world.com/health/neurology/sleepdisorders

Sleep Disorders: SSDI Eligibility Guidelines

Allsup
True Help is dedicated to simplifying the world of disability benefits for individuals and organizations with expertise in SSDI Representation, Return to Work, Veterans Disability, and Healthcare Assistance.
Website: www.truehelp.com/understanding-ssdi/guidelines-by-disability/sleep-disorders-and-social-security-disability-insurance

Sleep For Kids

National Sleep Foundation

This website by the National Sleep Foundation provides easily readable information about the importance of sleep, sleep disorders, and tips for getting a good night's sleep to children ages 7–10, their parents, and their teachers.
Website: www.sleepforkids.org

American Psychological Association (APA)

APA is a scientific and professional organization representing psychology in the United States, with more than 115,700 researchers, educators, clinicians, consultants, and students as its members.
Website: www.apa.org/monitor/feb04/sleep.aspx

Sleep Health

HealthyPeople.gov

Healthy People provides science-based, 10-year national objectives for improving the health of all Americans. Healthy People has established benchmarks and monitored progress over time in order to encourage collaborations across communities and sectors, empower individuals toward making informed health decisions, and to measure the impact of prevention activities.
Website: www.healthypeople.gov/2020/topics-objectives/topic/sleep-health

Sleep Problems

Caring.com

Caring.com is an online destination for those seeking information and support as they care for aging parents, spouses, and other loved ones. They equip family caregivers to make better decisions, save time and money, and feel less alone—and less stressed—as they face the many challenges of caregiving.
Website: www.caring.com/articles/sleep-problems

Sleep Problems In Teens

Kidshealth

KidsHealth provides information about health, behavior, and development from before birth through the teen years.
Website: kidshealth.org/en/parents/sleep-problems.html

The Sleep Doctor

Most people could improve their sleep and many others are dealing with disorders, such as insomnia. The Sleep Doctor has advice, news, and tools to help you.
Website: www.thesleepdoctor.com/2017/03/30/teens-need-sleep-think

U.S. Racking Up Huge "Sleep Debt"

National Geographic News
The National Geographic Society is a nonprofit scientific and educational organization that pushes the boundaries of exploration to further our understanding of our planet and empower us all to generate solutions for a more sustainable future.
Website: news.nationalgeographic.com/news/2005/02/0224_050224_sleep.html

Want To Sleep Better

Sound Sleep Health
Sound Sleep Health, founded by sleep medicine expert, Gandis Mazeika M.D., has been granted program accreditation from the American Academy of Sleep Medicine (AASM) and fulfills the high standards required for receiving accreditation as a sleep disorder center.
Website: www.soundsleephealth.com

Mobile Apps For People With Sleep Problems

Alarm Clock Xtreme
This app allows you to wake up in a way that works for you and even helps you sleep better with a built-in sleep cycle tracking and smart sleep monitor.
Website: play.google.com/store/apps/details?id=com.alarmclock.xtreme.free

Calm: Meditate, Sleep, Relax
Calm has guided meditation sessions and sleep stories, along with 25+ soothing nature sounds and scenes to use during meditation, yoga, or to help you sleep.
Website: play.google.com/store/apps/details?id=com.calm.android&hl=en_GB

Deep Sleep
This application is a guided meditation intended to help you overcome insomnia and get to sleep.
Website: itunes.apple.com/us/app/deep-sleep-andrew-johnson/id337349999?mt=8

Digipill: Sleep, Relaxation and Mindfulness
This app will help you beat insomnia, lose weight, reduce stress, be more creative, and much more. It uses a combination of psychoacoustics and neuro-linguistic programming (NLP) to help you unlock your subconscious in order to change your mood, perception, or even your behavior.
Website: itunes.apple.com/us/app/digipill-sleep-relaxation/id578068250?mt=8

Nature Sounds Relax and Sleep

This app has six different good quality nature relaxing sounds (sounds of nature) including thunder, ocean sounds, sea, birds sounds, rain, night in jungle, water sounds, waterfall, nature and start your personal audio therapy.
Website: play.google.com/store/apps/details?id=com.zodinplex.naturesound&feature=search_result

Pillow

Pillow is an advanced sleep tracking alarm clock that can measure and track your sleep quality. It can help you to wake up refreshed and learn more about the benefits of great sleep.
Website: itunes.apple.com/us/app/pillow-smart-sleep-cycle-alarm/id878691772?mt=8

Pzizz

Sleep at the push of a button! Fall asleep fast, stay asleep, and wake up refreshed. Now with "Focus" too!
Website: itunes.apple.com/ca/app/pzizz/id915664862?mt=8

Relax & Sleep Well

This is a hypnosis and meditation app consisting of four free hypnotherapy and meditation recordings and over 80 in-app purchase options covering insomnia, stress, anxiety, mindfulness, sleep, weight-loss, confidence, self-esteem, the solfeggio frequencies, binaural beats, spiritual healing, and much more.
Website: itunes.apple.com/us/app/relax-sleep-well-by-glenn/id412690467?mt=8

Sleep as Android

Smart alarm clock with sleep cycle tracking. Wakes you gently in optimal moment for pleasant mornings.
Website: play.google.com/store/apps/details?id=com.urbandroid.sleep&hl=en

Sleep Better with Runtastic

Sleep Better sleep tracker app offers you a simple and engaging way to get better sleep using a sleep tracker and sleep timer. Track moon phases, keep a dream diary and more using this preferred sleep app on your Android device.
Website: play.google.com/store/apps/details?id=com.runtastic.android.sleepbetter.lite

Sleep Cycle alarm clock

Sleep Cycle alarm clock monitors your movement during sleep using the sensitive accelerometer in your phone and then finds the optimal time to wake you up during a 30 minute window that ends at your set alarm time.
Website: play.google.com/store/apps/details?id=com.northcube.sleepcycle

Sleep Easily Meditations

Sleep Easily Meditation guides you through every step of the way to relax your whole body and mind. This meditation leaves you refreshed, renewed and resonating so much more from your heart and a place of stillness.
Website: itunes.apple.com/us/app/sleep-easily-by-shazzie-a-guided-meditation/id458059886?mt=8

Sleep Genius

Sleep Genius is a scientifically designed sound program for sleep. It was created following decades of research to develop algorithms that trigger your brain into sleeping faster, longer, and deeper than ever before.
Website: sleepgenius.com; itunes.apple.com/app/sleep-genius-revive-cycle/id873376319?ls=1&mt=8

Sleep Time: Sleep Cycle Smart Alarm Clock Tracker

Sleep Time uses the sensitive accelerometer in your Android to detect movements during the night. Its algorithm determines the phase of sleep, and sets off the alarm at the perfect moment. You will never wake up from a deep sleep feeling groggy again.
Website: play.google.com/store/apps/details?id=com.azumio.android.sleeptime

Sleep Tracker

PrimeNap is a sleep tracker and sleep cycle alarm clock with many features for you to graph your sleep patterns and wake up at the perfect time feeling refreshed.
Website: play.google.com/store/apps/details?id=com.primenap

Sleep Well Hypnosis

Sleep Well Hypnosis helps you reduce anxious thoughts and prepare your mind for deeper, more restorative rest.
Website: itunes.apple.com/us/app/sleep-well-hypnosis-free-cure/id720652207

SleepBot

The Sleepbot app includes motion and sound graphs, sleep debt log, statistics, trend graphs (averages, sleep/wake times, patterns), multiple custom alarms, and resources to help you fall asleep.
Website: play.google.com/store/apps/details?id=com.lslk.sleepbot

Sleepo

Sleepo brings great collection of HD sounds that can be mixed into the perfect relaxing ambiences. You can choose from different types of rain, nature sounds, city sounds, white noise or instruments. Save your favorite sound mixes so they are always by hand with you.
Website: play.google.com/store/apps/details?id=net.relaxio.sleepo

Sleeptracker-24/7

Sleeptracker-24/7 is a solution for the iPhone users that measures and correlates resting heart rate, includes advanced sleep cycle monitoring with smart alarms and power naps, and incorporates "Get Active" alerts.
Website: 4-7.motionx.com

White Noise

White Noise generates sounds over a wide range of frequencies, masking those noise interruptions, so you can not only fall asleep, but stay asleep.
Website: play.google.com/store/apps/details?id=com.tmsoft.whitenoise.full

Index

Index

Page numbers that appear in *Italics* refer to tables or illustrations. Page numbers that have a small 'n' after the page number refer to citation information shown as Notes. Page numbers that appear in **Bold** refer to information contained in boxes within the chapters.

planned napping, defined 22
PLMD *see* periodic limb movement disorder
polysomnogram
  defined **103**
  narcolepsy 135
  periodic limb movement disorder
  (PLMD) 152
  sleep apnea 98
positive stress, nightmares 160
"Postmarket Drug Safety Information For Patients
  And Providers" (FDA) 89n
posttraumatic stress disorder (PTSD)
  nightmares 160
  overview 75–7
pregabalin, restless legs syndrome 147
pregnancy
  fatal familial insomnia (FFI) 117
  nocturia 186
  restless legs syndrome 145
prion protein (PrP)
  fatal familial insomnia (FFI) 116
  sleep deprivation 212
procedural memory, napping 23
progressive relaxation, insomnia 111
Psych Central, contact 294
Psychology Today, website 299
psychotherapy
  depression 218
  insomnia 108
PTSD *see* posttraumatic stress disorder
puberty
  defined **242**
  sleep 36
  sleep bruxism 178
Pzizz, mobile app 304

Q

quazepam (Doral), insomnia 90
quinacrine, fatal familial insomnia (FFI) 118

R

RBD *see* REM behavior disorder
Ready Campaign, contact 286
reasoning
  memory 212
  slumber 45

relationships
  depression 218
  mood 70
  nightmares 159
  pain 189
  restless legs syndrome 143
Relax & Sleep Well, mobile app 304
relaxation techniques
  athletes 221
  insomnia 111
  stress 73
REM behavior disorder (RBD)
  described 156
  parasomnias 155
restless legs syndrome (RLS), overview 143–9
"Restless Legs Syndrome Fact Sheet"
  (NINDS) 143n
Restless Legs Syndrome Foundation (RLSF),
  contact 294
Restoril (temazepam), insomnia 91
RLS *see* restless legs syndrome
Rozerem (ramelteon), insomnia 91

S

S.A.F.E. Alternatives®, contact 295
Safe Teens, contact 295
SAMHSA *see* Substance Abuse and Mental Health
  Services Administration
school
  attention deficit hyperactivity disorder
  (ADHD) 208
  delayed sleep-wake phase disorder 120
  jet lag disorder 120
  night-time asthma 181
  non-24 hour sleep-wake rhythm disorder 120
  posttraumatic stress disorder 75
  restless legs syndrome 143
  snoring 9
  start times 241
"Schools Start Too Early" (CDC) 241n
seasonal affective disorder (SAD), circadian
  rhythms 19
Seconal (secobarbital), insomnia 91
self-esteem, bladder control problems 165
senses, hallucinations 133
shift work
  drowsy driving 227
  sleep deprivation 200